MW00399218

Praise for
Voice of the Wildcats

"He called the football games for Kentucky, the basketball games, and he went on to do Cincinnati Reds baseball—a three-letter man; they were hard to find, especially in the broadcasting business . . . and I kind of learned by listening to him."—Vernon Hatton, former UK basketball player and 1958 NCAA Championship team member

"Claude Sullivan taught me one thing: everything in life is based on preparation, because if you prepare, you will succeed. I never saw anyone work harder at preparing than Claude Sullivan did, which is what made him the great announcer and the great broadcaster that he was."—Jim Host, former announcer and president of Host Communications

"I grew up listening to Claude Sullivan call UK football and basketball on the radio. The radio play-by-play man was the ultimate communicator, painting a word picture as the action unfolded. None was better than Claude Sullivan, a true wordsmith who brought the scene to life. I am certain that my own broadcasting style has been greatly influenced by those early years of listening to Claude Sullivan and Cawood Ledford. Any Wildcat fan who has been enthralled by the vivid descriptions of great moments in UK sports will enjoy the story of Claude Sullivan, lovingly told by his son Alan."—Tom Hammond, NBC Sports

"He was the voice of the Kentucky Wildcats. His credentials were incredible for a young man, and he *was* a young man—he was twenty-seven when I met him, when I came to the University of Kentucky. When he started he was probably only a year or two older than some of the players."—Cliff Hagan, former UK basketball player, 1951 NCAA Championship team member, and former director of UK Athletics

"Alan Sullivan recounts the story of his father's broadcasting career covering University of Kentucky sports, horse racing, and Cincinnati Reds baseball at the midpoint of the twentieth century. The author has meticulously researched the details of the UK sports covered by his father and skillfully uses oral history interviews to provide insightful and entertaining stories."—Terry Birdwhistell, Dean of Libraries, University of Kentucky

"He did his homework, he went to practices, he talked to the coaches, he talked to Adolph Rupp and Bear Bryant and others, and he knew what it was about. I think the ones that came along later, like Cawood Ledford and J. B. Faulkner, also heard him broadcast. I think Claude was kind of the model."—C. M. Newton, former UK basketball player, 1951 NCAA Championship team member, and former director of UK Athletics

"What an absorbing tribute this is to this man who in his prime was a legendary figure in broadcasting a trio of sports within a geographical region that extends several hundred miles. The son has done his daddy proud, as he reminds his readers often of how his father prioritized family activities ahead of his passion for work. It is a fascinating read."—Jim Cox, author of *Radio Speakers*

Voice of the
Wildcats

To Chuck,

Enjoy the read + radio clips.
See attached information.

Go Cats!

[signature] 12.06.14

VOICE OF THE WILDCATS

Claude Sullivan and the Rise of Modern Sportscasting

ALAN SULLIVAN WITH JOE COX

Foreword by Tom Leach
Afterword by Billy Reed

UNIVERSITY PRESS OF KENTUCKY

Scholarly publisher for the Commonwealth,
serving Bellarmine University, Berea College, Centre College of Kentucky,
Eastern Kentucky University, The Filson Historical Society, Georgetown
College, Kentucky Historical Society, Kentucky State University, Morehead
State University, Murray State University, Northern Kentucky University,
Transylvania University, University of Kentucky, University of Louisville,
and Western Kentucky University.

Editorial and Sales Offices: The University Press of Kentucky
663 South Limestone Street, Lexington, Kentucky 40508-4008
www.kentuckypress.com

Frontispiece: Nineteen-year-old Claude at the mic for WAVE, Louisville, 1944.
Courtesy of WAVE Radio.

Photo opposite: Claude and Alyce at the mic. Courtesy of WVLK Radio.

Cataloging-in-Publication data is available from the Library of Congress.

ISBN 978-0-8131-4703-1 (hardcover : alk. paper)
ISBN 978-0-8131-4704-8 (epub)
ISBN 978-0-8131-4705-5 (pdf)

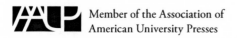

To Alyce and Claude Sullivan,
parents who were a dynamic team
and set an example for establishing
and balancing their family
and professional lives

Contents

Foreword

John Calipari refers to University of Kentucky basketball as the "gold standard" in the game. That phrase also applies to legendary voices such as Claude Sullivan, who brought the Wildcats' games into the homes of the Big Blue Nation via the radio airwaves.

Cancer claimed Claude in the prime of his career at the age of forty-two in 1967. I was six years old, so I don't remember listening to his calls of the Kentucky games. However, I was given a 1970 vinyl album called *Great Moments in Kentucky Basketball,* and it included audio clips of famous plays from the past. One that stuck out for me was the call of Vernon Hatton's unforgettable thirty-five-footer to tie Temple in a game at UK's Memorial Coliseum in the 1958 season. In the clip was a voice I had not heard before, and the call was as precise and descriptive as it was passionate. It was Claude Sullivan's voice.

When I was hired to announce the UK football games in 1997 and the basketball games later, legendary sports industry leader Jim Host was the decision maker because Host Communications held the broadcast rights. And one piece of advice Jim gave me was to go find some tapes of Claude Sullivan calling games and listen closely to his style. One item I still keep today in my football game-day package of broadcast notes is Jim telling me how one of Claude's greatest strengths was how he would set up the field for the listener like a chessboard, explaining how one move might impact another, such as a cornerback coming up to play tight on a wide receiver. During my first year as the play-by-play man for the UK radio network, I was able to secure a tape of one of Claude's broadcasts of a Kentucky–Tennessee football game from his son Alan. Once I listened to it, I became more keenly aware of what Host and others had told me about the quality of Claude's work. And I have always heard that the reason UK did not choose a single "voice of the Wildcats" until 1968 was that nobody wanted to pick between Claude Sullivan and Cawood Ledford.

There's a difference between a worker and a craftsman in any field, and Sullivan was an artist who painted with words. Obviously, there was an innate talent there, but those who knew him and worked with him will tell you that a key to the quality of his radio calls was his work ethic—the preparation of statistics, practice observations, and conversations with coaches that enabled him to add context to the description of the game action as it was unfolding before him. A radio call of a live sporting event usually involves two or more hours of unscripted words, but broadcasters such as Sullivan could seamlessly move from play to play as if they had written it out in advance, all the while painting the word pictures of the environment in which the game was playing out.

A few years before his death, Sullivan had been hired to call games for the Cincinnati Reds in addition to his UK duties. It was a tribute to Claude's versatility, in the mold of an announcer like Kentucky-native Tom Hammond of NBC in this era. We hear of "coaching trees" in sports, when the assistants of a certain head coach leave to launch their own successful careers. Sullivan had his own "broadcasting tree," with many successful Kentucky announcers tracing their success back to the seed of inspiration provided by Sullivan's work.

When speaking to groups of Big Blue fans, I always say that the Wildcats are our state's greatest common denominator. UK sports is the one topic almost any person of any background can use to find common ground for a conversation with anyone else in any city in our state. The quality of the broadcasts by early announcers such as Claude Sullivan served to enhance the Big Blue Nation's intense allegiance to the Cats at a time when few, if any, games were televised.

I have always said that I had the best training any young broadcaster could hope to have by being fortunate enough to grow up in central Kentucky. That's because of the quality of announcers I heard calling the action of the teams I followed, the Wildcats and the Reds. The same goes for an earlier time when young announcers here grew up listening to Claude Sullivan's calls.

Tom Leach

Introduction

Memories . . . and the Wheel

It was a warm September evening across the rolling pastures of Kentucky's bluegrass region. In Commonwealth Stadium in Lexington, Kentucky, more than 60,000 fans had gathered on a pleasant Saturday evening to cheer on a scrappy University of Kentucky (UK) Wildcat football squad, which was in the process of defeating Ole Miss en route to a 2006 season culminating in the team's first bowl victory in twenty-two years. Those fans had also gathered to honor six new members of the UK Athletics Hall of Fame.

At halftime, the selected inductees, along with family members, journeyed onto the beautifully manicured field and stood as public-address announcer Carl Nathe read through a brief summary of each honoree's accomplishments and the crowd welcomed the group into Wildcat immortality.

Among the six members of the 2006 class, the second Hall of Fame class in UK history, was Claude Sullivan. The most important people in Claude Sullivan's life—his sons, David and Alan, flanking the love of his life, Alyce—walked across the lush grass, smiled, and waved to the crowd in recognition of the applause that greeted them. Announcer Nathe summarized a career that included broadcasting

1

UK Athletics Hall of Fame induction ceremony, Commonwealth Stadium, 2006: David, Alan, and Alyce Sullivan. Courtesy UK Public Relations.

four Wildcat National Collegiate Athletic Association (NCAA) basketball championships, announcing many of the greatest moments in Wildcat football history, covering four seasons of Cincinnati Reds baseball, and winning the Kentucky Sportscaster of the Year award for eight years running over friendly competitor Cawood Ledford. On this occasion, Claude was joining not only his perceived rival Ledford in the Hall of Fame, but also close personal friends such as Wallace "Wah Wah" Jones, Paul "Bear" Bryant, and Adolph Rupp. The only person missing on this lovely late-summer evening was the subject of the honor himself—tragically now gone for almost four decades.

Some of the younger fans in the stadium that night wondered, "Who's Claude Sullivan?" Although the honors that surrounded Sullivan are astounding in length and breadth on the printed page, they cannot fully convey the significance or excellence of his career. The timing of that relatively brief career was significant—Sullivan found himself at a very young age broadcasting some of the greatest and most meaningful moments in Wildcat history. Alongside his four NCAA Championship broadcasts, he covered two other basketball squads that were as interesting and memorable as the title squads. He covered four Wildcat bowl squads, including the best team in the history of the program, and broadcast what may forever remain the greatest game in Wildcat football's century-plus history. Sullivan broadcast baseball at the time when it was essentially beyond challenge as the nation's greatest athletic pastime. He covered baseball players whose names resound as giants today—Aaron, Mays, Clemente, Musial, and Rose, among many others. There were also surprises—or accomplishments that only those well versed in radio history or inside Claude's closest circle of family and friends might know. But all of these accomplishments merely skim the surface.

Fellow UK broadcaster Ralph Hacker appreciated the hidden

depth behind Claude's accomplishments. When Sullivan's career was near its unexpected end, Hacker was just getting started as a young announcer. Hacker's career later included broadcasting two Wildcat NCAA titles and many seasons of football. However, neither the passing of years nor the ascendency of his own broadcasting star dulled Hacker's enthusiasm for his mentor.

Hacker recalled Sullivan in these words:

> Claude Sullivan was a radio play-by-play man, one who described the action in such vivid detail that you could feel the bitter bite of the cold winter wind during a football game, you could smell the popcorn in the stands . . . you could feel the "hit" of each play. His emotions were that of a fan, his reporting of every game . . . professional. Before the terms coined by Jim McKay, through the words that Claude Sullivan used, he let the fans feel the "joy of victory and the agony of defeat." He was for many . . . *the voice.*

However, when asked how Sullivan most impacted his own life, Hacker recollected a single specific incident—one he recalls in speaking engagements across the state and the nation—and words that Sullivan shared with him and that he has shared with multiple generations of announcers and fans.

The incident Hacker recalls occurred sometime in 1967. Cancer was ravaging Claude Sullivan's body, and although the public knew little of the extent of that battle, it is safe to say that Claude was very aware of his own mortality—if not aware of exactly how short his remaining life would be.

"He was very ill, and we were sitting in the back of a room at the Phoenix Hotel at one of Mr. Kincaid's banking seminar groups that he put on, and Claude asked me to sit with him," Hacker remembers. "He turned to me, having difficulty speaking, and he said, 'May I give you some advice?' And I said, 'I would love it from you.'"

As a young broadcaster, Hacker was probably not routinely offered the counsel of an established colleague who had been named Kentucky Sportscaster of the Year eight consecutive times. His interest definitely awakened, Hacker focused in tightly on what Sullivan told him next.

> Claude gave me this piece of advice I'll never forget . . . what you have to do in order to survive is you have a hub. Claude went on to describe that [on the] hub will be [sales at] WVLK. . . . That's one spoke, and then you do some programming at WVLK, that's another spoke. You're doing ball games at WVLK, that's another spoke, and then [you] go on and do regional television. Claude described building yourself a wheel by adding spokes to the hub, and if any of those spokes breaks, the wheel will continue to roll until you can get another spoke to replace it.

Years after that meeting, Hacker contemplated those words again. He admitted that "nearly everything I've done in life professionally came from that one conversation with Claude Sullivan." Every time another opportunity came his way, Hacker explained, he would add a spoke to his professional wheel. "I've never spoken to a group of young people," he confessed, "that I haven't given them that advice and told them where it came from."

Building a wheel was not just an isolated piece of advice that Claude Sullivan shared with young Ralph Hacker on that afternoon in 1967. It was a personal philosophy that enabled a meteoric rise and an amazingly full, if agonizingly brief, life. The idea of the wheel appears to have sprung from a childhood tragedy that caused young

Claude to reevaluate his life and for a time threatened to end that life before he had ever picked up a microphone.

From that initial battle, Claude Sullivan learned of life's duality—of the great achievements and beautiful moments that are possible, but also of the unpredictable and at times even cruel nature of fate or circumstance, which can topple ambitions, rearrange plans, and ultimately leave any person without time before expected. In forty-two years of life, Claude Sullivan reached personal and professional highs that defy the imagination. He also scratched, suffered, and worked relentlessly. From the chaos of life, Claude would impose order. He would build a wheel. And what a wheel it would be.

A loving and supportive family—first the one into which he was born and later the one that he would establish with his beloved wife, Alyce, and their sons, David and Alan—always functioned as the hub of the wheel. Next came the broadcasting. Sports was always a central part of Claude Sullivan's life, and that interest manifested itself in years at the top of collegiate sports, horse racing, and Major League Baseball broadcasting. Spokes were added, and spokes were taken out. Claude would add where he could and survive losses where he could not or where one activity subsumed another. But there was always more. Broadcasting innovations, production improvements, and network formation again placed Claude ahead of his time and showed the man behind the accomplishments—always looking for more and better ways to impose his ambition on his world. This is not to say that Claude Sullivan was single-minded. His quick and easy friendship and the deep and abiding love he shared with his family speak otherwise. For that matter, his adventures in international travel and even dalliance with something like espionage will amaze even many who knew him well.

The wheel was always in motion—always rolling on, with newer and stronger spokes, and carrying Claude Sullivan to places that he could hardly have dreamed of. It is no mistake that Ralph Hacker recalls Claude saying that "what you have to do to survive" is build that wheel. Perhaps the strongest testimony to the wheel of Claude Sullivan's life is that it still spins in the decades that Claude has been gone.

What Claude experienced as life is now, for the most part, history. Step back into that history and get to know Claude Sullivan—the man, the father, the businessman, the friend, the broadcasting legend. Watch the wheel be built and strengthened, the spokes added and multiplied. Marvel at a great life. For those who are too young to have witnessed those glory days, let Claude transport you once again to the best seat in the house. And watch the wheel continue to roll.

1

Building a Life

Claude Howard Sullivan announced his own entry to the world four days after Christmas of 1924. He was born in Winchester, Kentucky, the first child of Claude Ishmael and Ethel Mae Sullivan. As a child of the Great Depression, Claude Sullivan lacked extensive luxury in his young life. He shared the top half of a duplex with his parents, his younger brother, Charles "Buddy" Sullivan, and his German shepherd dog. The bottom half of the duplex was occupied by Claude's maternal grandmother and his uncle.

The wheel seems to have always been a central motif in Claude Sullivan's life. The first wheels he knew were probably those of the Texaco truck that Claude Ishmael drove. Relatives recall the elder Sullivan as a man who always had a twinkle in his eye and enjoyed spending time with young Claude. Indeed, family was always very important to Claude. Brother Buddy Sullivan was mentally disabled and in a less informed and forgiving society was essentially a secret known only to those closest to the Sullivan family. Claude learned from an early age to be patient with his brother, and an affection developed between them that extended for many years as Buddy constantly listened to Claude's later broadcasts on their grandmother's old Crosley radio set.

As an active and imaginative young boy, Claude had a happy childhood for the most part. His family doted on him, and he was eager to please. However, even in the most normal phase of his life, there could be little doubt that Claude was different from those around him. This difference manifested itself even in his physical appearance, as the black-haired little boy would fix a gaze on adults with his one gray eye and one green eye. It could be a bit unnerving, but the ultimate effect was a physical reminder that Claude Sullivan saw the world differently than everyone else. How appropriate, then, that he spent most of his adult life sharing exactly what he saw.

In many respects, young Claude was very much a product of his time and place. Winchester was a rural town of around 8,000, and Claude spent much of his childhood outdoors. He and his father hunted and fished whenever they could, often hiding the fishing from Ethel Mae, who was horrified of water. Claude Ishmael spent hours meticulously hand carving wooden bass fishing lures, and his son used those same lures for decades.

At the same time, although Claude's youth seems pastoral and quaint, he did come of age in a time when the automobile was flourishing—as were America's other pastimes. It was not unusual for Claude Ishmael to take young Claude on a day trip in the Texaco truck and stop off in a roadside bar for a beer. Again, Ethel Mae was generally kept in the dark as much as possible, but there is no doubt that the camaraderie of the adult crowd impacted young Claude. With the recent and exponential growth of mass media, sports became a common language that every truck driver and day laborer knew and shared. It is almost certain, Kentucky being a basketball haven, that many of those bar conversations Claude listened to centered around Coach Adolph Rupp, the new coach of the UK

Wildcat basketball squad. Although Claude had no way of knowing it then, Rupp would be a central figure in his life.

Claude grew to become an exceptional young man. He was active at Winchester High School, where his achievements included being voted senior class president, serving as captain of the football, basketball, and debate teams, and being a member of the drama club and the Rotes Club (student version of Rotary). According to family friend and prominent Lexington banker J. D. Reeves, he and Claude were members of the "Georgia Street Gang" back in Winchester in a more innocent age when a gang was merely a group of indefatigably active teenagers.

As with many Kentuckians of his age, Claude's first great love was basketball, and it was the center of his plans. Young Claude planned to play well enough at Winchester High to win a scholarship from one of Kentucky's major universities, perhaps even a roster spot on Coach Rupp's Kentucky Wildcats. In a pre–National Basketball Association (NBA) world, Claude planned not only to star in college basketball, but to become a physician. Unlike many young dreamers, he was skilled enough on the hardwood and in the classroom that his dreams were moving toward becoming viable realities.

All of that changed early in his sophomore year in 1939, when his team traveled to nearby Mt. Sterling, Kentucky, for a game with archrival Mt. Sterling High. During the week before the game, Claude had developed an infection or boil on his elbow but attempted to play through what seemed to be a relatively minor ailment. During the Mt. Sterling game, he took off ahead of the field for an open layup. As he jumped, a Mt. Sterling defender suddenly appeared from behind and forced Claude into the concrete block wall behind the goal. There was no padding on the wall, and he took a direct hit to his infected elbow. Claude fell violently to the hardwood floor, rolling in pain as the boil ruptured from the impact of his fall. Although he was in great discomfort, he came back to finish the game and was taken to Clark County Hospital for treatment when the team returned home.

It did not take long for complications to arise. Claude developed a high fever, and the infection in his elbow grew considerably worse. In an era before penicillin was commonly available, treatment of serious infection was still remarkably primitive. The infection moved quickly into Claude's left leg and knee. Two Lexington specialists, Dr. Scobbee and Dr. Williams, eventually assessed Claude as having osteomyelitis, a serious bone infection. The same condition would nearly cripple Mickey Mantle a decade later before penicillin, by then available at the largest and best hospitals, saved Mantle's career.

Claude was not as fortunate. Dr. Scobbee and Dr. Williams advised Ethel Sullivan that they had to perform surgery to remove infected areas of his left knee in an attempt to stall the disease and keep the infection from spreading. Claude's condition could become life threatening if the infection progressed, and possible amputation of the left leg was discussed. For Claude, everything he had worked for was crashing down. His health was failing, and he was too ill even to attend school, much less play basketball.

For the bright boy, two rounds of questions piled up on each other. The first was purely medical: Would he survive? Would he lose a leg? The second round of questions, although less immediately critical, undoubtedly wound around and around young Claude's mind: What would he become? If he couldn't be a basketball star, what would he be? How could he become a doctor when he was missing school and would do so for the foreseeable future? In his sickbed, Claude Sullivan pondered the question the great poet Langston Hughes would ask later—"What happens to a dream deferred?"

After Claude's surgery, his mother and grandmother homeschooled him for the remainder of his junior year of high school. Even if he healed enough to be allowed to return to school, he would remain under strict doctors' orders to avoid unnecessary exertion or activity. For the skilled athlete and school leader, this was bitter medicine indeed. Finally, Ethel Sullivan decided that it wouldn't hurt to let Claude attend a Winchester High basketball game. The emotional reunion boosted Claude's spirits and provided dividends that no one could have imagined.

In the crowded gymnasium, Claude, fresh off of greeting his former teammates and his friends, had trouble finding a seat. Someone noticed that the public-address announcer's usual spot was vacant and suggested that Claude fill in the role. Armed with ample knowledge of Winchester's squad and after a bit of preparation, Claude Sullivan began his career behind a microphone, this time as a public-address announcer. Relying on his background in debate and public speaking, young Claude was an instant success. Any nervousness melted away in pure enjoyment. Perhaps the most memorable moment of the night came when he ad-libbed an instant commercial for one of the team's sponsors—a funeral home—and then had a good laugh at the apparent commentary implicit in the announcement's coming immediately after a minor injury to a player had stopped the game.

Winchester High officials were thrilled. They begged Ethel Sullivan to allow Claude to become the regular public-address announcer. Although Ethel had a mother's protective reticence to contravene doctor's orders, she could not deny that Claude's new job had improved his spirits and restored his excitement about his future. Claude Sullivan's path as a superstar athlete had suddenly ended, but a new way was beginning to reveal itself.

Perhaps consciously and perhaps not, as young Claude reflected on the whirlwind of recent events, he realized that his old dreams of athletic stardom and medical education had been dangerously narrow. He had left no room for the unpredictable nature of human experience. For a child of the Depression, it was hardly news that adversity, whatever its shape and nature, unavoidably fell into every life. When it did, from here out Claude Sullivan would be ready. He would build his wheel—and the evening that his mother took him back to Winchester High's gymnasium he found the first spoke of that wheel behind a microphone.

Although high school basketball public-address announcing was a fine start, Claude quickly saw the bigger and better possibilities of life behind a microphone. Due to the extensive schoolwork he had completed during his recovery time from surgery, he graduated high school at the age of sixteen in the fall of 1941, six months ahead of his classmates. Almost immediately he sought out work as a radio broadcaster.

A sixteen-year-old Claude Sullivan badgered the manager of WCMI until he convinced the manager to hire him as its chief radio announcer, even at the less than princely salary of $12 per week. It was clearly the chance to gain experience, not money, that attracted Claude to WCMI. In later years, he would tell his family, "The pay was not great, but neither was I."

Claude's career was about to take off, however, due in part to events far beyond his control. Shortly after Claude graduated from Winchester High, the Japanese attacked Pearl Harbor, and the United States was drawn into World War II. As the war quickly escalated, a large pool of possible radio announcers either chose to join the armed services or were drafted into service.

For Claude, who had long since learned to compensate in daily life for the extensive surgeries that had left one leg forever shorter than the other and somehow avoided a tell-tale limp, there was no question of ability to serve in the war. He could not pass a military physical or obtain a medical release. He was clearly frustrated by being unable to serve his country, lobbying unsuccessfully for even a military desk job. However, it simply was not to be.

Being unable to serve in the military, however, meant that he was able to pursue gainful employment with larger radio stations. Claude quickly fixed his attention on WAVE in Louisville. He applied for a position as a morning news show host and assistant announcer to Don Hill in covering Louisville's minor league baseball franchise, the Colonels.

Ironically, WAVE did not consider Claude initially because its manager feared that he would be drafted. Although Claude knew he could not get into the military, he decided to inquire about his draft status and to his surprise found that he had somehow been placed on the "deceased" list. The error was corrected, and Claude awaited a possible call for service, but by this time WAVE no longer bothered to await military clearance prior to considering Claude (subsequently, Claude's status was classified as 4F, unfit for service). Although the war was still prominent in Claude's life, as it was for any other American of the era, it no longer held him back from starting his professional journey.

On May 3, 1944, in his most dramatic tones, from the WAVE offices, nineteen-year-old Claude Sullivan shared this news story:

> There was not a cloud in the skies over North Burma and that was bad . . . but the Japs liked to catch unarmed transport planes like ours, over the hump between China and India. . . . The radio operator had just informed us that four "zeros" were somewhere in the neighborhood. . . . Teetering on a board on a ration box, I thrust my head up into the glass bulge on top of the C-47 staring into the dazzling blue. . . . If we spotted the "zeros" first, we had a chance. . . . The pilot, Lt. George Hanna of Louisville, had slipped the camouflaged plane down low into the valley and tried to sneak away. . . . But if they saw us first, and came out of the sun, well, most likely another plane

number would be rubbed off the black board at the base in San India. And the boys that would fly over the hump would say, that would lead to the casual tone I had heard so many times, "Hanna got his today."

No, Claude had not ended up at the great war's front. And his careful delivery was not being broadcast to an audience of thousands hanging on his every word. Instead, he was reading copy from a recent *Reader's Digest* magazine as he auditioned for the announcing position at WAVE in Louisville. The recording was a particular favorite of Claude's, and he hung on to it and soon utilized the same recording to apply for national broadcasting positions at major markets, including at least one job in New York City. But in May 1944, once the WAVE hiring personnel heard Claude's recording, they were pleased and interested, and Claude was hired immediately. For a nineteen-year-old from a small town, Louisville would represent a definite adjustment. With its metro area boasting more than 300,000 in population in the 1940 census, it was a big-league town, figuratively if not literally. Living and working there would bring many changes to Claude Sullivan's life—including one change more notable than all the rest.

Claude had been at WAVE for only a matter of months when he went on a blind date arranged by a friend with twenty-one-year-old Alyce Lee Grubbs. Not unlike the instant attraction of announcing, Claude knew right away that he had met his match in Alyce. Although she was beautiful and in all regards ladylike, Alyce was no stranger to sports because she had grown up with three brothers and was the daughter of a former semipro baseball player. As the couple's first date wound on and as Claude basked in the glow of instant connection with Alyce, he knew what he had to do. Returning Alyce to her home at the end of the date, he assuredly, if abruptly, told her,

WAVE softball game with Claude (*left*) at third base in leg brace, July 30, 1944. Courtesy of WAVE Radio.

"You know, I'm going to marry you." Half surprised and half flirting, Alyce asked, "What makes you so sure?" Similarly half serious and half jocose, Claude replied, "Because I want to, and I always get what I want."

Some small matters, such as the two-year age gap between the couple, would have to be addressed. Claude took to wearing fake eyeglasses as he tried to stretch his nineteen years to twenty-one, like Alyce's. He even penciled in an earlier birth date on his résumé. Whatever tricks it took, Claude perfected them quickly. In only three months after that first date, he and Alyce were engaged. As the couple grew more comfortable, Claude worried less about surface details and shared his life completely with Alyce. One family photograph showed Alyce looking on as Claude played third base on a WAVE softball team, complete with a leg brace on his maladjusted left leg.

On November 25, 1944, Claude and Alyce united in marriage at the Bear Grass Christian Church in Louisville. In Alyce, Claude had reshaped the hub at the center of his career wheel and his life. She would be his wife for the remainder of his life, his most ardent supporter, his partner, and the mother of their two sons. Even more than that day in the winter of 1940 when he discovered announc-

WAVE baseball, with Alyce *(third from left)* cheering, July 30, 1944.
Courtesy of WAVE Radio.

ing, the date of his wedding would define Claude Sullivan's life and
career. Although he always loved his parents, brother, and extended
family, the hub at the center of his life would now be Alyce and the
family they would create. In newlywed bliss, the Sullivans began
Claude's assent up the broadcasting ladder.

Just as Claude's career was taking shape at WAVE in Louisville,
sixty miles to the southeast in Lexington Adolph Rupp was forming
the UK basketball program into one of the nation's finest. Claude

Claude wearing fake glasses to make him look older for Alyce, who was two years his senior. Courtesy of WAVE Radio.

was destined to make his broadcasting mark covering that program, but he and Alyce would have to take a circuitous route in making that transition.

Claude hoped for a more direct path to becoming a nationally renowned announcer and so made contact with Pat Kelly at NBC in

New York. Kelly could not offer Claude a job because he was holding large numbers of positions for returning service members, but he did encourage Claude to come to New York to see what he could pick up. For a young man who had never been on an airplane and who drove the roads in the era before interstate highways were very common, the journey was almost beyond comprehension—as was the Big Apple, the ultimate broadcasting jewel of the national market. His drive to move ahead was bigger than the barriers of fear and difficulty, and Claude determined he would make the trip.

Claude made the journey to New York, visiting Kelly at Radio City Music Hall. Kelly's position on giving Claude a job was unchanged. He simply had no jobs to offer because all positions were being held for the returning servicemen. He recommended that Claude attempt to gain a position in one of the other large markets, such as Pittsburgh, Chicago, Cleveland, Denver, or Washington. He further recommended that Claude work under a "constructively critical program manager" for a couple of years and smooth out his voice. Although Claude was disappointed in not obtaining a national position, he enjoyed seeing Radio City Music Hall, observing a few NBC programs in production, and obtaining all the information he could about announcing and production in the Big Apple. His curiosity was piqued by the mass of different cultures he encountered as well as by the first-rate facilities and performances he had witnessed at Radio City.

By the time Claude returned to Louisville, he realized that he had been a big fish in a small pond—that he remained a young broadcaster and needed experience in order to meet his career goals. He returned from New York even more focused and determined to learn as much as he could as quickly as he could. In fact, to that end he corresponded with Pat Kelly over the next year, continuing to stay in close contact in case a position in the American cultural capital suddenly came open. Although no such position materialized, Kelly

A radio drama from WAVE with *(left to right)* Marjorie Plank, Jack Bendt, and Claude, 1944. Courtesy of WAVE Radio.

and NBC had made a national position something tangible and real to Claude, and that reality would drive him harder toward his ultimate professional goal. And he soon found that he could satisfy both his professional drive and his personal life by staying closer to home.

In the meanwhile, back in Louisville, Claude's role at WAVE gave him experience in many aspects of radio, including programming and network news. Claude called Louisville Colonels baseball games but also worked on radio dramas such as *The Man in the Balcony*. However, the pay was often substantially less than the workload, and in November 1945 the Sullivans planned a move to Knoxville, Tennessee, where Claude received a raise to $50 per week from station KNOX and was allowed to work overtime for pay and to take on additional responsibilities with some of the new shows.

Claude at WMIX in Mt. Vernon, Illinois, 1946. Courtesy of WMIX Radio.

Claude saw KNOX, pay raise aside, as a stepping stone toward either station ownership or a network position in a much larger market. By mid-1946, he felt that neither possibility was strong and so moved along to WMIX in Mt. Vernon, Illinois, near St. Louis. WMIX ultimately proved to be something short of the opportunity

Claude at WKLX in Lexington, Kentucky, about 1947. Courtesy of WVLK Radio.

Claude had in mind. He had numerous discussions with East Liverpool Broadcasting of Ohio about a new station in Pittsburgh, which would both employ him and give him a share of ownership. However, with all of the Federal Communications Commission red tape, the establishment of the new station was not moving quickly.

Due to the era's open-door policies, Claude often managed to moonlight play by play for an additional station or two while still maintaining his principal employment at another station. After he passed on the Pittsburgh possibility, he and Alyce, by now doubtlessly rather road weary, moved on to WZIP in Covington, Kentucky. Claude was hired as the commercial manager of WZIP, but it appears that he may have doubled up between WZIP and WKLX in Lexington throughout 1946–1947. He began working full-time on UK basketball and football for Ted Grizzard at WKLX.

As Claude's career moved on, by 1948 he ended up broadcasting solely for WKLX in Lexington. Much of the attraction to WKLX was due to the presence of Ted Grizzard. Grizzard had come to the station from Nashville and sported a résumé that included being a featured performer on dramatic radio shows and time spent as a professional musician. He was a talent scout and manager at WKLX, and he had been familiar with Claude since his days back at WAVE. Grizzard recognized Claude's talent and desire to succeed. Given Grizzard's experience in radio, the two became fast friends. Ted Grizzard became the "critically constructive program manager" that Pat Kelly at NBC had mentioned to Claude, and the friendship that would develop between them lasted for the rest of Claude's life.

Through his work at WZIP and WKLX, Claude became fully versed in broadcasting high school basketball. The late 1940s was a golden era of Kentucky high school basketball, a time when the small, rural Kentucky schools specialized in acting as giant killers in the state tournament. Claude was front and center at several of the more memorable games.

He was behind a microphone for WKLX at the Jefferson County Armory in Louisville for the 1947 Kentucky state tournament, which Maysville won. He returned the next year when Carr Creek's little-engine-that-could chugged its way through to the

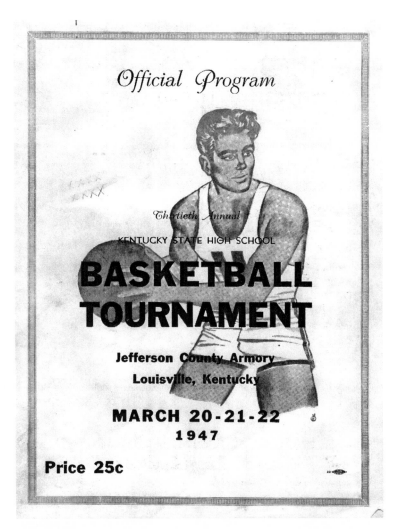

Official Program

Thirtieth Annual
KENTUCKY STATE HIGH SCHOOL

BASKETBALL
TOURNAMENT

Jefferson County Armory
Louisville, Kentucky

MARCH 20-21-22
1947

Price 25c

Kentucky High School Athletic Association state high school basketball
tournament program, Claude's first high school state tournament, at the
Jefferson County Armory in Louisville, Kentucky. From the Claude Sullivan
Collection.

semifinals of the tournament, losing to Maysville. Carr Creek's path ran through Covington Holmes High, and Claude called that game on WZIP, the Covington station. That local broadcast is the oldest-surviving complete game in the extensive archives of Claude's work. At just twenty-two years old when he called his first state tournament, he was barely older than some of the players in those games. A native Kentuckian through and through, Claude loved the tournament and returned for twenty-nine consecutive years, broadcasting all but a few of the sixteen games when there was a UK NCAA tournament or until his health would no longer allow.

Whenever the circumstances allowed, even within the regular season, Claude revisited the high school game. Not only was high school basketball where his career behind a microphone had begun, but it enabled him to stay close to his Winchester roots. A particular thrill came in 1951 when Clark County High, Claude's hometown school (he had gone to Winchester High, which merged with Clark County High in 1963 to become George Rogers Clark High), defeated Cuba High in the first state tournament held in Memorial Coliseum to bring home the state title to Clark County. Although Claude sought more prestigious spokes to add to the wheel of his career, he never forgot where he came from, figuratively or literally.

High school basketball held obvious charms for Claude, but the biggest stage in Kentucky sports had become UK basketball. In fact, so high was the demand for radio coverage of Kentucky basketball that even before Claude had set foot in Alumni Gym, UK's home court at the time, he had utilized the technology of the day to broadcast UK games in absentia.

Claude's first UK basketball broadcast was on New Year's Day in 1945, just three days after he turned twenty, when the Wildcats took on Long Island University in the venerable palace of big-city basketball, New York's Madison Square Garden. While the Wildcats were in New York, though, Claude was hundreds of miles away, sitting in a Western Union telegraph office back in Kentucky. He received a telegraphed play-by-play feed from Madison Square Garden, and, utilizing only that minimal account and a rich imagination, he described the action in vivid detail to his listeners.

The pitfalls of this method of broadcast were numerous. Telegraph operators who were not seasoned basketball fans could misstate pivotal information or simply provide untimely silence. Sometimes technical breakdowns could complicate the process. Future US president Ronald Reagan called Chicago Cubs baseball games via this method while he worked as a Des Moines, Iowa, broadcaster and often recalled for comic effect the day when the telegraph wire broke down in midgame and left him depicting foul ball after foul ball after foul ball until communication was restored, somewhere around more than a dozen imaginary foul balls later. Despite the difficulties inherent in the medium, Claude was excited to have the opportunity to cover Adolph Rupp's Wildcats. They won the first game of UK basketball that he broadcast, 62–52, with freshman Alex Groza pacing the Cats with 25 points. Claude later covered Groza's career in great detail over the next few years.

University of Kentucky sports were to become the next spoke in the wheel of young Claude Sullivan's career. And what a spoke they would be! Claude could scarcely have chosen a better time to set up shop in Lexington. Adolph Rupp had been in town since 1930 and was rapidly making Kentucky synonymous with college basketball excellence. Before Rupp, Kentucky basketball, although garnering minor success, was not particularly notable. Rupp's predecessor, John Mauer, had directed a slow, patterned offense that had made for plodding, dull basketball. But the Baron of the Bluegrass implemented a run-and-gun, aggressive, fast-breaking style of play that not only won games but put rear ends in seats—and around radios.

Claude (*center*), J. B. Faulconer of WLAP (*right*), and Phil Sutterfield of WHAS fishing at the reservoir in Lexington, mid-1950s. From the Claude Sullivan Collection.

In 1947, when Claude first garnered a full-time assignment covering Wildcats basketball, there was no single "Voice of the Wildcats." Rather than a single aligned network holding the rights to cover the games, in that time each individual radio station that wished to cover the Wildcats was given permission to do so as long as it complied with certain minimal requirements. It was not unusual for half-a-dozen central Kentucky radio stations to broadcast a UK home game. Claude, at the ripe age of twenty-two, joined a corps of experienced announcers such as Phil Sutterfield and J. B. Faulconer, who broadcasted games on Lexington's WLAP. Cawood Ledford, who was later dubbed the "Voice of the Wildcats," had not yet joined the competing squad of broadcasters. Given the number and high quality of competitors, Claude had entered a challenging situation, but he remained determined to prove his mettle. As he had told Alyce on their first date, he always got what he wanted.

Even the excited Claude or a less ebullient but equally focused Adolph Rupp could not be aware of quite what a run of basketball excellence the two were about to witness. In the mid-1940s, Rupp had attracted perhaps the greatest recruiting class college basketball had yet seen. Ralph Beard of Louisville Male High and Wallace "Wah Wah" Jones of Harlan, Kentucky, were two of the finest athletes Kentucky would ever see. Talented post player Alex Groza joined them. Shut out by additional veterans Cliff Barker and Kenny Rollins, eager newcomers to the program such as Joe B. Hall and C. M. Newton wound up as benchwarmers.

Only the more astute fans and followers realized that Claude was also coming into his position in time to catch yet another golden era. University of Kentucky football had floundered in relative mediocrity for years, with coach A. D. Kirwan compiling an up-and-down record of slightly above or below a .500 season. In 1946, athletic director and head football coach Bernie Shively, looking to hire the Wildcats' next coach, took a chance and hired an outsider—Paul "Bear" Bryant, a thirty-two-year-old Alabama alumnus with exactly one year of head-coaching experience. Kentucky basketball manager Humzey Yessin recalled his memories of the breaking news in a recent interview. "We [the basketball team] were on a road trip, and we had just gotten back," Humzey said. "Somebody got a newspaper for Coach Rupp, and they said, 'Bear Bryant has been hired as football coach.' And everybody says, 'Well, who in the hell is he?' They didn't know anything about him." Humzey, Adolph Rupp, and college football would learn who Bryant was soon enough.

Bryant posted a 7–3 mark in his UK debut in 1946. This was an encouraging sign, but the Wildcat football program had still never played in a single bowl game. However, change was in the air, and Claude Sullivan had positioned himself perfectly to be right in the middle of it. Here he was—younger than many of the players he

would cover, barely of legal age to vote or purchase an alcoholic bev-
erage, and living his dream—getting ready to bring every glorious
basket and touchdown into households in and around Kentucky.
It took a young man, a dreamer, a visionary even, to imagine what
would come next. And even then imagination could not match the
reality.

2

The Best of Times

Although broadcasting high school sports had been a pleasant and productive step in Claude Sullivan's career, his sights were set much higher when he was twenty-two. When he settled in at WKLX, Claude was given his next great opportunity—although few would have appreciated the magnitude of that opportunity. The next spoke in Claude's wheel was UK football. Then, as now, Southeastern Conference (SEC) football was some of the best in the nation. The name "Kentucky" did not yet put fear in the hearts of many foes at the time, but that began to change in 1946, when Bear Bryant came to town and led a 7–3 season.

In 1947, Claude was on board, covering Bryant's second UK squad over the entire season. In only his second year, Bryant was already something of a legend for his intensity, his superorganization, and the physical nature of his practices. But Bryant had to push his teams hard. Kentucky's negligible football tradition was obvious by so many measures. When Bryant was hired, UK had spent a total of two weeks in the Associated Press's (AP) top twenty-five poll—in the poll's history. The Wildcats were 0–14–1 against ranked opponents. Three more losses to ranked teams had followed in 1946, although they were Kentucky's only three losses.

Kentucky's football home was McLean Stadium at Stoll Field. McLean Stadium was a magnificent poured concrete structure with arches covered in ivy, towering above Euclid Avenue, providing a scenic backdrop on campus, and creating a classic venue for football. The stadium expanded in 1947 and 1948 and had two concrete sides, and during Claude's tenure bleachers added another 4,000 seats in the end zones between them. The field was the location of the first college football game in the South, played in 1880. Transylvania, then known as Kentucky University, defeated Centre by the unusual score of 13¾–0.

The first game Kentucky played at Stoll Field was versus Vanderbilt in 1916. During World War I, the area was utilized for military training rather than for football. McLean Stadium was built later in 1924, named for Price McLean, an engineering student who was fatally injured in a UK football game in 1923. The historic stadium also hosted the first SEC football game, played there in 1933, when Kentucky defeated Sewanee, 7–0.

The band's practice field and the university's botanical gardens ran along the west end of the stadium. After one particularly dull half, Bryant, instead of delivering a lecture, famously utilized the halftime break to have his team scrimmage each other on the band practice field. Alan Sullivan remembers the stories Claude told about Bryant as they sat in the booth on game day. Quarterback Vito "Babe" Parilli confirms the story by recollecting the lecture from their coach for playing too well. During a halftime 40-point lead against North Dakota State, Bryant took the starters out to the band field to scrimmage. The second string went out to play the second half and won 83–0. Parilli also confirmed that after the North Texas opening-game win, when the fans had left the stadium, the Bear had the team run wind sprints on the field.

Stoll Field press box showing the number of competing radio banners in the 1950s. Courtesy of the *Lexington Herald-Leader.*

Stoll Field's press box stood at the very top of one side of the stadium, a climb of more than thirty rows of seats. On game days, Claude ambled up the steps, heavy briefcase full of equipment in hand, in rain and shine and snow, to bring his audience the next chapter in Bryant's ongoing football saga.

In 1947, Claude witnessed Kentucky football history. Unimposing 1946 quarterback Phil Cutchin was replaced by a young man who went on to become a football legend—the great George Blanda. With Blanda under center and returning All-SEC end Wah Wah Jones (he would be called a wide receiver now), Kentucky was primed for a successful 1947 campaign. Bryant's hard-hitting defense also made Kentucky a force to be reckoned with.

Claude's first game as a full-time UK football announcer was a tough 14–7 loss at Ole Miss. From there, however, Bryant's Wildcats reeled off five straight victories, including three shutouts, highlighted by wins over a number 9 Georgia squad and a number 10

Vanderbilt team. One play that particularly impressed young Claude came courtesy of the Wildcats' Don "Dopey" Phelps, who followed up a three-and-out by UK's defense to begin the Georgia game by returning Georgia's first punt for a touchdown en route to the 26–0 shellacking. The play impressed Claude so much so that he remarked on Phelps's play two years later when broadcasting the 1949 Kentucky–Georgia matchup.

Although Kentucky did lose home games to Alabama and Tennessee, Claude broadcast a gallant Wildcat team posting another 7–3 mark. This time, on the strength of the two victories over ranked teams, Kentucky was given a bid in the Great Lakes Bowl in Cleveland, Ohio, against Villanova. The bowl berth was intended as a reward, but Kentucky's experience with the swirling winds off of Lake Cuyahoga in December was not very pleasant. Miserable weather led a crowd listed at 14,908 to show up for the one and only Great Lakes Bowl in Cleveland's cavernous Municipal Stadium. Blanda kicked the only field goal of his UK career, and after two rushing touchdowns and an interception return for a score, UK opened up a 24–0 lead, which they held for a 24–14 final. Although Claude was elated to cover a bowl-winning UK football team, it probably took him the majority of the winter to regain the feeling in all of his extremities. Fortunately, the first Wildcat basketball season for Claude was under way, and it was red hot. If Claude's good fortune at adding such a viable spoke as UK athletics to his professional wheel was difficult to believe, it hardly compared to the basketball season that was just starting up as football finished.

Adolph Rupp came to Kentucky in 1930, just three years after Lindberg's historic flight, and Rupp was just a year younger than Lindberg as Claude opened one of his broadcasts with his game setup. The squad Rupp unveiled in the fall of 1947 knew no equal—not only in Kentucky history, but in college basketball history. In the spring of 1946, Kentucky won the National Invitation Tournament (NIT), which was the school's first major championship. With the NCAA Tournament only six years old at the time, the NIT was the most prestigious title. Adolph had convinced freshman Ralph Beard, who had joined Wah Wah Jones as a football Cat before his shoulder injury sent him to Louisville briefly, to come back to UK to play basketball.

Ralph made the winning free throw to clinch the NIT. In early 1947, just before Claude became the full-time voice of the Cats, UK returned to the NIT finals but was upset by Utah in the title game, with Beard being held to just one point. Rupp advised a devastated Beard to work on his outside shot, which the great guard did to devastating effect. Claude noted the Utah loss in a pregame introduction in later years by stating, "Among those that witnessed that game, most still carry some deep feelings for the officiating," which was his subtle way of saying it was not up to par.

Beard, featured as a cover boy on the first issue of a national magazine called *Sports Illustrated* (not the same magazine as the one known by that title today), was already blessed with blinding speed, terrific ball-handling skills, and quick hands on the defensive end of the floor, creating numerous steals and fast breaks. Fellow junior Alex Groza was an effective post scorer and at six feet seven inches was a physical force to be reckoned with in this era. Baseball, football, and basketball star Wah Wah Jones could score when needed and was a rugged, if slightly undersized rebounder and generally a superb complementary player. Kenny Rollins and Cliff Barker made up the rest of the group that composed the "Fabulous Five." Rollins was the squad's defensive stopper, and Barker rivaled Beard in ball-handling skills and sharp passes.

Although Kentucky's roundball excellence was much the same then as it is now, many facets of it were quite different in the fall of 1947. Home games were played in cramped Alumni Gym, which seated about 2,400. Equipment manager Humzey Yessin remembers that student tickets were assigned on an alternating basis, with blocks of students getting tickets for either one half of the season or the other half. In later years, Alyce Sullivan recalled the raucous atmosphere of Alumni Gym. The facility was "very loud and confined," the noise even "deafening" at times. Alyce remembered getting to games early and sitting by broadcaster J. B. Faulconer on press row in order to manage to have a chair.

In an effort to share Kentucky basketball with those outside of the fortunate few who could fit in Alumni Gym, the team played three games in Louisville at the 6,000-plus-seat Jefferson County Armory during the 1947–1948 season. Humzey Yessin related that the team stayed at a nearby hotel and, in a precursor to UK football's modern "Cat Walk," walked to the armory from the hotel before the game, amidst much excitement and pomp from Wildcat backers. Kentucky played several games a year at "the Armory" and compiled a 61–11 record there.

Only eight teams were chosen for the NIT and the NCAA Tournament in 1948. Selections were purely a matter of invitation, and the only qualifications that mattered were those that the selection committee decided upon. The easiest path for the Fabulous Five was to leave no argument as to their excellence.

Kentucky lost once at Temple in December and once at Notre Dame in February. Otherwise, they won, and for the most part they steamrolled the opposition. Claude shared some absolute roundball demolition with his broadcast audience—for instance, before losing to Temple, UK began the season winning by 39, 39, 54, 49, 24, 36, and 42 points in the preceding games. Not only did the Wildcats have an undefeated SEC season, but they did not win by less than 10 points in any conference game.

Like Claude's first UK broadcast, the two biggest games of the season took place in New York's hallowed Madison Square Garden.

Of course, unlike the teletype rebroadcast in 1945, Claude was front and center for an NCAA semifinal matchup with Holy Cross and their star, the legendary Bob Cousy. Kenny Rollins and Dale Barnstable hounded Cousy relentlessly, holding him to 5 points, as Groza scored 23, Beard 13, and Jones 12 points for a 60–52 UK victory.

Three nights later, on March 23, 1948, Claude was at the microphone for UK's first NCAA Tournament title via a 58–42 win over an outmatched Baylor squad. Alex Groza was the tournament MVP, with 14 points to lead the Cats. The rookie announcer with the veteran team had witnessed possibly the greatest season in college basketball history. And what's more, the season was far from over.

The year 1948 was an Olympic year, and basketball was among the events taking place at the Games in London. Unlike in the modern Olympics, basketball at this time was still restricted to only amateur players, and as the current NCAA Tournament champions the Wildcats were placed in a tournament in Madison Square Garden to determine the team that would represent the United States in the summer Games. Kentucky was first matched up with the University of Louisville Cardinals, who had won the National Association of Intercollegiate Basketball (NAIB) Tournament Championship. Kentucky thrashed its intrastate rivals 91–57 and then matched up with the same Baylor team that it had defeated by 16 points for the NCAA crown only six days earlier. This time, UK bested Baylor by 18 points, 77–59. This set up a match with the Phillips Oilers for the tournament championship.

The Oilers were an Amateur Athletic Union (AAU) dynasty in an era when the AAU remained a viable alternative to the NBA. Phillips Oil sponsored the team, and players would choose to forego professional basketball to play on the Phillips team while working jobs within the Phillips Oil infrastructure. The best and most notable of the Oilers was Bob Kurland, who had starred at Oklahoma

A&M (now Oklahoma State), where he had helped win the 1945 and 1946 NCAA titles. Forward Vince Broyla, who had played at Notre Dame, was another standout on the team.

Several commentators have referred to the Olympic Trials Tournament final matchup between UK and Phillips Oil at Madison Square Garden as "the greatest game ever played," and Phillips edged the Wildcats 53–49. Kurland was the difference, posting 20 points and holding UK's Groza to a mere 4. Ralph Beard poured in 23 points for the Wildcats, who came up just short. In a compromise, five Oilers, five Wildcats, and a hodgepodge of other players were chosen for the Olympics. Phillips coach Omar Browning was the head coach, and Rupp would serve as the assistant. Indeed, in a recent interview, Wah Wah Jones recalls Rupp storming into the locker room after "the greatest game" and angrily thundering, "Well, you boys just made me the *assistant* coach of the Olympic team."

Claude was front and center for "the greatest game" as well as for a series of three subsequent exhibitions between Phillips and UK that were played a couple of weeks before the Olympics, primarily to raise money to send the team to England. The exhibitions were played in Tulsa, Kansas City, and Lexington on a temporary court placed down on Stoll Field. Kentucky managed to win the exhibition game in Kansas City but lost in Tulsa and the final tune-up in Lexington. UK team manager Humzey Yessin recalled how the temporary court came from the Louisville Armory and stretched between the 35-yard lines at Stoll Field. The game was played in front of a then full house estimated at 14,000 fans, which was the largest crowd to see a basketball game at the time.

Claude did not travel to London for the Olympics due to the trip's prohibitive cost—but also to a new addition in Kentucky. Alyce gave birth to their son David two months before the Olympics, and so the Sullivan family—now three in number—followed the Games from home in Kentucky.

Pre-Olympic exhibition game score card from 1948 game at Stoll Field. From the Claude Sullivan Collection.

Phillips "66" Oilers
VS.
University of Kentucky

Stoll Field

July 9, 1948
8:30 p. m.

PRICE
10c

Pre-Olympic exhibition game at Stoll Field, July 9, 1948. Kentucky and the Phillips Oilers played on a portable court from the Jefferson County Armory in Louisville. Kentucky lost the game to Phillips 56–50. From the Thoroughbred Press Fabulous Five Brochure, 1948.

Claude's family maintained a special position at the center of his life, and the joy and excitement of David's birth emphasized those critical bonds. David was born in Cincinnati, and while Claude was traveling back and forth from northern Kentucky to Lexington in those days, his love for and devotion to his new son and his wife were apparent. His relationship with Alyce and David, particularly in these busy days, sometimes lacked quantity in time together but was always of the highest quality. Whenever Claude was on the road for more than a few days, he wrote to Alyce, and many of those letters survive today, demonstrating an affection that transcended the miles between him and his family at any given time.

The birth of David drew notice within Claude's professional associates at UK, probably helped by a generous share of paternal bragging. Shortly after the birth, Adolph Rupp stopped by the Sullivans' apartment with a gift for the family—a child-size leather UK basketball, autographed by the coach himself. Fatherhood forever changed Claude's life—and he couldn't have been happier.

While domestic bliss reigned in the Sullivan household, over in London at the Olympic Games the Phillips and Kentucky contingents alternated playing time as units for team USA. With the exception of a close call in a two-point win over Argentina, they stormed through the Olympics. Back home in Kentucky, Claude made a tape recording of a BBC interview with Adolph Rupp after one of the games. Never at a loss for words, Rupp told the broadcaster, "I don't want the people back home to think we are over here on a picnic." The broadcaster countered by noting, "You have been winning by 30 points but say you're not playing well. . . . If you were flat-footed today, I would hate to see you when you are playing on your toes!" The US team was on its toes more often than not, winning the gold medal over France 65–21 in a game in which Alex Groza was the high scorer.

Even the normally impossible to please Rupp admitted to

Claude that seeing "my boys stand on the podium at Wembley Stadium . . . was one of the memories that I'll never forget." Although Claude was disappointed at not being present, he had followed the Games closely and had to be thrilled with a year that had culminated in broadcasting UK's first bowl game, UK's first NCAA Tournament title, and the Olympic trials—as well as with the off-field and court triumph of becoming a father. For a twenty-three-year-old Claude, this combination would be difficult to follow.

Indeed, Bear Bryant's 1948 football squad was not up to the challenge of following the memorable hoops campaign. The team did experience a bit of a drop-off from the previous season. The squad posted a 5–3–2 record in George Blanda's senior season and did not return to a bowl. Blanda threw for 967 yards and seven touchdowns, both of which were apparently UK records, and Wah Wah Jones, fresh off a third season of being an All-SEC basketball player, led the team in receiving for a second straight year, catching five of the scores from Blanda. One of Claude's 1948 broadcasts survives, and it includes an excited call of a Blanda-to-Jones scoring strike, leaving no doubt that both Claude and the Kentucky fan base appreciated the potent offense. But whereas the offense gained more than 40 yards per game more than in 1947, the defense forced thirteen fewer turnovers, and that decline was responsible for the team's struggles. Quarterback Babe Parilli watched from the sidelines because, under the rules of the time, he could not play as a freshman. Talented players such as Bob Gain and Bill Leskovar had not yet established themselves. Bryant's time would come, but not in 1948.

The 1948–1949 UK basketball squad, in contrast, picked up right where the defending champions of the previous season had left off. Kenny Rollins had graduated, but Beard, Groza, Jones, Barker, and Dale Barnstable were a year older, stronger, and even more ready to defend UK's title. Mostly, the Fabulous Four (the prior season's Fabulous Five less graduate Kenny Rollins—not to be confused with the long-haired Englishmen who surfaced a decade and a half later under the same moniker) steamrolled anyone in their path. Kentucky won fifteen games in the 1948–1949 season by 30 points or more. There were occasional close games—UK survived a tough December rematch against Bob Cousy and the Holy Cross team they had beaten in the previous season's Final Four and dropped a game to St. Louis 42–40 in late December. Otherwise, Alex Groza, who scored more than 20 points per game in his senior season, laid waste to the competition, and the rest of the team followed his lead. It was a talented, veteran group, and there was no reason to doubt its greatness.

In fact, in order to understand precisely how veteran—and how unique—the group was, it is perhaps best to consider the subject within the context of one of Claude's broadcasts. At halftime of the season's final game in Seattle, Claude profiled senior Cliff Barker. He told of the twenty-eight-year-old Barker's service in World War II and how Cliff had been a prisoner of war for sixteen months. He recounted how Barker had found a volleyball in the prison compound where he was held and had started playing games with his fellow prisoners. Barker's story is unquestionably remarkable, but just as remarkable was that it was being recounted by a twenty-four-year-old Claude Sullivan. Not only Barker but 1947–1948 starter Kenny Rollins was also older than Claude. In case Kentucky's basketball exhibition was not remarkable enough, the wunderkind behind the microphone added something extra to the show.

After the Wildcats won that season's SEC tournament in four games by margins of 37, 31, 39, and 16 points, Kentucky, then with a record of 29–1, decided to attempt a Grand Slam, trying to claim both the NIT and NCAA Tournament titles. Claude and the squad headed to New York's Madison Square Garden for the NIT, where the team was playing for the ninth time over the past two seasons.

Despite being a heavy favorite over Loyola of Chicago, the Wildcats lost a shocker, 67–56, their second loss of the season. Babe Kimbrough, writing in the *Lexington Herald,* commented that the Wildcats "lacked the fire which has characterized their play." At the time, Claude was quoted as saying that Kentucky "did not look sharp," and two years later he and J. B. Faulconer stated that they merely thought Kentucky was having an off game. Just how off that game was and what it meant to the UK program were not apparent for some time.

Meanwhile, the Wildcats returned to Lexington for a few days and then headed back again to Madison Square Garden, where they promptly dispatched Villanova and Illinois to earn a spot in the NCAA Tournament Championship for a second straight season. The title game against Oklahoma A&M would be played in Seattle, Washington. For Claude, this distance was nearly as formidable as traveling to London the previous summer, but WKLX put the funds together to send him to the game. He would be the only Kentucky broadcaster present at the Edmunson Pavilion.

Claude opened the broadcast by acknowledging that, to his knowledge, this was the farthest broadcast (Seattle to Kentucky) originated by a local independent station, and he thanked Purcell's Department Stores and Dixie Ice Cream for making it possible. The broadcast was transmitted, in accordance with the technology of the time, via a telephone line. Because the game was being played on the West Coast and a consolation game was played first, it was around midnight local time in Kentucky when the game tipped off. Claude would later recount an airline pilot telling him of flying over Kentucky in the late hours of the night and seeing so many lights on that he radioed Louisville to see what had happened. The game, the pilot was told: those lights were the many households hanging on Claude's every word to bring them UK's fate.

Although it was a late night for many across the Common-

Adolph Rupp with trophy *(far right)* and UK Wildcats beside airplane after the 1949 NCAA Tournament. Claude is next to Adolph. Courtesy of the UK Athletics Department.

wealth, it was ultimately a happy night. Playing in his final college game, Alex Groza continued to be unstoppable. He poured in 25 points, muscling the Wildcats through a tough title game. Just before 2:00 a.m. Eastern time, fans in Lexington heard Claude render this call: "Five seconds to play, the Wildcats leading 46–36, this will probably be the last shot of the ball game. And Line misses, and it comes off. . . . One second, one second to play, and Yates shoots and drops the ball on the floor as the game ends. The Wildcats are the defending champions!"

The NCAA Tournament trophy would remain in Lexington, courtesy of the 10-point victory over Oklahoma A&M. Alex Groza was named not only Most Outstanding Player of the tournament,

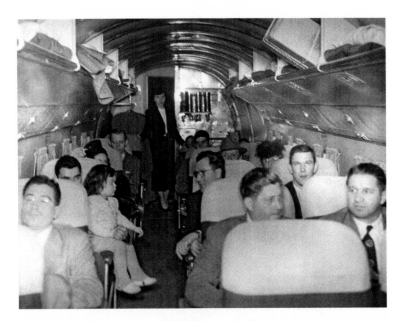

Claude on airplane with the basketball team in 1949. Assistant coach
Harry Lancaster is front right, with Claude in the second row behind him.
Lancaster is sitting next to Larry Boeck of the *Louisville Courier-Journal*.
Courtesy of the UK Athletics Department.

but also Helms Player of the Year, making him UK's last consen-
sus Player of the Year until Anthony Davis in 2012. He finished his
career as the university's all-time leading scorer and was everyone's
All-American, an honor that was also bestowed almost as universally
on Ralph Beard and Wah Wah Jones.

Shortly after the championship season in 1949, Larry Shropshire wrote a column in the *Lexington Leader* discussing how much
mileage Claude had piled up during the 1949 campaign. After
announcing the races at Keeneland, Claude declared to Larry, "I can
think of a better way to travel," referring to air travel. Claude was
asked to take a pencil to the number of miles traveled in both football and basketball and came up with 19,335 miles. He went to New

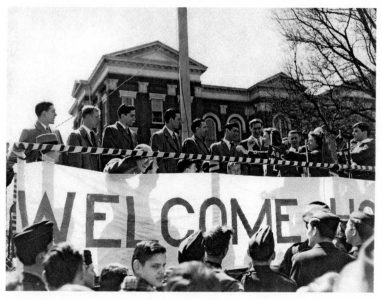

Celebration at UK in front of the administration building on campus after the 1949 NCAA Championship. Courtesy of the UK Athletics Department.

York for the NIT, came back to Lexington and covered the Sweet 16 in Louisville, went back to Manhattan for the NCAA regional, and then flew to Seattle for the championship!

Following the NCAA Championship, Groza, Beard, and Jones ended up on the NBA's Indianapolis Olympians together, where they were joined by Wildcats Cliff Barker and Joe Holland. Claude continued to associate professionally with the Fabulous Four in the NBA because he frequently broadcasted the Olympians' games via teletype. He received many postcards and letters with positive comments on the broadcasts as Kentucky fans stayed abreast of the NBA careers of their favorite sons, then as now. At the time, UK was more or less on top of the athletic world. That reign continued only temporarily, however, before the NCAA dropped a bomb that would shake the very foundation of the Wildcat nation.

3

Glory Days

In mid-1949, Claude Sullivan was twenty-four years old. He was married and had a young son. He had climbed to the top of his profession—calling his second consecutive NCAA basketball championship game and broadcasting Paul "Bear" Bryant's Wildcats gridiron exploits. Where could things possibly go but further up?

Not everyone was as optimistic. At least one person didn't think much of the 1949 football squad's chances, and that was Coach Bryant himself. In 1948, Claude had begun conducting a weekly coach's show with Bryant on WKLX. Claude and "the Bear," becoming fast friends, discussed the previous week's games and looked ahead to the next matchup. That said, these interviews, probably some of the earliest weekly coach's shows ever broadcast, are a far cry from the politically correct mindlessness that passes for such shows today. Bryant, aided by Claude, shot straight from the hip, predicting the week's games and giving his candid thoughts on opposing players and teams.

Although none of the 1948 coach's shows have survived, most of the 1949 season's broadcasts have been archived. In the week before Kentucky's season opener against Mississippi Southern (the school now known as Southern Mississippi), Claude asked Bryant to assess the SEC.

"In my opinion, there are four outstanding teams in our league this year," Bryant answered. "I think Mississippi and the University of Tennessee, the University of Georgia, and Tulane are definitely in a bracket by themselves—that is, as to strength. . . . I think there's another bracket with Alabama and Vanderbilt and Georgia Tech. And in the lower bracket would come Florida, Kentucky, LSU [Louisiana State University], Mississippi State, and Auburn. . . . I don't think there's any doubt but Tennessee, Mississippi, and Georgia definitely have the rest of the league outmanned—outmanned with the exception of Tulane."

Indeed, with one bowl appearance in the school's history and the great George Blanda now gone from Lexington, there was no apparent reason for outsiders to expect much from Bryant's 1949 Wildcat team. However, behind the scenes Claude saw reason to doubt Bryant's negative assessment of his own squad.

Although Blanda was gone, he had been replaced as quarterback by a young sensation from near Pittsburgh, Vito Parilli, henceforth known as "Babe." Parilli, who was as determined to escape from Pittsburgh's steel factories as Wah Jones had been to escape from a life of coal mining, proved to be a program-making quarterback—tough and deceptively athletic and skillful. He had watched and learned behind Blanda in 1948, and beginning in 1949 he led Kentucky to an unparalleled three-year run. In 1949, as a sophomore, Parilli threw eight touchdowns and passed for more than 1,000 yards. Those statistics are humble by modern standards, but at the time Parilli led the SEC in passing, Kentucky led it in scoring with 27.6 points per game.

Junior tackle Bob Gain, whom Bryant grudgingly admitted in a 1949 preseason coach's show to be "a great tackle," was named to several All-American teams in the 1949 season. Running back Bill Leskovar benefitted from Gain's blocking and Parilli's passing threat by putting up a single-season rushing record that stood until Sonny Collins broke the mark in 1973.

On the defensive side of the ball, defensive back Jerry Claiborne (who thirty-three years later became UK's head football coach) had nine interceptions—a single-season record that still stands at UK. Kentucky allowed only 71.6 yards per game rushing to its opponents and held them to 4.8 points per game in the regular season. The defense also forced fifteen more turnovers than the offense made, and the results could be breathtaking.

In the season opener, Kentucky dispatched Mississippi Southern 71–7 in Lexington. The team's second contest was a road game at LSU and the first meeting in football between the two SEC schools. Bryant, on the coach's show the following week, was concerned about the Tigers. He admitted in an interview with Claude, "If I knew that Mississippi Southern was not going to be that strong a team, I would have overlooked them for the LSU game." He advised that he would "only . . . practice hard until Tuesday and then taper off." However, concerned about the September bayou heat, he practiced the team on Friday night to make sure they were prepared. Parilli admitted in a recent interview, "We just were afraid to lose because [Bryant] put the fear in you!"

Bryant could have rested easy. The Wildcats dealt a 19–0 thumping to their hosts. By now, the Bear was in rare form in continuing to downgrade his own squad. On the following week's coaches show, he predicted that a veteran Ole Miss team would beat Kentucky by four or five touchdowns. The beating went in the opposite direction, with UK winning 47–0 at Ole Miss. Kentucky intercepted six passes in the game and returned them for 240 total yards, setting an NCAA record. When the squad flew back to Lexington, hundreds of excited fans were there to congratulate the team, and

Celebration of the 1949 UK football team as it arrives home after beating Ole Miss 47–0 in 1949. Claude can be seen in the center of the photo interviewing Coach Bryant. Courtesy of the *Lexington Herald-Leader*.

Claude was engulfed by celebration when he interviewed Bryant at the airport.

After two more shutouts, UK was number 7 in the nation with a 5–0 mark. Kentucky then lost to Southern Methodist University (although SMU star Doak Walker was out with an injury), but the Wildcats' only other defeat was a 6–0 setback to Tennessee in the season's final home game. That loss cost the Cats an SEC championship, which went to Tulane.

After a 9–2 regular season, Kentucky was chosen for the 1950 Orange Bowl in Miami on January 2 against the University of Santa Clara. Bryant's squad, which was ranked number 11 in the nation entering the game, had certainly given Claude a bowl destination superior to the December 1947 trip to Cleveland.

Unfortunately, the beautiful scenery of Miami proved to be the best part of the 1950 Orange Bowl for UK. Leading 7–0, Parilli

connected on a long pass play to Bill Leskovar down to the Santa
Clara 3-yard line as time was running out in the half. Kentucky had
time for two plays, but two running plays were stopped just short of
the goal line, and the clock ran out. Parilli remembered, "The Bear
came running down the sideline, and I went running the other way
to the locker room because I did not want to face him." The missed
opportunity was the difference in the game as Santa Clara took over
in the second half, winning the game 21–13.

For Claude, the season, despite the troubling ending, had
been almost nothing but positive. Leading up to the Orange Bowl,
Claude had a chance to visit with Mel Allen, the longtime voice of
the New York Yankees, who was in Miami to broadcast the game
for CBS. Despite his happiness in Kentucky, Claude still dreamed
of being a national radio announcer. In those days, baseball was
the predominant professional sport, being far more popular than
pro football or basketball. Accordingly, no sportscasting position had more prestige than that of the men who broadcast Major
League Baseball. Claude had grown up following the Cincinnati
Reds, whose broadcasters had included the legendary Red Barber,
who called Reds games for five years during Claude's youth. The
Reds would be the most choice spoke to add to Claude's professional wheel. In 1950, however, veteran broadcaster Waite Hoyt
was entrenched in Cincinnati, calling the games on his own, and
Claude wondered if he could ever break into the major leagues. For
the time being, he made Mel Allen's acquaintance and renewed his
own larger broadcasting goals.

Meanwhile, not only was the Wildcats' on-field work a pleasure, but Claude's relationship with Bear Bryant continued to grow
closer. Babe Parilli confirms that he perceived the closeness between
UK's top announcer and the head coach. In a recent interview, Babe
indicated that Bryant would sometimes talk more to Sullivan than
to his own team. He recalled his old coach and admitted, "He did

not confide in many people. In fact, [Claude] was one of the very few. . . . We just loved [Claude]. He was *it;* he was *the* voice of the Wildcats."

Both Sullivan and Bryant were driven young men who were earning their stripes in their respective trades, and a mutual respect and friendship developed between them. Alyce Sullivan recalled one difficult loss, after which she and Claude had gone to see Bryant at his home because there was no real postgame press conference area at the time. Bryant had been morose, but when Claude and Alyce rose to leave, Claude shook his hand, and Bryant told him, "You know, Claude, I appreciate you coming out tonight. . . . None of the other SOBs had the nerve to come here."

Although both Bryant and Claude were focused, neither was above a good practical joke. Late in his life Claude recounted for a newspaper interviewer that before a particular home game the Bear decided to tell him the first three plays of the game so Claude could impress his radio audience. Claude jotted them down, and then when the game started, he "predicted" those first three plays, with the third going for a Kentucky touchdown. He recalled that after the game fans were calling in asking how the announcer knew more about the plays than the coach.

While Bear Bryant was busy trying to build a dynasty in Lexington, Adolph Rupp was tackling the even more difficult task of maintaining one. Two straight NCAA Tournament Championships left little room for less than greatness for UK's 1949–1950 basketball squad. Legends such as Beard, Jones, and Groza were long gone. Seniors Jim Line and Dale Barnstable had played supporting roles on the 1949 team but were now expected to become stars. But the biggest star of this bunch, figuratively and literally, was Bill Spivey.

Kentucky's first seven-footer, Spivey had been a rail-thin recruit from rural Georgia who took advantage of mandatory fresh-

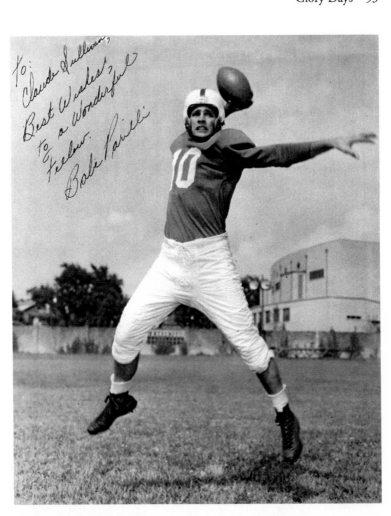

Babe Parilli in UK press photo, passing, 1950. The inscription says, "To Claude Sullivan, Best Wishes to a wonderful fellow, Babe Parilli." Courtesy of the UK Athletics Department.

man ineligibility to lift weights, eat bigger meals, and generally try to look more like a basketball player and less like a bean pole. To say that he succeeded would be understatement. Given that he was a full five inches taller than Alex Groza, who had been his predecessor as

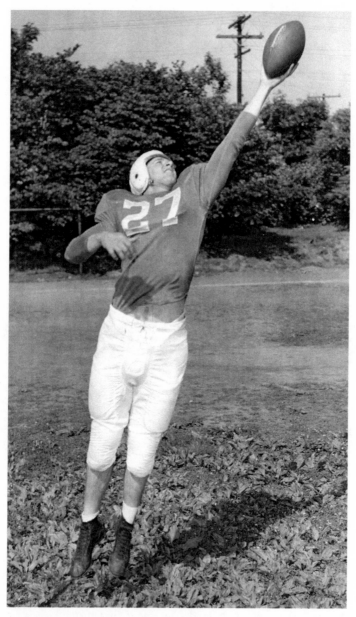

Wah Wah Jones UK football photo, 1949. Courtesy of the UK Athletics Department.

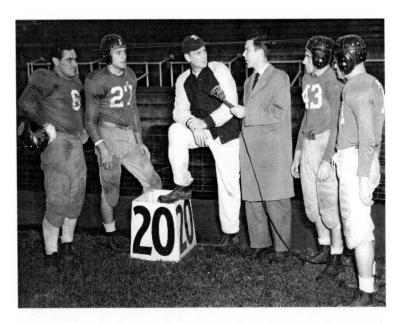

Claude interviewing Bear Bryant with players looking on, 1949. Courtesy of the UK Athletics Department.

UK's low-post presence, Spivey's size astounded teammates and confounded opponents. In the 1949–1950 campaign, only twice would he fail to score in double figures. He had a deft touch and was a solid rebounder and intimidating shot blocker. With Spivey drawing the focus, Line and Barnstable could chip in solid games, and sophomore newcomers Bobby Watson and Shelby Linville added further punch. Kentucky, as it turned out, would be almost as much of a force this year as it had been in Claude's first two UK basketball broadcasting campaigns.

Claude's third full UK basketball campaign would also be his last in Alumni Gym. Despite much public consternation and handwringing over the "white elephant" that was being planned, the university was putting the finishing touches on Memorial Coliseum in preparation for the 1950–1951 campaign. Kentucky's top basketball team had been deemed worthy of equally unrivaled facilities, despite the $3.925 million price tag. Although Claude was undoubtedly impressed with the new construction, it is worth noting that he never broadcast a UK defeat from Alumni Gym, which is the sort of record that could build a healthy dose of superstition.

The 1949–1950 squad did their part to uphold Claude's perfect record. With Spivey, Line, and Barnstable leading the way, UK again was perfect at home. On the road, they did suffer a December loss at St. John's and a trio of January losses within the conference. However, by tournament time Rupp's squad was again humming.

Life was not always easy for a traveling sportscaster. Claude recalled one infamous game, at Georgia Tech on January 16, 1950, for the rest of his life. He was meticulous in pregame preparation and always made sure that the relevant accommodations were prepared for his broadcast. This involved reserving space and paying a small fee to the home institution. This particular game was a bit unusual because it was being televised—a rare feat and perhaps one that explains the chaos that ensued. Claude and J. B. Faulconer appeared to broadcast the game for stations WKLX and WLAP, respectively. Georgia Tech, however, decided it had no space for them, despite its indications to the contrary and acceptance of Claude's earlier payment. Claude was eventually placed in the arena concourse, viewing a television screen to depict play-by-play to his listening audience. To make a difficult situation even more intolerable, the *Atlanta Journal* picked up the story the next day, running a photograph of Claude, who, the story indicated, had been conveniently assisted by the kindly Georgia Tech authorities into a much more comfortable broadcasting setup. Claude completed his broadcast, and UK won 61–46, but the "bush-league performance" of Georgia Tech's athletic department was one story that Claude shared many times over the years that followed.

The 1949–1950 season was eventful, but usually in more pleas-

LEXINGTON WKLX STAFFER DESCRIBES SPORTS ACTION VIA TV AT WSB
From Left: G. Sutton, Engineer; Claude Sullivan, Don Stevens, Engineer; Ray Rast, of Tech

TV Enables Radio 'Casters To Put Ball Game on Air

By WAYNE ANDERSON

The space problem at the Georgia Tech gym is somewhat acute. Ask any Tech student who tries to find tickets to basketball contests.

But this space problem isn't confined to basketball fans. No less than two Lexington, Ky., radio stations came to Atlanta Monday night prepared to broadcast the Tech-Kentucky basketball game only to find that there just wasn't any place to set up.

John M. Outler Jr., general manager of WSB, came to their rescue making room in the WSB studios for one of the two stations to permit an announcer to describe the cage action by watching a television screen.

The other station installed their equipment in a local radio store.

So, both WLAP and WKLX were able to fulfill their broadcast commitments, via the television screen and the WSB-TV picture.

* * *

This article appeared in the *Atlanta Journal* on January 17, 1950, following the game between UK and Georgia Tech. Georgia Tech pushed WKLX out of its paid-for press table space to accommodate television broadcasting so that all students would have an opportunity to view the game. Claude broadcast from the lobby using a TV to monitor the game. Courtesy of the *Atlanta Journal*.

ant ways. In the third-to-last UK game in Alumni Gym, Spivey set a school single-game record of 40 points in a win against Georgia Tech. Later Claude frequently referred to the final game in Alumni Gym, which was a challenge when Vanderbilt jumped to a 41–29 halftime advantage, but Jim Line and Dale Barnstable rallied the Cats to a 70–66 victory. Kentucky had an eleven-game winning streak going into the SEC Tournament, in which they throttled Mississippi State, Georgia, and Tennessee by 10, 16, and 37 points, respectively.

At 25–4, UK was ranked third in the nation and accepted a berth in the NIT, where they would play lightly regarded home-town heroes City College of New York (CCNY). Against an athletic and determined CCNY squad, Kentucky fell behind at the outset. Although Spivey's bulk meant that the team was a bit more deliberate than the Fabulous Five, it was still a bizarre sight to see an opposing team running and gunning Rupp's squad out of Madison Square Garden. CCNY took a 13–1 lead. By halftime, the lead had stretched to 25, and at the buzzer it was 39 points, with UK crushed 89–50.

Rupp was embarrassed and devastated. With this loss, Kentucky was not among the eight-team 1950 NCAA Tournament field selected to play two weeks later. In 1964, Claude recalled this defeat during an interview and remembered staying up with Rupp in his hotel room after the game, the coach pacing up and down the room, muttering, "Thirty-nine damn points," over and over. The slight over being left out of the NCAA Tournament stung nearly as badly, and Rupp's complaining may have played a real part in the tournament's expansion to sixteen teams a year later. He felt that Kentucky had been snubbed by the NCAA selection committee and that it should have been automatically invited back for a possible "three-peat."

Although some drop in results was inevitable, Claude was stunned when after two brilliant championship seasons the 1949–

1950 crashed to a sudden halt. This was nothing compared to what was looming in the wings.

Back on the gridiron in the fall of 1950, one thing indisputably clear was that the 1950 Wildcat football squad shaped up to be the best that Claude had broadcast. No longer could Bryant claim that his team belonged at the rear of the conference. The AP sportswriters ranked the Cats thirteenth at the beginning of the 1950 season.

Parilli was a year older and more experienced, as was Gain, who was now everyone's All-American selection and a force on both the offensive and defensive lines. Walt Yaworsky was another stalwart on the offensive line. Not only was the Wildcat backfield talented, but the receiving corps thrived as well. Al Bruno, also a teammate of Wah Wah Jones on the basketball squad, had a season that went unmatched until Hal Mumme's Air Raid came to town nearly half a century later.

Bryant was always at the center of the program's success. His vigorous training camps, his intense practices, even his infamous midgame scrimmage all became the stuff of legend. In the same way that Adolph Rupp's name has become synonymous with the history of Kentucky basketball, Bryant was writing a similar mythology surrounding the football program.

Now that he had put together a collection of top talent, the results were amazing. Whereas the UK offense had been dominant in 1949, in 1950 the passing game clicked even more efficiently. Not only did Parilli lead the conference in passing again, but he was one of the top passers in the nation. Kentucky scored 34.5 points per game in 1950, a mark that again would take half a century and a few football revolutions to be equaled.

Claude referred to Bryant's "stout" defense that was up for another season of ball hawking. The Cats went plus-13 in turnover margin, intercepting twenty-nine passes for the second consecutive season. UK allowed 5.7 points and 176.8 yards per game. The question wasn't merely whether this squad was good; it was whether it was the best.

Kentucky opened with four consecutive shutouts, destroying North Texas State, LSU, Ole Miss, and Dayton by a combined count of 106–0. Indeed, only three times all season would UK score less than 25 points—and only twice would it allow more than seven.

Although Cincinnati finally put up a touchdown on UK in its 41–7 loss that moved 5–0 Kentucky to fourth in the national AP poll, the Bearcats were decimated by Parilli and Bruno. That day Claude broadcast a game that was simply ahead of its time. Against Cincinnati, Parilli went eighteen of twenty-nine passing for 338 yards and five touchdowns. The touchdowns tied the SEC record, and the yardage set a new conference mark. Al Bruno caught three of Parilli's passes for touchdowns in the game.

Wildcat fever raged as win followed win. Villanova (34–7), Georgia Tech (28–14), and Florida (40–6) were dispatched. Mississippi State brought the top defense in the nation to Lexington and left with a 48–21 loss, as Parilli again tied the league record with five touchdown passes. After the 83–0 senior-day win over North Dakota, UK was 10–0 and ranked third in the nation.

Tennessee, 8–1 and number 9 in the nation, awaited UK in the SEC finale. Bryant's nemesis struck again, stunning UK in a 7–0 defeat that prevented a perfect season. Still, Bryant won the SEC Championship outright and had little time to fret over the Tennessee loss—the Sugar Bowl and Coach Bud Wilkinson's undefeated Oklahoma team awaited.

Calling Oklahoma "undefeated" was like calling Claude's listening audience passionate. Not only was Oklahoma a perennial power, but it had not lost a game since the 1948 season opener. It had won thirty-one straight games with a power running attack—including halfback Billy Vessels, who went on to win a Heisman

Trophy as a Sooner two years later—that ran roughshod over the competition. Oklahoma had been held at less than 27 points only once all season, in an early 14–13 win over number 4 Texas. Vessels himself ran for fifteen touchdowns in the season. Few gave the Wildcats much of a chance in the 1951 Sugar Bowl.

But Bryant, given a month to prepare, crafted a brilliant game plan. In front of 82,000 fans in New Orleans and many more back in Kentucky tuned in to Claude's broadcast on New Year's Day 1951, Bryant's Wildcats played a wide-set defense, daring Oklahoma to break big plays on the edge. When Vessels and his Sooner teammates tried, they met a stone wall. Time and again Oklahoma quarterback Claude Arnold was hurried into poor decisions, or Vessels was cut down in the backfield. Particularly impressive coaching again came in the decision to insert Walt Yaworsky into the UK defensive line, despite the fact that he had played almost exclusively on offense all season. Yaworsky, who was honored as the game's Most Valuable Player, recovered an Oklahoma fumble deep in Kentucky territory in the first quarter. On the next play, Parilli hit a 22-yard scoring strike to Wilbur Jamerson, giving UK a 7–0 lead. In the second quarter, Parilli drove the Cats 81 yards, with Jamerson plunging in from a yard out for a shocking 13–0 halftime advantage.

In the second half, Oklahoma took the opening kickoff and drove to a first and goal at the UK 3-yard line, before Yaworsky rose up again, dumping an Oklahoma third down play for a loss of 5 yards. The drive ended with Oklahoma turning the ball over on downs. Kentucky's game plan went conservative, with the Wildcats being content to run the ball into the line and eat up the clock. Parilli recalled Bryant telling him at halftime not to throw the ball in the second half. Oklahoma managed a score with seven minutes to go, cutting UK's lead to 13–7, but it came no closer. When the game ended, UK had pulled the upset, knocking off everyone's number 1 team. Although UK was not recognized as a national champion at the time, statistician Jeff Sagarin would later award the team his mythical national title for 1950. UK's 10–1 record has been equaled only once in the six decades of UK football since then. UK went 10–1 in 1977, but at the time it was not eligible for the SEC title or postseason play because it was on probation. In the 1950–1951 season, Parilli was fourth in the Heisman Trophy voting and was named SEC Player of the Year, and Gain won the prestigious Outland Trophy, awarded to the nation's top lineman.

The season was a triumph—the best in Kentucky football history. From his prime spot in the Sugar Bowl, Claude took it all in. These were halcyon days that even Claude sometimes struggled to believe were real.

Bryant's gridiron glory had astounded Kentucky's fans, but Adolph Rupp was not a man to be outshone. His 1950–1951 squad picked up where Bryant's gridiron warriors left off in creating probably the best year of UK athletics ever. Juniors Spivey, Linville, and Watson were joined by a particularly tough group of sophomores that made the squad elite. Rugged Cliff Hagan of Owensboro could control the low post at six foot four, although as a midyear high school graduate he would not be eligible until the season's second semester. Madisonville guard Frank Ramsey was such a great player that even unabashed UK loather Bobby Knight was still praising Ramsey as his favorite Kentucky player ever six decades later. Reserve forward sophomore Lou Tsioropoulos eventually became the third great player of the class and was a particular favorite of Claude's.

For his part, Tsioropoulos recalled his admiration for Claude in a recent interview. "He was very friendly," Lou said, "I think I liked the way he dressed and acted, and he personified . . . the Kentucky gentleman." With Claude at a mere twenty-five years old when the season began, it is little wonder that Tsioropoulos had little difficulty relating to the broadcaster, who was much closer to his age than the stern taskmaster who ran the Kentucky program.

Tsioropoulos and Claude, the "Kentucky gentleman," spent a great deal of time together in Kentucky's legendary practice sessions. It was an intense scene for one and all as Coach Rupp ruled with unquestioned authority. Tsioropoulos recalled, "There was never any talking. [Coach Rupp's] expression was, 'You can only talk if you can improve on the silence.' . . . The people that came in could not talk. I think he admonished one of the UK officials that came in there and talked. That was his territory, and as long as you knew about that, you would get along fine."

The practices began at 3:15 p.m. Tsioropoulos elaborated, "It was an hour and a half of continuous movement and basic fundamentals, knowing your position and everybody doing what their position should do. So he would work on people and their position, not on the whole team. . . . Adolph tried to interject some humor into it. He tried to be humorous at times, and sometimes it worked, and sometimes it did not because we did not know when the hell to laugh!"

If Rupp had realized what a juggernaut he was about to unleash, perhaps everyone could have enjoyed a few more laughs.

With Spivey in the middle and Watson and Ramsey scoring from the guard spots, Hagan and Linville added grit and depth to a daunting Kentucky squad. The Wildcats began the campaign and inaugurated Memorial Coliseum in front of a crowd of 8,000 with a 30-point drubbing of West Texas State. They simply improved from there. The second game of the year, a home contest with Purdue, featured the formal dedication of the Wildcats' new basketball palace in front of a crowd of more than 11,000.

Memorial Coliseum held up to five times the crowd that old Alumni Gym had managed. Claude recalled Rupp warning him that the facility was still too small; at the time, the words were

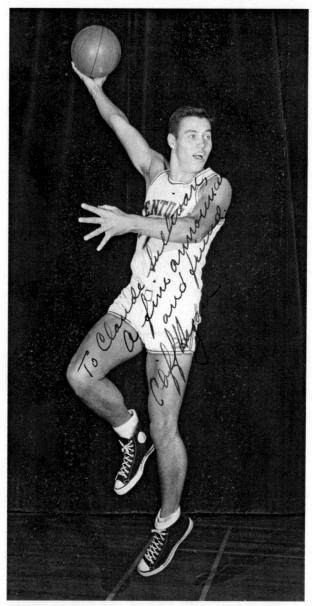

Cliff Hagan, UK photo, 1951. The inscription reads, "To
Claude Sullivan, a fine announcer and friend, Cliff Hagan."
Courtesy of the UK Athletics Department.

Frank Ramsey, UK photo, 1951. The inscription reads, "To Claude Sullivan, a good announcer and wonderful friend, Frank Ramsey." Courtesy of the UK Athletics Department.

unbelievable, but hindsight proved Rupp correct. That said, college basketball in the 1950s was a very different environment than it is today. Lou Tsioropoulos recalled that the band was not present at the games back in Alumni Gym or in the early days of Memorial

Lou Tsioropoulos, UK photo, 1951. The inscription reads, "Good luck, Claude. Lou Tsioropoulos." Courtesy of the UK Athletics Department.

Coliseum, and, according to Lou, even the cheerleading was different, and it was mostly quiet. Adults dressed up for the games in sport coats and dresses, and male students wore ties. The whole environment was very sedate; the lights did not go down during introduction, and there was generally much less hoopla involved.

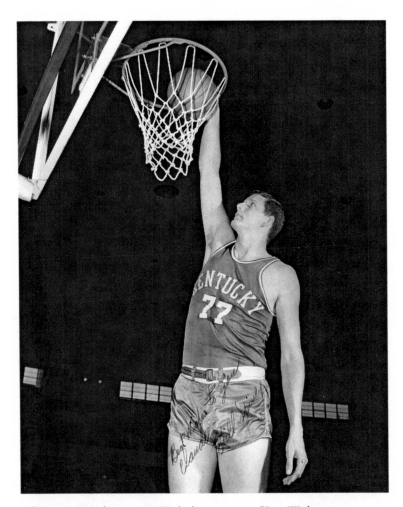

Bill Spivey, UK photo, 1951. With the inscription "Best Wishes to you, Claude. Bill Spivey." Courtesy of the UK Athletics Department.

The Coliseum did not need trickery to be impressive. A solid cream-colored brick structure with an impressive high facade, the facility was dedicated to Kentuckians who had served in the US military and had passed away in World War I, World War II, and the Korean War. It was built on Euclid Avenue, straight across the street from Stoll Field and McLean Stadium. Claude immediately took up residency at center court with WKLX's banner flying in front of him. Although he had enjoyed the charm of old Alumni Gym, he quickly adapted to the new facility.

The Wildcat squad also adapted very quickly. The team lost only twice—once on December 29 by one point to St. Louis in the Sugar Bowl Tournament in New Orleans and again in the SEC Tournament in a 4-point decision to Vanderbilt 61–57 at the Armory in Louisville after twenty-one straight wins. Claude referred to that Vandy win years later: "That loss seemed to shock Kentucky . . . for the Cats beat Loyola Chicago in a postseason game on Match 13 by 97–61. Then in the NCAA tournament [they] beat Louisville, St. John's, Illinois, and Kansas State for the Championship." That is to say, UK was a mere 7 points from an undefeated season. In the meanwhile, Rupp's squad won by 30 or more points no fewer than ten times in the 1950–1951 season.

Spivey was the best player in college basketball, scoring 19.2 points per game. Linville, Watson, and Ramsey were also double-figure scorers, with Ramsey making a few All-American teams and all three earning All-SEC honors (Linville being second team). Hagan and senior Walter Hirsch were nearly also double-figure scorers.

Early in the 1950–1951 season, the team provided a memorable moment as Rupp hosted his alma mater, Kansas, taking on Coach Phog Allen in a clash between the game's two best big men, Spivey and Kansas center Clyde Lovellette. In front of a record crowd of 13,000 packed into Memorial Coliseum, UK won the game 68–39 as Spivey dominated Lovellette, outscoring him 22–10 and leaving no doubt who the better player was.

In March, UK defined itself as the power of college basketball. The team was without Hirsch in the NCAA Tournament; he had played as a freshman and thus was ineligible for postseason play. Hagan was forced into the starting lineup, but no let-up occurred among the Wildcats. Shelby Linville pitched in 23 against Louisville in the first-round win at Raleigh when Spivey was double-teamed. The next rounds were at Madison Square Garden against St. John's and Illinois. Against St. John's, with the score tied and less than three minutes to play, Linville hit three straight goals to put Kentucky up to a 16-point thumping of number 9 St. John's.

Claude agreed with other media that the last game UK played again Illinois at Madison Square Garden was one of the greatest games played. Spivey had fouled out with the score tied. Linville hit two more shots to tie the game again after Rupp moved him to the pivot spot. Kentucky got the ball with the game tied, and, according to Claude, C. M. Newton was pinned in the corner, where he leaped and hit Linville at the free-throw line. Linville put the winning jumper away for a 76–74 squeaker over the number 5 Illinois team. In the final seconds, with Spivey and two other starters having fouled out, Tsioropoulos found himself double-teamed, which helped Linville get open. Tsioropoulos recently reflected on his talented teammates and laughed, "Some scouting report they had, double-teaming me!"

In the 1951 tournament finals, UK's biggest foe might not have been the tenacious Kansas State Wildcats, but the medical staff. Spivey had a cold and was definitely under the weather. Hagan had strep throat and was not allowed to start. In fact, many didn't expect him to play. In a recent interview, he jokingly recalled stories of pestering Rupp on the bench, asking if he could play. Kansas State's Lew Hirsch outplayed Spivey, and Kansas State led 29–27 at the half.

Rupp, who had been ill for much of the tournament, had little sympathy for his players. He delivered a paint-peeling tirade and utilized Hagan heavily in the second half. Buoyed by the outburst from Rupp and some clutch play from Hagan, UK outlasted Kansas State 68–58, mostly by virtue of 22 points and twenty-one boards from

Spivey and Cliff Hagan's crucial 10 points off the bench. Rupp had led Kentucky to its third NCAA Tournament title in four seasons. Groza had given way to Spivey, who seemed likely to give way to Hagan—but probably only after another title. Claude had to think he had stumbled into an NCAA hoops dynasty, which has been equaled only by the one that John Wooden put together a decade and a half later at the University of California, Los Angeles (UCLA). The truth was much less simple and much more painful.

The year 1951 was a time in which the accomplishments and changes in Claude's personal life nearly outflanked all of the Wildcat triumphs he had covered. He founded the Standard Oil Network that year. J. B. Faulconer was already broadcasting Wildcat sports via the Ashland Oil Network at the time, and Claude's wheel-and-hub plan for obtaining his business goals had encouraged him to make the entrepreneurial move toward bigger spokes.

At the time he established the Standard Oil Network, he had just moved from WKLX to WVLK with his mentor and friend Ted Grizzard. Claude remained associated with WVLK for most of his UK broadcasting career. Even when he later moved to WINN in Louisville, it was in the Bluegrass Broadcasting Network, and his broadcasts were still carried on WVLK by a special contractual arrangement. During his tenure at WVLK, Claude was eventually appointed director of programming for the station.

The Standard Oil Network was a master stroke purely on a business level. Broadcasting cost money; although the details from the first days of the network are no longer available, records from the 1960s demonstrate that a home broadcast cost around $1,800 to $2,000 to create. Accordingly, each network affiliate in that era paid a nominal fee of around $75 to $100 per home game, with the fee being greater for a road broadcast or to include the postgame interview with Coach Rupp. In essence, then, Claude was deferring his

Claude at the WVLK mic in the Phoenix Hotel studios in 1958. Courtesy of WVLK Radio.

operating costs by spreading them across a dozen and a half or more affiliated stations across Kentucky.

But the more significant effect of creating the network was that Claude had ensured that Wildcat backers all across the Commonwealth and not just within the range of his home station would be able to tune him in for the next round of Wildcat battles. More than a temporary influx of income, the network enabled Claude to gain a foothold across Kentucky as the accepted and known voice of the Wildcats. In essence, although talent, dedication, and skill had brought the twenty-six-year-old Claude this far in his career, the business savvy in establishing the network helped make him famous and enabled him to compete with WHAS, which had extended coverage outside of the state of Kentucky as a one station beacon.

The Standard Oil Network, which eventually included more than twenty affiliates, enabled Claude to stay ahead of J. B. Faulconer, Dee Huddleston, Phil Sutterfield, Cawood Ledford, and many other competing broadcasters. As mass media grew, Kentucky was the Commonwealth's team, and on the basis of the Standard Oil Network Claude Sullivan became and remained its primary announcer. He became Kentucky's voice for Kentucky's flagship teams, and it was a position he maintained for the rest of his life.

In addition, 1951 was a special year for yet another reason for Claude and Alyce. A few weeks after the NCAA Tournament triumph, the Sullivans celebrated again as son Alan arrived into the family. By a strange coincidence, the births of both David and Alan came shortly on the heels of a Wildcat NCAA Tournament championship.

Like David before him, Alan was quickly inducted into a way of life in which Kentucky sports were a pivotal component. Although both boys grew accustomed to Claude's being busy on Fridays and weekends throughout football and basketball season, they also grew accustomed to the insider's life that they were accorded. For instance, one of Alan's earliest babysitters was Wah Wah Jones's longtime friend and former UK basketball manager Humzey Yessin. Claude always viewed his broadcasting career as a family enterprise, and as David and Alan grew older, this became even more true.

In the summer of 1951, Claude and Alyce had a three-year-old David and a newborn Alan to occupy their time. As in 1948, the combination of great expense and the pull of family life kept Claude at home while the Wildcat basketball squad traveled. This time, Rupp's destination was Puerto Rico, where his NCAA champions played a brief series of outdoor contests on dirt courts. While Claude was at home playing the doting father, Rupp kept him up to speed, sending along a postcard telling him about the games and reporting that the Wildcats were "living like kings."

It was a royal existence for Kentucky athletics. In Claude's four seasons on the radio dial, he had broadcast three NCAA Championships, three bowl seasons, and only an odd handful of losses, almost none of those at home. Claude rode the wave, sure that it could be only a short while until the national exposure he sought would come his way. However, within the next few years Bryant was gone, Kentucky was under NCAA probation, and Claude's ticket to the national position he sought still had not arrived.

4

The Fall

By mid-1951, the previous few years of Claude's career had left him wondering how much better his professional life could get. A national position had not yet come his way, but the basketball and football Wildcats had reached unparalleled success; he had established the Standard Oil Network; and away from work he had become a father twice. However, adversity was preparing to rear its head again. If the rise of the past few years had been sudden and amazing, the fall of those to come would be even more drastic and unexpected. Fortunately, Claude's wheel plowed through the difficult times, and better days would come again.

As the fall of 1951 rolled around, football season dawned again. With Kentucky coming off of a 10–1 season and a Sugar Bowl upset over Oklahoma, the SEC wouldn't be sleeping on Bear Bryant's 1951 Wildcat squad. All-American quarterback Parilli would return for his senior season. However, Bob Gain had completed his eligibility, as had Sugar Bowl hero Walt Yaworsky and ace receiver Al Bruno. The squad did not figure to be at the same level as the previous year's squad, but it still proved to be entertaining.

Some of the entertainment came away from the public's pry-

ing eyes. In the fall of 1951, Bryant prepared for his annual fall preseason camp. On August 31, 1951, Claude received a letter from
Bryant inviting him to join the team in Millersburg for an eight-day
training camp with two-a-day practices. In the letter, Bear Bryant
stated: "I personally hope that it will be possible for you to be our
guest during the entire eight day period while we are at camp. . . .
I sincerely would like to have you come up and stay as long as possible." Babe Parilli recalled Claude's invite and noted, "That was a
feather in [his] cap. . . . I don't think there were any other media people there." The preseason camp was a time of intense physical workouts, and Bryant was all business.

As the invitation to fall camp attests, the relationship between
Claude and the Bear was as close as ever. Claude attended the full
camp, and his correspondence includes a return note from Bryant
after the camp ended, thanking him for coming.

Claude was back behind the microphone for his fifth year with
Bryant, this time via the Standard Oil Network. Once again Kentucky had a high-powered offensive attack, with Parilli leading the
SEC in passing, totaling 1,643 yards and nineteen touchdowns, the
latter mark a school record that stood for more than forty years.
Defensively, Kentucky took a step back, allowing more than 35
yards and almost 5 more points per game.

After a 72–13 thumping of Tennessee Tech to open the season, Kentucky dropped three straight heartbreakers, a 7–6 loss
at Texas, a 21–17 disappointment at Ole Miss, and a 13–7 home
loss to number 11 Georgia Tech. UK had not lost three straight
games since 1948, and a third straight bowl game looked nearly
impossible.

However, a 27–0 beating of Mississippi State followed, and
the Cats closed out October by beating number 12 Villanova 35–13
and winning at Florida, making the team record 4–3 thus far. Three
more wins opened November, highlighted by a 32–0 blanking of

number 19 Miami. UK was now 7–3 and had won six straight when it hosted top-ranked Tennessee.

Although Tennessee, en route to a national title, again humbled Bryant 28–0, Kentucky's steady improvement led to an invitation to the Cotton Bowl against number 11 Texas Christian on January 1, 1952. In front of more than 75,000 fans in Dallas and countless others back in Kentucky via Claude's broadcast, Babe Parilli finished his Wildcat career with two touchdown passes to Emery Clark, leading UK to a 20–7 win over the Texas Christian Horned Frogs.

Parilli led the offense, and Kentucky's defense turned Texas Christian away on four first-half drives inside the Kentucky 25-yard line. Bryant was ecstatic with a third consecutive bowl appearance and a second consecutive victory. To put the matter in perspective, no other college football program had played in bowl games in each of the past three seasons—aside from Kentucky, only a handful of other schools even made two bowl games over the three seasons.

Another year and another warm-weather January locale had to spoil the twenty-seven-year-old Claude Sullivan. Of course, he might have paused to savor New Year's Day in Dallas had he realized that he himself would not broadcast another Kentucky bowl appearance—or that it would be a day shy of a quarter-century before UK made another bowl appearance.

Meanwhile, in the weeks before the 1951–1952 basketball season began, a bombshell was dropped on UK athletics. On the evening of October 20, 1951, investigators from the New York City District Attorney's Office seized former Wildcats Dale Barnstable, Alex Groza, and Ralph Beard. Groza and Beard were in Chicago, as was Coach Rupp, who was to coach in an All-Star Game there. A former UK football player named Nick Englisis had befriended the three players while they were still Cats, probably on the basis of being

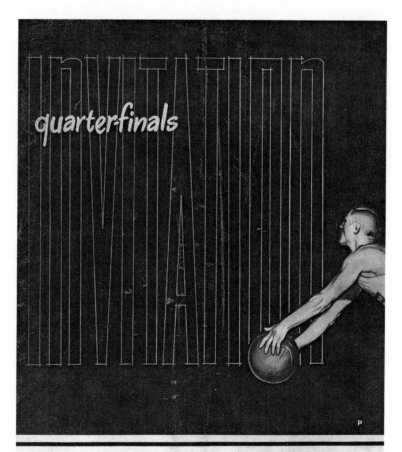

quarter-finals

BRADLEY vs. WESTERN KENTUCKY
U. OF KENTUCKY vs. LOYOLA

MADISON SQUARE GARDEN · MARCH 14, 1949 · 25c

24c N. Y. C. SALES TAX 1c

NIT program, March 14, 1949. Kentucky lost to Loyola in the first round. It was one of the games that supported the accusation of point shaving. From the Claude Sullivan Collection.

Beard's teammate on the 1945 UK football squad. Englisis had enticed the three Cats during the 1948–1949 season initially to play over the point spread, running up the score so that gamblers who had bet on Kentucky to cover the spread would profit. Once Englisis had gained the three players' confidence, he then coerced them into shaving points—which is to say, the opposite behavior, trying to win the game by less points than had been projected. This apparently took place in a regular season game against Tennessee, which UK still won despite the point shaving, as well as in the shocking NIT loss to Loyola. The point shaving had apparently extended into the 1949–1950 season as well, and several other players were eventually implicated.

In a recent interview, Humzey Yessin, who was the team manager during much of the era in question, gave his explanation of how Kentucky's role in the scandal was uncovered:

> The [point spread] lines were getting so big that if you bet on Kentucky, the lines were up thirty or forty points. And then Rupp would take a team out, and they'd never play the second half. They wouldn't even be dressed and sitting on the floor, and then [those who bet on Kentucky] got beat because they didn't cover the line on the game. . . . The big gamblers were the ones that called in the authorities and said, 'Something's going on at these games because a lot of money . . . used to be on Kentucky, and then it started showing up against [them]. . . . The gamblers blew the whistle. . . . That's what happened, and [this kind of thing] was going on in New York all the time.

Indeed, Kentucky was hardly alone in the scandal; the investigation touched on thirty-one players from seven schools. Judge Saul S. Streit of New York made headlines by calling college football and basketball a sordid big business. Meanwhile, according to Russell

Rice's book *Kentucky Basketball's Big Blue Machine,* when investigators arrived on campus to continue their investigation, former players refused to answer any questions.

The investigation dragged on into the 1951–1952 UK basketball season. A virtual shoe-in to repeat as champions, the Cats instead became a team with a black cloud hanging over it. Spivey, the best player in college basketball as a junior, was slated to miss the beginning of his senior season due to off-season knee surgery. Even with Spivey on crutches to begin the season, Cliff Hagan returned to dominate the low post. Fellow juniors Frank Ramsey and Lou Tsioropoulos also played major roles, as did senior guard Bobby Watson. This group was such an offensively talented squad that they averaged about 7.5 points per game more than the previous year's national champions had.

UK had a tough road loss at Minnesota in the third game of the season and for the second straight season dropped a one-point decision to St. Louis in the Sugar Bowl on Claude's birthday, December 29. Otherwise, they just won. Hagan averaged 21.6 points per game, which was a UK record, and also totaled 16.5 rebounds per game. Ramsey chipped in with 15.9 points per game, and Watson added 13.1 per night. Kentucky won fifteen games by 30 or more points—including an impressive 81–40 thumping of nationally respected St. John's, a squad that UK would meet again.

On the day after Christmas, with his knee healing but the point-shaving scandal continuing to draw national attention, Bill Spivey asked that he be removed from eligibility pending resolution of any participation by him in the scandal. Spivey later testified under oath and even took lie-detector tests in an effort to clear his name. These efforts didn't help.

It was a Jekyll-and-Hyde existence for Kentucky basketball in 1951–1952. On the court, another fabulous Wildcat team remained ranked number 1 in the nation for most of the season and seemed likely to win a fourth NCAA Tournament Championship. Off the court, the rumors grew louder, and although Rupp initially defended his players tirelessly, the scandal became an albatross that could not be thrown off.

Spivey had been implicated when two former players testified that he had shaved points. Spivey denied the allegation but admitted that he had been asked to shave points and had not reported the plot to university officials. The university's athletic board eventually voted to remove Spivey from the eligibility list. Spivey had hoped to return for the NCAA Tournament, but he did not.

Of course, Kentucky had been number 1 without an injured Spivey, and there was no reason for things to change. On March 22, 1952, Kentucky played the East Regional Final in Raleigh, North Carolina, presumably en route to the Final Four in Seattle. Just prior to tipoff, Claude received a telegram from Ted Grizzard that Cuba had defeated Clark County in the semifinals of the state high school tournament in Lexington. Claude had left the state tournament site prior to the semifinals to join UK in Raleigh.

At Reynolds Coliseum in Raleigh, the opponent was the same St. John's squad that UK had destroyed by 41 points earlier in the season. This time, however, Coach Frank McGuire's squad shocked UK 64–57. Hagan had 22 points but was outplayed by St. John's center Bob Zawoluk, who finished with 32 points. St. John's continued on to the Final Four, and a disappointed Kentucky squad's season was over. Kansas went on to defeat St. John's in the NCAA that year and then placed the bulk of the players on the USA team at Helsinki. Ed Ashford, writing for the *Lexington Herald* after the game, noted, "The Wildcats in the eyes of the nation's sportswriters and coaches were the best team in the country." Ashford went on to describe that "the saddest sight was the expression on the faces of sportscasters J. B. Faulkner [*sic*], Claude Sullivan and Phil Sutterfield as they canceled their flights

Fabulous Five player Alex Groza with game ball and MVP trophy from the 1949 NCAA Tournament, with Wah Wah Jones, Cliff Barker, and Ralph Beard. Courtesy of UK Athletics.

to Seattle." There would, unfortunately, be much sadder sights in the months to come.

Ralph Beard, Alex Groza, and Dale Barnstable pled guilty to conspiracy in New York court. Each was given a suspended sentence by Judge Saul Streit, who apparently used the gambling trials to crusade against what he saw as the uglier elements of big-time college athletics. The NBA, where Beard and Groza had starred, suddenly was no longer interested in them. Beard told author Charley Rosen for his book *Scandals of '51* that Judge Streit had also told him that if he "so much as touched a basketball in a YMCA" during his three-year suspended sentence, "he'd throw my ass in jail." That more or less ended

Beard's and Groza's promising pro careers. Groza had ranked second in the NBA in scoring in each of his first two seasons and had been named an All-Star in 1951. Beard had been in the top ten in the league in scoring and assists in his two seasons and likewise had been an All-Star in 1951. Neither played another second of NBA basketball. Russell Rice indicates that Groza and Rupp never had any real relationship after the scandal and that only near Rupp's death in 1977 did he and Beard bury the issue and make peace. Humzey Yessin stated in an interview that Beard had told him that he never actually played at less than his full ability. Humzey further derisively spoke of the small amount of money involved as "chicken feed."

As for Spivey, he maintained his innocence not only privately, but also publicly. Unlike the other players, he did not plead guilty. He fought the charges against him, and after indictment his trial ended in a mistrial, with the jury voting 9–3 in favor of his acquittal. The prosecutor did not attempt a second trial, but in the climate of the times Spivey was tainted by association. NBA commissioner Walter Kennedy banned him from the NBA. Spivey would eventually sue Kennedy, and the league settled with him, but far too late for Spivey to play in the NBA. Like Beard and Groza, he became something of a basketball vagabond, a name that was alternately remembered in celebration and in cursing.

When Judge Streit sentenced Beard, Groza, and Barnstable, he ordered the Kentucky State Welfare Commission to investigate the situation. Although that investigation apparently amounted to much of nothing, the SEC and the NCAA also began poking about in Kentucky's garbage. The SEC examined the situation and in August 1952 ruled that Kentucky basketball would be banned from SEC play for the 1952–1953 season. That is to say, Kentucky could not play against any of the other teams in the conference. The vote was near unanimous, with only the University of Tennessee voting against the ban.

Accordingly, Rupp went ahead with plans to play solely a non-conference schedule in 1952–1953. At that point, the NCAA reared its head. As is not entirely out of keeping with its modern character, the august governing body of collegiate athletics, realizing the difficulty of ever sorting out point shaving or controlling it when there was no law against it in Kentucky or most states, chose other grounds for action against Kentucky. Kentucky would be banned from play for the 1952–1953 basketball season based on a number of small payments from boosters or directly from the university to players from 1946 through 1951. UK president Herman Lee Donovan, likely tired of the entire business, chose not to appeal the findings, but to enforce the one-year ban, along with some minor penalties in football, where illegal benefits had also apparently been paid.

From this period, Claude's notes include a preliminary statement from the university in which the school pointed out, "It seems that Judge Streit attributes the athletics scandal at Kentucky to 'the inordinate desire by the trustees and alumni of Kentucky University for prestige and profit from sports.'" Even in 1952, that accusation sounded absurd when Kentucky basketball's annual budget was a mere $107,000. The university also noted that at no point in the NCAA's sixty-seven-page report was any mention made of "organized gambling in New York, or the criminals that produced the scandal."

Rupp was furious, famously vowing that he would not rest well until the NCAA president had to hand him another championship trophy. As noted earlier, he had been emphatic in his defense of his players and in arguing that cancelling the season for a team that had nothing to do with the point shaving or illegal benefits was too harsh a penalty. Meanwhile, President Donovan was for the most part meekly submitting to the penalties despite the fact that NCAA athletics in general, then as now, was hardly a bastion of propriety.

Of course, for most of the proceedings Claude Sullivan was as confused as any Kentucky supporter. Unlike most people, he had a platform and a voice to share his thoughts with the nation. In late December 1952, doubtlessly after much deliberation, he did just that, reading this editorial on his daily *Wiedemann Sports Eye* radio show:

> At this Christmas time we're caught wondering. Wondering how some other folks are feeling. The president of Michigan State, Mr. John Hannah, has been condemning the big-time athletics right all along. His football teams, however, have been tearing everything in the country apart. Then the day before the big game with Notre Dame, his first-string quarterback, Don McAuliffe, was robbed of sixteen tickets the athletic department had GIVEN him. At the going rate, they were worth $560. He was robbed of them when a phone caller asked him to come to an apartment if he wanted to sell them.
>
> Remember the main reason the University of Kentucky was suspended from basketball? They had given some players $50 spending money before a Sugar Bowl tournament in New Orleans. Not tickets, but money which couldn't be spent since it was left over from a subscription to send a couple of boys to the 1948 Olympic Games.
>
> How [do] the people connected with the NCAA feel this Christmas Eve watching CCNY play basketball when the school had to fire the basketball coach for what they called fixing grades and paying money? Grades were altered to get the boys in school and then fixed to keep them eligible according to the university.
>
> Yet CCNY is still playing basketball, while a fine bunch of Kentucky boys who had nothing to do with the scandal other than read about it in high school are not permitted to play.
>
> It was interesting to note yesterday where the president of

the NCAA, Mr. Hugh Willett of Southern California, lost a
key man just before the Rose Bowl game with Wisconsin. It
seems the boy had been playing a few years too long. Yet Mis-
ter Willet jumped on Kentucky and threw them out.

We also wonder how [banned UK football player] Gene
Donaldson feels this Christmas Eve when he thinks of the
great year he was robbed of because he got a job paying a dollar
an hour. Not quite what sixteen tickets to the Michigan State–
Notre Dame football game on Friday night would bring!

Maybe the chickens are coming home to roost, but nothing
we might say will make much difference to the NCAA because
most often a word to the wise is infuriating.

Claude's cataloging of NCAA inequities undoubtedly struck many
nerves in and around the Commonwealth. Unfortunately, it looked
as though he would have plenty of time to think about the matter because after the 1952 football season it would be a long winter
indeed.

Claude undoubtedly was glad to be back to covering the playing
field instead of the legal beat when the 1952 football season rolled
around. The aforementioned banned lineman, Gene Donaldson
(who was chosen in the third round of the National Football League
[NFL] draft a year later despite missing his senior season), proved
to be a significant loss to the team. Babe Parilli was now plying
his trade with the Green Bay Packers, who had taken him with the
fourth overall pick of the 1952 NFL draft. Dick Shatto was the leading passer in 1952 for UK, and his 221 yards in the season were less
than Parilli had managed in the Mississippi State game alone in
1951. Wide receiver Steve Meillinger was talented, accounting for six
of UK's eight passing touchdowns, but he couldn't throw the ball to
himself. Kentucky fielded the weakest offense in Bryant's UK ten-

ure. The defense had lost much of its talent as well, so UK ended the season at –14 on turnover margin.

In a particularly ironic twist of fate, UK opened the season against Villanova. Kentucky had blasted Villanova the previous season, 35–13, on the day that Beard, Groza, and Barnstable were arrested and the point-shaving scandal materialized. This time around, Kentucky was thumped 25–6 in its opener. After four more games, UK's lone win was a 10–7 triumph at Texas A&M, and the team was 1–3–1.

At the point when Claude had to begin to wonder if his job had gone from blessing to curse, Bryant's squad responded, winning four straight games over Cincinnati, Miami, Tulane, and Clemson, bringing the squad into Knoxville at 5–3–1. Tennessee continued to be Bryant's personal nemesis as Kentucky played well but left with a 14–14 tie rather than with a win.

Still, at 5–3–2, UK edged into the top twenty on the basis of its solid second half of the season. However, in the season finale, it was drilled 27–0 at Florida, ending the season with Bryant's worst UK mark at 5–4–2 and certainly without a bowl bid as Florida, by virtue of its final victory, earned a spot in the Gator Bowl.

In a normal year, a disappointing football campaign would have been just that—disappointing—but with no basketball on deck the question for Claude was what exactly he would do next.

Of course, for a sportscaster, earning pay is contingent on broadcasting games. Without UK basketball, Claude's situation was at least somewhat in limbo. Imagine the surprise, then, when a search through Claude's correspondence years after his death yielded an official-looking letter from WVLK, which stated as follows:

As you are aware, your duties at WVLK included the broadcasting of University of Kentucky Basketball. The weekly payment to you by WVLK was based upon your fulfilling such duties and since there is to be no basketball, we believe you will agree that it is only proper that your salary be reduced in proportion to the amount of work of which you have been relieved. Therefore, commencing November 15, 1952 your weekly salary check will be reduced to $20.94. This has been figured carefully, and is in accord with the Kentucky wages and hour law pertaining to your profession.

The letter was signed (in pencil) by station owner Garvice Kincaid and general manager Donald Horton. Alyce Sullivan, many long years later, laughed when she was shown the letter and said that Claude and Don Horton loved to play practical jokes on each other and that this letter was one such joke. She assured that there was no reduction in pay.

In actuality, Claude was hardly idle; what with his sales and programming duties at WVLK during the 1952–1953 season, he managed to call a selection of games involving the Eastern Kentucky University Maroons, Transylvania University, and local high schools to supplement his play-by-play needs. The inventory of score cards indicates that Claude stayed busy with an expanded schedule of high school games as well as the usual state tournament games. The "lost season" also provided Claude with another chance to shore up yet another spoke in his professional wheel.

Since at least the early years of his time at WKLX, Claude had supplemented his sportscasting work by covering Kentucky's other signature sport—horse racing. He had broadcast the April and October meets at Keeneland, Lexington's horse-racing facility, at least as far back as 1948, when he was calling the feature race. Along with baseball, horse racing was one of his biggest challenges.

Claude would rehearse calling the race based on reading the

racing program the day before the race, memorizing the jockey's color and the horse's name and number. This preparation was based on his early realization that when the horses were in a pack, the race announcer might glimpse only one of the three identifiers in question, and he had just a split-second chance to name the horse, his position and relationship to the field, and the distance from the finish line. Horse racing was an unforgiving sport to broadcast.

One fellow broadcaster, Ray Holbrook, recalled producing commercials for Claude at Keeneland and then in the booth later in Claude's horse-racing career. Ray said he always admired how Claude could announce horse racing, stating, "It was the most difficult thing I ever did. . . . Claude was very, very meticulous in his preparation for the race of the day in everything he did, the same as other sports, basketball, and football. . . . I tried to call a race one day, and I tried it one time . . . I screwed up enough that I never went back to it!" Another announcer of the era, Dee Huddleston, when questioned about broadcasting horse racing, admitted, "I have never tried it, and I have often wondered how they keep up with those horses. You can't take your eyes off the race to look at your notes or anything; you have to stay with it."

Claude did stay with it. Although Cawood Ledford soon became the major name in horse racing in his position at WHAS, Claude stuck with the sport throughout the years. Perhaps his most famous call, Tim Tam's 1958 Bluegrass Stakes win in a photo finish, was years away, but, given the lost basketball season, Claude could spend more time focusing on the ponies. For the remainder of his career, he covered the races and featured them in his daily *Wiedemann Sports Eye* radio show.

Despite staying busy at the horse track and the NCAA's ban on Kentucky basketball, Claude did manage to call a bit of UK basketball during the lost 1952–1953 season. Adolph Rupp remained furious

about the unfair punishment inflicted on his team and was determined to use a year without the distraction of games to hone his
squad into a razor-sharp unit that he would use to slash throughout the national scene in 1953–1954. Cliff Hagan recalls those days,
noting, "It was just drills, drills, drills, drills, drills, and it gets very
long when you don't have games to break it up." In part, to relieve
the boredom and, Hagan believed, to obtain publicity, Kentucky
scheduled four scrimmages in Memorial Coliseum from December
to February. Claude was there for each of the games and apparently
broadcast them all on the Standard Oil Network.

The scrimmage format initially was varsity and freshmen, but
when a talented freshman squad was drilled by 31 points, Rupp
broke the remaining games into Frank Ramsey's team versus Cliff
Hagan's team or else the Blues and Whites, with a relatively even
distribution of the squad's talent.

Claude wrote about the experience in an article penned for the
1953–1954 UK fact book, the early equivalent of the modern media
guide. From the best seat in the house, he penned the following
words entitled "Wildcatting":

One of the strangest seasons in the history of collegiate sports
was written into the annals of athletics last winter during the
suspension of the nation's top-ranked basketball team—University of Kentucky—from intercollegiate competition. . . .
   Charging no admission and adding the incentive of clin-
ical explanations of the Kentucky system, the exhibition
series of four intra-squad scrimmage games, between divided
groups of Wildcat cage candidates drew surprisingly large
crowds. While attendance at sporting events, particularly
basketball attractions, fell off around the country over the
last winter under the competition of television and other
undetermined causes, the quartet of public practice sessions

attracted a total audience of nearly 35,000 into UK's spacious Memorial Coliseum.

The workouts drew, successively, crowds of 6,500 (on the worst night of the winter); 9,000; 10,000 (probably the largest crowd in the South that year); and 9,200. The average of approximately 8,750 for the four-game season likely was some sort of record—especially considering the intramural nature of the affairs. At any rate, the large turnouts were interpreted by most observers as loyalty to Coach Rupp and the scandal-rocked UK team, which unjustly bore the brunt of punishment for something that they had no connection with whatsoever.

Claude went on to write about the squad, naming Ramsey and Hagan as obvious standouts, and Lou Tsiropoulos as the odds-on pick for most improved player. He then talked strategy, quoting Rupp as noting, "There's a lot of lost time in the usual practice schedule, but . . . we didn't lose any." Claude hinted at new plays and new strategies and generally gave notice that when Kentucky finally took to the court again in intercollegiate activity, the result would be something to behold. College basketball would taste Adolph Rupp's wrath.

Meanwhile, when football rolled around again in the fall of 1953, there was a palpable sense of relief in Lexington. However, all was not well with Bear Bryant's program. In 1952, likely under serious prodding from the higher levels of the university, Bryant had announced that UK would stop recruiting players outside of Kentucky and would utilize only five scholarships annually to non-Kentuckians, which would be awarded to players who sought out UK rather than vice versa. Of course, two Wildcats, Gene Davidson and Chet Lukawski, had been suspended in the NCAA investigation, and Bryant could not have been very happy about that either.

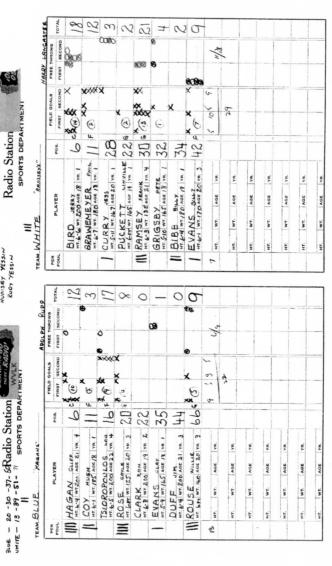

Cliff Hagan's team versus Frank Ramsey's team in the Blue–White Game, January 13, 1953, during the canceled season. From the Claude Sullivan Collection.

But perhaps more than any of those issues, Bryant was likely sick of being in Rupp's shadow. Years later in his own book, Bryant stated, "We were too much alike, and he wanted basketball No. 1 and I wanted football No. 1. In an environment like that one or the other has to go." Indeed, Bryant told *Sports Illustrated* in 1966 that he traced his departure to an incident in 1951, when the university had given Rupp a car after UK won the SEC in basketball again and gave Bryant a watch for winning the SEC for the first time. Funny enough, according to research on the subject, Rupp wasn't awarded a car until March 1955, but the governor of Kentucky and twenty-five UK boosters awarded Bryant a car after the 1952 season, with the governor proclaiming him a lifetime Kentuckian.

This story of an alleged battle for supremacy between Rupp and Bryant eventually gained public acceptance due in part to Bryant's own comments, but those closest to the situation doubt it. Jim Host recalled Bryant asking Rupp and a few media members to his home after Rupp's last game at Alabama in 1972. Host recalled the legends sharing a fifth of bourbon and calling each other "Paul" and "Adolph" and swapping friendly stories. Although there was doubtlessly some rivalry, a deep and abiding affection between the two was apparent to those who knew them best.

In any case and for whatever reasons, Bryant was not very contented when the 1953 season began. After UK opened the season by losing to unranked squads from Texas A&M and Ole Miss, even an optimist would have been looking on the dark side. But with All-Americans Ray Correll on the offensive line and Steve Meillinger catching passes at end, sophomore quarterback Bob Hardy improved week to week. The Kentucky offense, although not back to the glory days of Parilli, improved its scoring average by nearly a touchdown per game from the previous year, and the defense led to a +3 turnover margin on the season.

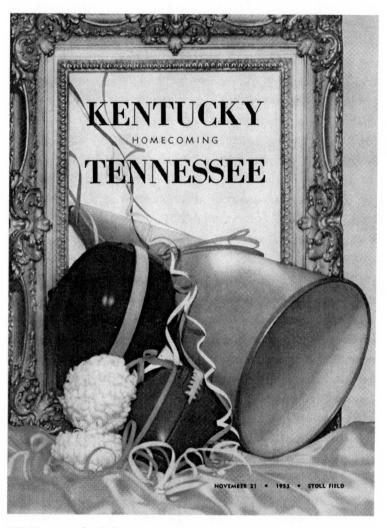

UK–Tennessee football game program, November 21, 1953, from Bear Bryant's last game at Kentucky and his only win over Tennessee. From the Claude Sullivan Collection.

Kentucky won six of the next seven games after their tough start, with the lone exception being a tie with number 14 LSU. UK was 6–2–1 when Tennessee came to Stoll Field to end the regular season. UK had risen steadily to number 13 in the national rankings, but Tennessee always seemed to kill off whatever momentum UK could muster. It had been eighteen years earlier, in 1935, that Kentucky had last won an annual matchup with the Volunteers. Claude had been ten years old at the time. Since then, with the exception of ties in 1948 and 1952, Tennessee had carried the day. With the winless streak threatening to reach adult status, both the Wildcats team and the man behind the microphone were ready for the late November showdown.

Claude's radio call from that day survives and is a masterful example of his talent at setting a scene. Thousands huddled around the radio and tuned in to the Standard Oil Network heard him say:

> Good afternoon, football fans everywhere, from Stoll Field on the campus of the University of Kentucky in Lexington— where the skies are perfectly clear with not a cloud in sight, brilliant sunshiny day, where the fans here on the southern side of a jam-packed Stoll Field and McLean Stadium in the shade with coats on and across the way in the sun-bathed northern side of the stadium many, many fans in shirt sleeves for the big game this afternoon. Because this is it! Kentucky versus Tennessee—a game that comes once a year and packs a wallop of Christmas. It has been the same story since 1893, a gridiron rivalry that carries more color, more glory, more prestige than any football game around the country. . . .

These two great neighboring universities have acquired friends and followers in distant parts of the nation that probably never have seen the two states but nonetheless rise up for the annual November battle. This afternoon's game has only one strange aspect—the Wildcats of Kentucky are favored to win. . . . Everyone here this afternoon is doggedly pulling for Kentucky or Tennessee. We imagine there are very few fans in the stadium that are just looking for a good football game, and the prize to the winner will probably be their pick of the Cotton or the Sugar Bowl.

Kentucky was ready to make history, scoring two early touchdowns to stake itself to a 13–0 advantage. Tennessee answered, as it always had for the past seventeen years, responding with two scores of its own to gain a 14–13 advantage. From there, it was back and forth. Kentucky scored after another long drive and led 20–14. Tennessee answered and reclaimed a 21–20 advantage. Late in the game, Harry Kirk blocked a Tennessee punt, and three plays later Bob Hardy pitched out to running back Ralph Paolone, who scored a 22-yard touchdown, putting UK back on top at 27–21.

Tennessee had time for one final drive and converted two first downs, the second on a fourth-and-5 play that defied logic because the Tennessee quarterback looked to be cornered but still converted a first down. Tennessee had second and 4 at the UK 46, when two penalties dropped them back across midfield. Bob Hardy, killing the Volunteers on both sides of the ball, intercepted a third-down pass inside the final two minutes, and suddenly Kentucky had nothing to do but run the clock out.

In the final seconds, Claude sounded as if his Christmas metaphor from the pregame were a reality. Counting down the final seconds, his elated call was, *"Has Kentucky beaten Tennessee? Have they? THEY SURE HAVE!"* Claude went on to add, *"A lot of folks are being carried off the field, and especially Bear Bryant."* As Claude signed off for the season, he noted that the fans were tearing up the goalposts by their roots. He advised listeners who planned to travel by Stoll

Field the following morning that he suspected there would be no goal posts standing.

The drought was finally over, and Bryant had slain the giant that was Tennessee. Russell Rice indicates in his book *The Wildcats* that Kentucky was offered a bid in the Gator Bowl and that Bryant brought the news to the training room, where the team was eating. When he asked, "How many centers want to go?" no one raised a hand in support of the idea. He repeated the exercise, asking the guards, and again no one was interested. Bryant proclaimed, "Hell, we can't play without centers and guards." No bowl bid was accepted, and Kentucky would be shut out of the bowls for the next twenty-three years.

Meanwhile, Bryant's name remained on the hot list for schools searching for a new head coach. The LSU Tigers came calling in January 1954, and Bryant turned them away. Russell Rice quotes the Bear as saying on that occasion, "I . . . hope I am fortunate enough for Kentucky to be my home forever."

It wasn't. A month later Texas A&M apparently made Bryant an offer that he couldn't refuse. Maybe his incentive for leaving was gaining the athletic director post, which Texas A&M gladly ceded to him. Maybe it was getting out of the vicious SEC or away from the stigma of NCAA sanctions. Or maybe it was the shadow of Rupp, as Bryant later contended. Alyce Sullivan recalled Claude telling her that Bryant's departure was a matter of money. She knew that Bryant had been happy in Lexington. Claude told her that Bryant had incredulously told him that Texas A&M offered him not only large amounts of money, but also ownership of oil wells. Regardless of what story was accepted, the Bear would no longer be the head coach of the Kentucky Wildcats. Kentucky football would simply never be the same.

As for Kentucky basketball, as his writing showed, Claude remained optimistic. But how would the team react after a year off from competition? Had the game passed Adolph Rupp by, or would Kentucky emerge as a team on a mission and soar to even greater heights? Claude, like his audience, had many questions and few answers.

5

A Return to Normalcy

In the winter of 1953, Adolph Rupp's Wildcats prepared to play their first game since the disappointing NCAA Tournament loss to St. John's twenty-one months earlier. The team was anchored by Hagan, Ramsey, and Tsioropoulos, as well as by a head coach with something to prove. Rupp yearned for another NCAA Tournament Championship, and with a year of practice he had assembled perhaps his best squad yet.

Thirteen thousand fans turned out in Memorial Coliseum to see Kentucky's opener with Temple. Kentucky led by 17 at the half and routed Temple 86–59. The big story, however, was an individual performance. Cliff Hagan, giving a welcome-back gift to the Kentucky fan base, dropped a Wildcat record 51 points on the Owls. With Hagan hitting his deadly hook shot, Rupp's Wildcats looked to have picked up exactly where they had left off.

Indeed they had. In an effort to compensate for not exposing his squad to the bright lights and big cities that had been an environment for trouble in the past, Rupp and athletic director Bernie Shively began the University of Kentucky Invitational Tournament (UKIT). The aim of the new tournament, according to Claude in one of his pregame introduction spots, was to return big-time basketball to the campus and "to provide the public with a view of top-flight basketball as it is played in different sections of the country." Claude also noted the secondary goals of "furthering the high ideals of an on-campus tournament and rejecting overemphasis of commercialism [as the] net proceeds of the UKIT are divided among the teams."

The first UKIT field included ranked Duke and LaSalle squads and a UCLA team led by a young coach named John Wooden. Kentucky beat Duke by 16 and LaSalle by 13 in winning the event, which became an annual tradition. In a recent interview, Hagan was poetic about the UKIT, recalling how it provided tough competition and allowed fans who did not normally attend games a special opportunity at tickets over the Christmas break. The annual tradition continued for another three and a half decades.

The 1953 UKIT games were some of the more competitive matchups UK played. For the season, Kentucky posted ten victories by 30 points or more, topping the 100-point mark in six games. Hagan averaged 24 points per game, Ramsey added 19.6 per outing, and Tsioropoulos, who was second in rebounding to Ramsey, averaged 14.5 points per game himself.

UK fluctuated between the number 1 and number 2 spots in the polls but did not lose a game. In fact, the team rarely came close. Only in a 6-point win over Xavier did an opponent play within single digits of the Wildcats. Meanwhile, the rest of the SEC dwindled away, until only one challenger remained.

LSU was led by All-American forward Bob Pettit and also refused to lose, at least in SEC play. Although a great player, Pettit never beat Kentucky, losing in Louisville, Lexington, and Nashville. When the season was completed, both LSU and UK arrived with undefeated marks in the conference. Because the SEC Tournament had been discontinued during UK's probation season (and would remain so for decades), the schools reached a compromise. They would meet in Nashville's Memorial Gym for a playoff to decide the SEC champion—and to decide the squad that would gain an NCAA Tournament berth.

Meanwhile, even during a glorious 1953–1954 season, which marked the "Golden Anniversary" of the UK basketball program, the last vestiges of old controversy swirled around the Wildcats. Hagan, Ramsey, and Tsioropoulos, the trio that had scored 58 of UK's average 87 points per game, might be ruled ineligible. Because the three were seniors and, due to the NCAA's ban, had completed an "extra" season with no game competition, all three were now graduate students—still enrolled at the university, but having already completed their undergraduate degrees. There was talk that the SEC or the NCAA might sideline the trio for their unusual "crime" of completing their degrees too quickly, which would doubtlessly cripple the Cats.

For the LSU game, the rumors remained just that. The SEC allowed the game to go forward as planned. Although Hagan had been the hero to begin the season, Ramsey had the stellar night in the SEC playoff game. LSU forward Pettit and Hagan had 17 points each and four fouls. The two stars basically offset each other, with neither having his best game. However, Ramsey managed 30 points, and Kentucky slowly stretched a 2-point halftime lead into a 63–56 triumph. Rupp had his sixteenth SEC championship, and Claude's broadcasting record extended to a perfect six SEC titles in six seasons with the Wildcats. Kentucky was back on top, but only briefly. After the game, the NCAA announced that Hagan, Ramsey, and Tsioropoulos were ineligible for the NCAA Tournament based on their status as graduate students. The three seniors had not only been robbed of a season due to the crimes of others, but now they were being punished because they had taken care of business academically and gained their diplomas.

Memories differ as to the scene in the locker room. Some insist that Rupp allowed the team to vote as to whether they would accept the NCAA bid without their three senior stars. Others deny that such a vote even occurred. Even those who say there was a vote assert that Rupp disregarded the vote. Both Tsioropoulos and Hagan agreed that a vote occurred and that the vote was 9–3 to accept the NCAA bid. Hagan recalled Rupp angrily overturning the vote, announcing, "No! I'm not going to take you bunch of turds . . . and ruin our perfect season!" Tsioropoulos was thankful, saying that going to the tournament would have been a mistake that destroyed the perfect season. LSU accepted the NCAA bid, and Kentucky returned to Lexington, undefeated but denied the national championship.

One of the few advantages of not making the NCAA Tournament trip was that Claude's social calendar was a bit more open than usual. A few weeks later, in April 1954, he found himself spending an afternoon with one of America's premier entertainers, the great Bob Hope. He played a round of golf in a foursome with Hope, local businessman Ralph Carlisle, and former Kentucky governor and Major League Baseball commissioner A. B. "Happy" Chandler. Golfing aside, Claude took advantage of the situation to interview Hope, who was complimentary of Claude's broadcasting work and expressed his happiness to be in Lexington for a performance at Memorial Coliseum that evening. Chandler could not resist hamming it up for Claude and insisted on singing a couple of songs with Hope.

That evening Claude and Alyce found themselves at the concert and enjoying a postshow cocktail party and dinner with many of Lexington's most prominent citizens. A photograph of the two with Hope, Carlisle, and Chandler preserved the memories of the evening and appeared many years later in a 2003 magazine article as Hope was celebrating his one hundredth birthday. From Rupp and Bryant to Hope, Claude's career voyage continued to amaze, particularly con-

At the Lexington Country Club, May 1954. Claude played golf with Bob
Hope and interviewed him and Governor Happy Chandler. *From left to
right:* Ralph Campbell of the Campbell House Hotel, Chandler, Claude,
Alyce, and Hope. Courtesy of *The Lane Report* 2003.

sidering that he was still in his twenties. Hope continued on to Louisville, where he enjoyed the Kentucky Derby. Claude moved forward
with his career, unaware that he was destined to follow in Hope's footsteps again soon, but this time on the other side of the world.

Soon enough the 1954 football season rolled around, with Blanton
Collier assuming the unenviable position of replacing Bear Bryant
as head coach on the Wildcat sideline. Collier, who was a transplant
from the NFL's Cleveland Browns, brought an excellent coaching
staff with him and seemed to be a solid fit for Kentucky. Quarterback Bob Hardy returned, and a young receiver named Howard
Schellenberger, who would go on to do great things as a head coach

himself in a few decades, gave UK a potent attack. The Kentucky defense was almost as stout as it had been under Bryant.

After the team began 0–2, they went 7–1 for the rest of the season. The turning point was likely week four of the season, when the 1–2 Wildcats faced an Auburn squad that had played in the Gator Bowl in 1953 and, in fact, returned to the same postseason berth in 1954. The teams traded scores until the game was tied at 14 in the fourth quarter. Kentucky drove deep into Auburn territory, bidding for an upset of the Tigers. An excited Claude brought the crucial play of the game home to the Kentucky fan base: "Eight minutes and fifty-five seconds to go. Auburn has a tremendous defensive job on its hands now. Kentucky, two feet away, on second down, with a 14–14 score on the boards. Kentucky led 7–0, then tied; they moved ahead 14–7 and caught once again. Hardy takes, moves to the right, outside guard, HE MADE IT, TOUCHDOWN, Bob Hardy!"

The Wildcats' 21–14 upset of Shug Jordan's team gave them the momentum needed to withstand the rest of the season. The squad went on to beat a ranked Georgia Tech squad and won the season's last four games, including a 14–13 thriller at Tennessee. Indeed, Collier, whatever his flaws were, proved to be the Tennessee killer. His 5–2–1 mark against the Volunteers is by far the best record posted by any UK coach against Tennessee. Unfortunately, he was not quite as sharp against the rest of the competition. That 7–3 UK team did not receive a bowl invitation. It did earn Collier the SEC Coach of the Year award. Not only was the 7–3 record Collier's best UK mark, but it was the best record the team would post for the next twenty-two years.

The 1954–1955 Wildcat basketball squad had some big shoes to fill. But, of course, Rupp didn't rebuild; he simply reloaded. Junior college big man Bob Burrow was new to the team but was talented enough to manage to join the 1,000-point club in only two seasons—a feat only a handful of Wildcats have achieved to this day. Billy Evans and Gayle Rose returned from the unbeaten squad and were joined by Jerry Bird and Phil Grawemeyer, two junior forwards who could also score in bunches.

This Kentucky team would become famous not for winning, although it won all except three games, but for losing: on January 8, 1955, Kentucky fans witnessed an event that they had not seen in some twelve seasons—a home loss. Claude, a couple of weeks past his thirtieth birthday, had been a teenager the last time such an event had transpired.

Unranked and poorly regarded Georgia Tech was a surprising team to end the streak, but the Tech team did indeed beat its talented hosts 59–58 and then beat them again later in the season at Georgia Tech. But it was the home loss, ending a streak of 129 straight wins at home, that everyone would remember.

Ferrell Wellman, now a Kentucky Journalism Hall of Fame member, was a child then, but in a recent interview he remembered that infamous broadcast. Ferrell recalled:

I can remember we had just moved into our house, and I was taking a bath listening to the Georgia Tech game when the winning streak was broken. I mean, I remember that perfectly.

[I was] staying in the bathtub even after the water was cold to see how the game came out. And it's funny. I can't remember hardly anything about most broadcasts, but I remembered that one because I was stunned, and I think that came through in Claude's broadcast at the end. People were just stunned. I remember telling my mother that Kentucky lost, and she said, "But no, you've got it wrong." I said, "No, the game's over. Georgia Tech's won." I remember . . . the stunned manner in [Claude's] voice and maybe in the crowd, and certainly in my bathtub . . . Kentucky lost to Georgia Tech.

Despite the most memorable event of the season being that loss, there was still a great moment of personal pride for Claude later in the year. On February 28, the Wildcats took on Alabama. Claude signed on with perhaps even more than his usual gusto that evening, telling his audience: "Good evening, basketball fans everywhere. This is Claude Sullivan, speaking from Memorial Coliseum on the campus of the University of Kentucky in Lexington. Tonight, basketball fans, the championship of the Southeastern Conference may be decided in this game between the U of K Wildcats and Alabama, here in Lexington—a game, incidentally, which is being short-waved to our armed forces around the world."

For this game, not only was Claude a national broadcaster, he was an international broadcaster. The Armed Forces Radio network, with seventy-seven stations worldwide, carried every word of the broadcast. Claude was especially proud of sharing the game with American soldiers serving overseas at the time. Although he was still saddened that he had not been able to serve during World War II, by means of this broadcast he was doing his part for Uncle Sam. The Wildcats cooperated with a 66–52 win over the Crimson Tide and did indeed win the SEC Championship.

Two weeks after that game, Kentucky's season ended via a first-round NCAA Tournament loss to Marquette. Burrow had been an All-American, and UK's 23–3 record had placed it at number 2 in the national polls before the tournament. However, a broken leg had sidelined Grawemeyer and weakened the squad. Another SEC Championship and a top-ten ranking would be a highlight for some programs, but Kentucky did not play the game merely for solid regular seasons. The year would ultimately go down as a disappointment.

As 1955 rolled along, Claude was looking to branch out in his career. There was no question of being fulfilled by broadcasting Wildcat sports. Although Claude loved the job, it was not the sort of national work about which he had dreamed. It is unclear when and how often he made overtures to national sports networks. Media, then as now, are ruled by tightly controlled secrets, and although Claude's correspondence from the era contains some hints and suggestions, the true facts were kept private between Claude and Alyce.

What is known is that in 1955 Claude suddenly saw an opportunity where one had not existed before. Ten years after the conclusion of World War II, world political relations were if not comfortable, at least grudgingly improving. Russia, determined to flex its muscle on the world stage, indicated that it would be opening its borders to American travelers in 1956. For a journalist, a young man, and a born adventurer such as Claude, the opportunity was simply too good to pass up. Quietly he began to make inquiries. He spoke with Pan Am Airways, which would make the first American flights into Russia. Determined to absorb as much preliminary education as possible, he also began taking Russian classes at UK.

It is impossible to guess exactly what Claude hoped to gain from his travel plans. Sponsoring a tour group through WVLK was a vehicle not only for the adventure and experience, but also for the journalistic reporting because the tape recordings he made were his main reason for making the trip. It is unlikely that he intended to grab international news scoops or dabble briefly in governmental spying. It is clear that he intended international travel to be another spoke on the wheel of his career, and the results, like everything else he touched during this period, were astounding.

Meanwhile, the day-to-day work of covering UK athletics continued into football season in the fall of 1955. Both Hardy and Schellenberger were back, and the latter had such a great season that he would be chosen first-team All-American. Both the offense and the defense recorded slightly better seasons than they had the previous year.

Yet somehow Kentucky failed to parlay this improvement into

more than a competent year. Oddly, the team went 2–0–1 against teams in the top twenty-five over the course of the season. However, the same team lost by 34 at Vanderbilt and dropped a home game to Mississippi State. Kentucky climbed as high as number 17 in the national polls but eventually faded back.

Still, for anyone who had broadcast as many tough losses to Tennessee as Claude had, the finale in Lexington had a chance to provide a highlight. Kentucky, gunning for a third straight victory over Tennessee after an eighteen-year drought without a single win against that team, powered the ball down the Volunteers' throats with running back Bob Dougherty. Tennessee star (and future Volunteers head coach) Johnny Majors was injured late in the first half and could not return to the game. There would be no suspense this year—just excitement. Claude called it like this:

> Tennessee, single wing left. Kentucky loosens the defense a little more. Carter, the tailback, takes it, rolls out, the pocket collapses, and he fumbles. A fight for the ball at the 45 yard line. . . . Kentucky GOT THE FOOTBALL. It was Ray Callahan, the left guard, who is playing his last game. Seven seconds to go, the chant starts, as Kentucky apparently will not run a play. Two seconds, one second, it's all over. Ladies and gentlemen, there you have it, as Kentucky has, for three straight years, beaten Tennessee. . . . Blanton Collier is being carried from Stoll Field.

The 23–0 shutout of Tennessee meant that Kentucky finished the season at 6–3–1, although the Wildcats ended up again outside of the bowl picture or the national rankings. Blanton Collier's days of triumph unfortunately would not last.

As the winter transitioned from the cold final weeks of football to the beginning of the 1955–1956 basketball season, there was again room for optimism in the UK camp. All-American post player Bob Burrow was back for his senior campaign, and not only did Bird and Grawemeyer return, but sophomores Vernon Hatton and John Crigler gave Rupp a talented, if not particularly deep, squad.

Still, this group would never gel like Rupp's other recent squads. In the first four games of the season, Kentucky lost a game and won the other three by only 1 point, 2 points, and 10 points. The loss had come to Temple, and the Philadelphia school would quickly establish a white-hot rivalry with the Cats.

Another clue that all was not well in Lexington came when Dayton beat UK in the UKIT finals 89–74 four days before Christmas. That loss would prove to be UK's worst UKIT loss in the seventy-four games UK has played in the history of the tournament.

To be sure, SEC competition showed that this UK team was no laughingstock. Wins over Georgia Tech by 53, over LSU by 42, and over Georgia by a mind-blowing 77 points (143–66) showed that on a given night UK could hang with most teams. But, by the same token, a 101–77 loss to Alabama on February 25 ensured that the Crimson Tide and not UK won the SEC Championship. Discounting the lost season, UK's last year of not winning the SEC Championship had been 1942–1943, which began when Claude was just seventeen years old.

Alabama declined an NCAA Tournament invitation based on the university's Jim Crow policy against playing racially integrated opponents, and so UK played in its place. After a victory, the Cats dropped to 20–6 and bowed out of the tournament with an 89–77 loss to Iowa. UK finished the season ninth in the AP poll. Burrow had been superb, averaging 21.1 points per game, and Hatton and Crigler had shown particular promise, with the former being named SEC Sophomore of the Year (an award given because freshmen were not eligible for competition).

After that season wound down, Claude was given the go-ahead to plan to enter the Soviet Union. He would be leading a touring group from New York, an unlikely proposition that had begun through Paul Grubbs, Alyce's brother, who worked at the Kentucky Chamber of Commerce. An article in the *Louisville Courier Journal* in 1956 indicated that the folks in Louisville were not coming to the travel agencies in droves to book tours of Russia. Although Claude was understandably nervous due to the political tensions that continued between the United States and the Soviet Union, he looked forward to a three-week trip in August 1956, where he would be one of the first Americans allowed into the country in years. He was intellectually curious about the Communist stronghold, and he perceived the broadcasting opportunities, perhaps in sending tapes back to WVLK to air.

Claude would add another spoke to his professional wheel and would take a break from covering touchdowns and foul shots in order to dive deeply into the world political scene. Suffice it to say that the twists and turns that he would encounter were at least as amazing as any provided by Adolph Rupp's and Bear Bryant's squads. In fact, on at least one occasion the stakes were higher than anyone might imagine.

6

Kentucky Broadcaster, International Man of Mystery

In August 1956, on his Pan American flight Claude Sullivan crossed over eastern Europe from Sweden to Helsinki, Finland. He had hoped to travel with the UK players to Helsinki as part of the 1952 Olympic Games. Those plans were canceled when St. John's upset UK in 1952, but now, four years later, he found himself with his first tour group headed on a train from Helsinki to Leningrad, Russia. The full itinerary of the 1956 trip is in Claude's diary, the details telling us the six members of the first WVLK tour group visited twelve countries. Claude worked the better part of a week to secure the six visas needed to enter the country. On August 12 at 7:15 a.m., Claude entered Communist Russia through the Iron Curtain, which amounted to two ranger-type towers with spotlights.

Russia was in a transitional phase, with Stalin's death in 1953 gradually giving way to Khrushchev's Thaw, a period when some openness with the rest of the world was promoted, and a gradual decline in censorship coincided with a general improvement in the typical Russian lifestyle.

It was into this tentatively opening world that Claude arrived only a few weeks after Bob Hope had undertaken a similar journey. By all indications, the Russians were as interested in Claude as he was in them. He later recalled being shown "state-of-the-art" Russian broadcasting facilities, which in reality were generally of substandard quality compared to the technology and equipment Claude was utilizing in America. Particularly noteworthy was the lack of any real manner of mobile technology. Claude's broadcasts had no equivalent within Russian life. Although the Russian culture was softening on a free press, again Claude was struck by the contrast to what he knew in America. He told the *Louisville Courier-Journal* in 1957, "One thing that is hard for me to take is their lack of news. Newspapers are cheap but they're just one big editorial page, printing mainly what the government, who owns them, wants printed." He also noted that a television station he had toured gave no coverage to news such as fires and accidents and that when he had asked about this, he was asked in turn, "Who would want to hear that?"

The most memorable moment of Claude's first trip, which was still a rather cautious venture, was being allowed to view the bodies of Stalin and Lenin, lying in state under the Kremlin. Although there were long lines to view the bodies, Claude recalled his tour director saying, "You are foreign visitors, and when I say, 'You go to the front of the line,' then you go to the front of the line." Claude willingly complied.

Lenin had died in 1924, the year Claude was born, so there was much curiosity in America as to how Russia maintained a thirty-two-year-old corpse. For his part, Claude could offer little technical insight into the preservation. He did say on his return that there was no doubt that the bodies of Lenin and Stalin were certainly real and that they were apparently being preserved by some manner of refrigeration system from below because the cold air was tangible within the vault. Bob Hope, who had made the Russian expedition a few weeks ahead of Claude, had viewed the bodies of the two leaders and jokingly dubbed them, according to Alyce, the "Cold Cuts." Claude recalled in his diary that Lenin's ears had gone black, but he also noted that his hands had been placed on his stomach and that he looked as if he could sit up and shake hands with his viewers.

The three weeks flew past, and Claude found himself planning to return to the Soviet Union, hopefully for a longer visit, next time with Alyce joining him in 1957. He also planned to use his second visit for broadcasting purposes. Having completed the grunt work of making contacts and establishing a good first impression, Claude looked forward to his return trip. He would share the trip, through WVLK, with his listening audience—even if one story would prove to be so interesting that it could not be shared.

Back in the states, Claude and WVLK had pioneered mobile broadcasting in Kentucky with the creation of the WVLK mobile unit. Paul Dunbar was the station engineer who adapted the technology for the mobile unit, and Claude worked closely with him in assembling the finished product.

Soon after his return from Russia, Claude had one of the mobile units installed in the trunk of his car so he could report "on the go." The equipment was very bulky, and the space it required compared to today's technology was extreme. The notes from the concepts that Claude worked on stated that the intended purposes of the mobile unit were public service, promotion, news, and goodwill. Examples he gave were covering a Kentucky–Tennessee football game and news events such as a drowning. The unit was projected to be live sixteen hours a day for seven days a week. Station engineer Paul Dunbar was responsible for maintenance, and a complete budget was prepared.

Retired broadcaster Ray Holbrook remembered the technological marvel that Claude assisted in developing. Holbrook recalled,

Mobile unit with reporter Paul Warneke, 1957. Claude was program manager of WVLK at the time and spearheaded the concept for community goodwill and news coverage. Courtesy of WVLK Radio.

"The mobile unit went out every morning at 6:00 a.m. That is when we started to cover news . . . with it. I think they had two turntables. It was a great PR unit. There were some mobile units in the country, but WVLK was on the cutting edge." There is no doubt that the ability to go mobile helped WVLK stay on the cusp of developing local news.

The mobile unit allowed Claude and his colleagues both to broadcast from remote locations and to stay in touch with WVLK from the road. Sportscaster Tom Hammond remembers growing up in the shadow of Lafayette High School and seeing Claude drive down Reed Lane with the "whiplash" antenna coming out of his trunk. Paul Warneke was one of the first mobile-unit reporters pho-

(Above) Claude broadcasting in his Oldsmobile convertible, with remote equipment in the trunk and a long "whiplash" antenna for sending and receiving. Courtesy of WVLK Radio. *(Below)* Claude's trunk showing the bulky equipment required to transmit remotely back to WVLK. Courtesy of WVLK Radio.

WVLK studio showing bulky equipment in the production studio at that time, around 1958. Courtesy of WVLK Radio.

tographed in the late 1950s when the unit came out. David Sullivan later became a mobile-unit team member, as was NBC's Tom Hammond in the late 1960s.

Claude was pioneering the use of mobile broadcasting locally for WVLK, and internationally he was breaking down barriers with delivery of firsthand overseas news to his audience at home. Concurrently he was program director at WVLK and had duties in Lexington to pay attention to. Jim Host was a new hire of Claude's and began as a disc jockey. Jim, then a young radio novice, remembers his early work as a disc jockey working for Claude. One time while working at night, Jim saw the red light on the control-room monitor come on, and he knew it was Claude calling in to check on something. "I hated Elvis," Host laughingly recalled. Given his position as a disc jockey, Host was expected to adhere to the station's top-forty format, playing the hits of the moment on an endless loop. When he conveniently failed to play one of Elvis's records in the appropriate slot, the phone immediately lit up. It was Claude, calling from his car. "Did you forget something, Jim?" he asked. Host feigned innocence, and Claude told him, "You know what I mean, and if you skip playing Elvis again, it will be the last thing you ever do for me." The two remained good friends, and Host refrained from skipping Elvis in the station's playlist from then on.

Claude's pursuits during the fall eventually turned to the more familiar role as voice of the Kentucky Wildcats gridiron hopes. As the 1956 football season arrived, Claude was back once again on the Standard Oil Network. Blanton Collier's 1956 Wildcats squad was led by tackle Lou Michaels. Named All-American as a junior in 1956, Michaels was one of the increasingly rare out-of-state Wildcat recruits, hailing from Swoyersville, Pennsylvania. His brother, Walt, had been a Pro Bowl–level NFL player and had played under Blanton Collier with the Browns. Accordingly, when Collier was hired for the UK job, Lou Michaels chose to spend his collegiate days in Lexington.

Michaels was singled out by his contemporaries as being virtually unblockable as a defensive lineman. At six foot one, 230 pounds, he was also a handful as a lead blocker on running plays. In case that was not enough, he also served as the Wildcats' punter and field-goal kicker. He had to be great—the 1956 UK offense, averaging just 208.4 yards and 11.9 points per game, could not win many games. Kentucky passed for only 360 yards all year, and Michaels was given the difficult task of bailing the Cats out again and again.

In the season opener, a 14–6 home loss to number 4 Georgia Tech, Claude had a new football experience—competing head to head with television. NBC broadcast the game nationally, but if the

Standard Oil Network worried about competition, it didn't show. Television was still something of a rarity, and the Standard Oil Network extended into Kentucky's rural back roads, places where NBC was only a myth.

Despite the team's offensive woes, Kentucky managed a 6–4 mark in 1956. Michaels and his defensive teammates held LSU, Maryland, and Xavier scoreless, and Vanderbilt, Georgia, and Florida managed just 6, 7, and 8 points respectively in three other close wins. In essence, that was it. In the games when opponents put up 13 points or more, UK went 0–4. Included in this category was a 20–6 loss to Tennessee—the first such loss in five years. Although Blanton Collier's three-year record was overall a winning one at 19–10–1, there were grumbles within the Kentucky fan base. At Texas A&M, Bear Bryant had taken the A&M squad from a 1–9 mark in his first year to a 9–0–1 mark in his third season. The question that would have decades to flourish was already taking root: "How did we let Bryant get away?"

Meanwhile, as the 1956–1957 basketball season dawned, there was no danger of Adolph Rupp's leaving Lexington. The Baron of the Bluegrass was firmly entrenched. Rupp is often noted to have half-jokingly cited Psalm 121 in defense of his policy of looking to the hills for his help. In this instance, Hazard sophomore Johnny Cox was ready to come to Adolph's aid. Cox, a six-foot-four scoring machine had been part of eastern Kentucky's run of three straight mountain schools collecting the state tournament hardware. With Cox and junior Vernon Hatton, Rupp had shooters. He also had some great component parts, such as juniors John Crigler, Adrian "Odie" Smith, and Ed Beck. What he did not have was size. At six foot seven, Beck was the sole Wildcat taller than six foot four to play significant minutes. Still, there was room for optimism. Claude, writing for *TV in the Bluegrass* (the local TV guide magazine that

Wah Wah Jones produced, featuring articles on movie stars and local sports, which Claude contributed to many times), noted in a preseason column, "[Rupp] has had tougher jobs of rebuilding. . . . Each time he's met the challenge with what the nation has come to call the 'Yankees' of basketball. So we're not willing to 'bury' the 'Cats."

Cox proved to be all that Rupp had expected. Claude, in another column in *TV in the Bluegrass,* this time two weeks into the season, compared Cox to Wah Wah Jones and admitted, "In comparing the two forwards, you will have to give Cox the edge in this early stage of his career." High praise, indeed, especially from a man who considered Jones a good friend. Only once in his entire sophomore season was Johnny Cox held to a single digit in scoring. In his fifth varsity game, he tallied 34 points in a win over Maryland. On three separate occasions during the 1956–1957 season, he scored 20 or more points in each of four consecutive games. On his way to All-SEC honors, he scored 19.4 points and grabbed 11.1 rebounds per game. Senior Gerry Calvert was solid, as was Hatton, although he missed nearly a month of the season due to an appendectomy. Adrian "Odie" Smith, a junior college product, had a remarkably inconsistent season. He barely played for nearly two months, scoring only 22 points as of January 19, when the Cats played Tennessee. He caught fire in the next seven games, though, scoring in double figures in each, with 24 points against Georgia Tech. He then cooled again, scoring only 22 points combined in his last five games.

After the previous year's brief hiatus, the SEC title again returned to Lexington. Kentucky won the UKIT and the Sugar Bowl Tournament in New Orleans. Although the team scattered four regular season losses into its results, it was number 3 in the nation when it reached the NCAA Mideast Regional final. The Wildcats faced number 11 Michigan State in a game played in Lexington. UK held a 12-point halftime lead, but Spartan star "Jumpin'" Johnny Green pulled eighteen boards and led a comeback to an 80–68 win for Michigan State.

Claude was quick to give credit where it was due, despite the disappointing loss. With befuddlement in his voice, he admitted: "They just whipped Kentucky by 12 points here in the Coliseum, and the thing that makes it even more phenomenal is that to do it they had to beat Kentucky by 24 points in the second half of play. Well, it's an unusual sort of ending to what looked like a tremendous start for the Wildcats based on first-half play."

Although Johnny Cox had scored 17 points, he shot three of twelve from the field and fouled out of the game. Center Ed Beck grabbed sixteen boards, but shot two of ten himself, and the Cats could not match Michigan State's inside game.

Kentucky's season was over, but Claude's was not. After the tough UK home loss in the Mideast Regional, he went on to broadcast the NCAA Championship game, his fourth such NCAA broadcast. Claude kept his scorecard but did not divulge in his notes why he chose to go to Kansas City without his Kentucky team to follow. Whatever his reasons, he selected a great game to cover as the title was decided in a triple-overtime thriller between Kansas and North Carolina. Carolina won the battle 54–53, although Claude was impressed by Kansas's freshman center, who was the game's high scorer with 23 points. Wilton Chamberlain, as Claude's scorecard referred to him, would have better days in basketball. Some were starting to wonder whether Kentucky basketball would as well.

It had now been six seasons since Kentucky had won an NCAA Tournament title—or even contended for one, truth be told. Rupp's vow to make the man who had banned UK from play hand him the NCAA trophy was starting to look a little shaky. Conventional wisdom suggested that Kentucky was feasting off of a mediocre SEC and that although Rupp could win a title with a great team, he could

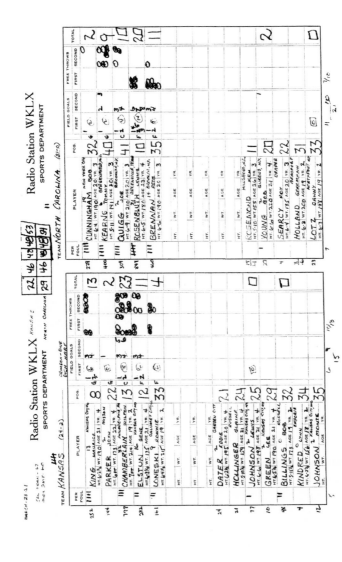

NCAA Championship game score card, Kansas versus North Carolina, who won 54–53 in two overtimes, March 23, 1957. Wilt Chamberlain is listed third on the left side of the card. From the Claude Sullivan Collection.

not direct a flawed team into playing its way into a title. The 1957–1958 UK basketball team looked like it would have plenty of flaws because it was essentially the same collection of players, less second-leading scorer Calvert. But, then, conventional wisdom can be wrong, and that is ultimately why the games are still played.

With the 1956–1957 season completed, games were the farthest thing from Claude's mind. His second tour of the Soviet Union was scheduled with a group from WVLK, and the journey would end up in Brussels, which was preparing to host the World's Fair a year later, in 1958. Alyce planned to join her husband for some rest and relaxation, and this time around Claude looked forward to honing his news-reporting skills by covering the trip for his flagship station. Although it was not the national job he wanted, it could be a stepping stone toward that job. Meanwhile, beautiful scenery and unequalled sightseeing sounded like a nice way to spend the summer of 1957.

It still sounded that way in early June, a few weeks before departure, when a pair of unexpected visitors arrived at the Sullivan household on Lafayette Parkway in Lexington. The two men identified themselves as officers with US Naval Intelligence and asked to speak with Claude. They had become aware of his travel plans and after preliminary small talk asked him if he could obtain some photographs of a Russian ship called the *Aurora*. The vessel was being billed as a new superstructure war ship, and although the American intelligence community had heard of the ship, no one could confirm its existence or provide significant details.

The officers asked Claude to gather any possible information, and if he could sneak a few photographs without being seen, all the better. The officers emphasized that they did not want Claude to endanger himself in any way, but they also reiterated that it was very important to them to learn more information about the *Aurora*.

The winds of fortune were apparently shifting Claude Sullivan—thirty-two years old, married father of two, and professional broadcaster—into yet another role: international man of mystery. It was the sort of news that didn't seem real, the sort that Claude could not and would not tell anyone. But at the same time, Claude's inability to fight in World War II had always annoyed him, and after careful consideration he decided that he would indeed try to gather the requested information—if he could.

The 1957 route is much easier to retrace than the 1956 route, based both on Claude's broadcasts and on his diary. Claude and Alyce landed in London and enjoyed a few days there before they left Britain on July 2. The group moved on to Germany and by July 6 into Soviet-occupied East Germany. From Germany, the group moved on to Poland and on July 9 into Moscow.

Three days later, on July 12, the group traveled into Leningrad (now St. Petersburg), which was a major Russian naval hub on the Baltic Sea. Interestingly enough, it was Navy Day in Leningrad, and Claude Sullivan wondered what he might see. The Soviet guide whom Claude's group was traveling with was a man named Igor Struvnik. He had served as the local guide on Claude's previous tour. Claude enjoyed Igor and later recalled that Igor had fancied himself as quite the connoisseur of American culture, although he noted that one of his favorite popular American songs was "Pistol Packin' Mama," which had indeed been a hit—fourteen years earlier. Claude cultivated a good relationship with Igor, and that was about to become important.

On Navy Day, Claude asked Igor if he might take a few photographs, and Igor saw no harm in the request from his friend. Meanwhile, Soviet regulations had carefully restricted what could and could not be photographed by international visitors. Firmly on the list of off-limit items were trains, bridges, ships, and planes. Nevertheless, Claude wandered off from his touring group to take a closer look at the ships. To his surprise and delight, he found one that he thought might meet the description of the ship that the naval officers had asked about.

Scanning the scene and doing his best to look casual, Claude pulled out his camera and began clicking picture after picture. Suddenly, out popped a Soviet official, frantically waving his hands and shouting, "NO PICTURES, NO PICTURES!" The man raced up to Claude and grabbed his camera.

The worst possible scenario was coming to pass. The angry Soviet official began to open Claude's camera, intending to rip out the film. As for Claude, who knew? Stalin was dead, of course, but his body was still being preserved for visitors, and in 1957 Russia was hardly an inviting human rights state. Would Claude's little mission spark a response from any government officials?

Fortunately it didn't, in large part because Igor happened on the scene just as matters were coming to a head. He promptly marched up to the Russian official with Claude's camera and gave him a verbal dressing down. As Claude watched, the two exchanged heated words, and eventually the official handed the camera back to Claude and stormed off. Claude later asked Igor what he had said. His friend answered, "I told the guy that I am in charge of these people and for him to go blow; I am running this show."

Claude managed to appear sufficiently innocent and puzzled about why the official had been so angry, which was probably quite an act, and to seem quite relieved, which undoubtedly was not an act. The trip wound on through the Ukraine and Georgia. Claude took the opportunity to see broadcasting equipment and sets, but he also was treated to a Russian farm, among other sites. Throughout both trips, Claude took delight in daily meetings and discussions with the Russian people. In an article that ran a few months after his return, he told the *Courier-Journal*, "Russia's youth are the prime hope of the free world. If Americans keep touring and the young

Russians keep meeting them, asking questions and making comparisons, the young Russians are bound to wonder if Communism is the right answer."

The prescience of those words is startling. Claude enjoyed being a cultural ambassador not only for WVLK and for Kentucky, but for the United States. His dabbling in lower-level espionage aside, he had a genuine interest in the people and places he saw. That interest came through in a series of brief newscasts aired on WVLK and called *Sullivan and the USSR*. The broadcasts opened dramatically with the chiming of the Kremlin clock, and each program, running around twelve minutes, took the listeners through the sights and experiences that Claude and his fellow travelers had shared. Or at least most of those experiences.

When Claude flew back to New York from Paris on August 2, there remained one piece of unfinished business. At home, he hurried to develop the film he had taken during his trip, and as soon as the photos came back, he contacted Naval Intelligence. The two naval officers who had seen him in June came by the house on Lafayette Parkway again. When Claude showed them his photographs, the officers were delighted. He had indeed photographed the elusive *Aurora,* and the intelligence officers were very grateful for his hard work. Indeed, it is impossible to say if Claude clandestinely completed other such missions for the United States. The *Aurora* and its secrets have remained well kept for more than fifty-five years. In any case, Claude was proud, relieved, and ready to go back to being a sportscaster.

After Claude's summer adventures, the 1957 Wildcat football season was probably destined to be something of a letdown. Lou Michaels was back for his senior season, and although he could tackle, block, and kick, there was no apparent way of also allowing him to throw, catch, or run with the ball. The 1957 season was fated to be remembered as one of great futility.

With Michaels pressuring backs constantly, the UK defense remained fairly stout, allowing more than 15 points only twice all season. However, after five weeks into the season UK was 0–5 and had scored only 7 total points. Kentucky had played against four teams in the AP top twenty in those weeks, and although it stayed in most of those games until the final minutes, if not the final seconds, it had not lost five consecutive games in more than a decade.

Eight weeks into the season, UK stood 1–7, with only a 53–7 thumping of Memphis State keeping the squad from the list of winless teams. A 27–0 win over Xavier in the season's penultimate game gave Coach Collier a bit of breathing room, and then only number 20 Tennessee remained on the schedule.

Then, as now, there remained a portion of UK supporters who accepted a poor season so long as it included a win over the Volunteers. Collier's track record was proven, and in the week leading up to the Tennessee game he made a move that caused Claude and much of the Wildcat Nation to wonder if it should have been made sooner.

Throughout the season, Michaels had been productive and sometimes dominant from his spot at defensive tackle. The only problem was that opponents tired of running into a brick wall and planned their offense to run away from Michaels as often as possible. Collier realized that he should give Tennessee no such option.

He inserted Michaels at middle linebacker. In *The Wildcats*, Russell Rice recounts Collier telling Michaels that against the conservative Tennessee attack he had no pass coverage responsibilities whatsoever and should simply swarm the ball on defense. It did not take long for the results to be apparent.

With the game scoreless in the first quarter, Tennessee took possession deep in its own end. Claude reported what came next: "Tennessee lines up for the first time in the game. Single wing to the left, on their own 13, first and 10. Wing back in motion, there's a

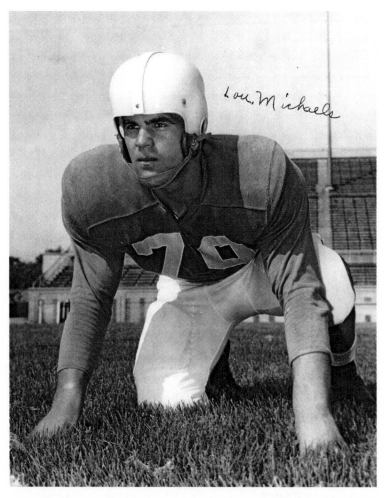

Lou Michaels, All-American football player, 1957, and College Football Hall of Fame inductee. Courtesy of the UK Athletics Department.

fumble in the Tennessee backfield, the ball goes down to the Tennessee goal line, there's a fight for the ball. Who got it in the end zone? It's either a touchback—OR A TOUCHDOWN, KENTUCKY!"

In the pandemonium of the moment, Claude couldn't tell

which Wildcat had recovered for the touchdown, but in fact it was the new linebacker, Lou Michaels, scoring his first and only Wildcat touchdown. Michaels made the extra point and then prepared for the ensuing kickoff.

Again, Claude brought that moment to his listeners: "Michaels lines up to kick off, and here it is. Michaels's kick is high and deep to Bobby Gordon at the Tennessee goal line. He goes back a yard to get it, out to the 5, the 10, the 15, the 20, the 25, the 30, FUMBLES THE BALL, AND KENTUCKY HAS GOT IT. . . . And Gordon is down and hurt as the Wildcats go mad."

It was Mr. Everything Michaels again, covering his own kick-off, and laying such a shot to Gordon that the fumble flew 10 yards forward. UK turned the fumble into another touchdown and never looked back, beating Tennessee 20–7 in Michaels's final game.

Despite leading a 3–7 squad, Michaels finished fourth in the voting for the Heisman trophy. The winner, ironically, was Kentuckian Paul Hornung, who himself had played for a Notre Dame team that also suffered through a losing season—the only Heisman winner for a losing squad. Michaels was chosen as the eighth pick in the following year's NFL draft. Unfortunately, his brilliance did not disguise the worst UK season since 1945.

The upset of Tennessee at least left the season in a positive light. Lightly regarded underdogs that packed more wallop than expected became a common theme around Lexington, and Claude was soon to have perhaps the most exciting season of his career.

7

Fiddlin' and Travelin'

The 1957–1958 UK basketball team was not very highly regarded—even by its own coach. Bert Nelli and Steve Nelli recount in *The Winning Tradition* that when Rupp was asked about the squad before the season began, he said, "We've got fiddlers, that's all. They're pretty good fiddlers; be right entertaining at a barn dance. But I'll tell you, you need violinists to play in Carnegie Hall. We don't have any violinists." Although Rupp thought his team was short on talent (figuratively and literally—as, again, only Ed Beck was taller than six foot four), he could not deny that the group was long on experience. Vernon Hatton, John Crigler, Ed Beck, and Adrian Smith were seniors, and all but Smith had started for multiple prior seasons. Johnny Cox would be the fifth starter, and the junior was coming off a great season.

Although these names resound in history today, at the time there was little reason to fear the group. Hatton and Cox were proven scorers, and Crigler and Beck had experience as quality supporting players. Smith, with his junior college roots and up-and-down previous campaign, was something of a question mark. The team was small, had minimal depth, and frightened essentially no one. However, by the end of the 1957–1958 season college basketball was singing a different tune—and it was one that the Fiddlin' Five, as this group came to be known, played.

After opening the season with wins against Duke and Ohio State, UK hosted Temple on December 7, 1957, in Memorial Coliseum. The Owls, with heralded guard Guy Rodgers, figured to be a tough matchup. Not only was Temple ready for the fight, but it countered impressively, and the ensuing contest was among the best games that Claude ever called.

Temple jumped out early, leading the Cats 21–13 in the first half, before UK trimmed the halftime deficit to a single point, 35–34. Temple again threatened to pull away, opening up a 47–42 lead in the second half. But Vernon Hatton connected on two free throws inside the final two minutes of regulation, which resulted in a 65–65 score, for the ninth tie of the game, which continued into overtime.

In overtime, Temple again jumped ahead, 69–65. In the last two minutes, Kentucky answered by rallying to tie the score once more, but Temple held the ball to the end of overtime, hoping to get a last shot for Rodgers. Claude described the action to his audience: "Temple appears to want just the last shot. There are now sixteen seconds to go. Rodgers out, fakes to break, turns and leaves Smith, now comes to the left side, comes back out deep with ten seconds to go, he moves to the left, there are eight seconds to go, here he makes his move for the shot, spins to the left, and shoots. IT IS GOOD! It is good, and Temple wins. Adrian Smith gets it with one second to go and time-out Kentucky."

Now, with Kentucky facing a 71–69 deficit with one second left and the length of the floor to be traversed, the atmosphere was tense. But Claude settled back in for the last second, as did his audience:

The fans now begin to pour for the exits. They have sat through forty minutes of regulation play, four minutes and fifty-nine seconds of overtime play, and they walk out. This could be the most thrilling play of the season, you know? This time John Crigler will put the ball in play for Kentucky, Ed Beck's under the basket, one second to go, pass to Hatton from thirty-five feet, it's GOOD! HOW ABOUT THAT? HOW ABOUT IT? VERNON HATTON DID IT! And it's tied up, ball game's over, ANOTHER OVERTIME COMING. Stand by, stand by! [long pause] It looks as if Sputnik just went off— coats, hats, sweaters, jackets, everything flying through the air as Vernon Hatton, from forty-five feet, has hit a shot with one second to go in the overtime, that leaves the ball game Kentucky 71, Temple 71, and stand by for another five-minute overtime. We had just finished saying, with the people beginning to walk out, that they were walking out on what could be the most thrilling play of the season, and, by golly, the 12,500 who saw it will never forget it.

Not only the lucky few inside the Coliseum, but many of those listening on the Standard Oil Network also would never forget Hatton's basket.

With the historic buzzer-beater on their side, Kentucky looked to take advantage of their new life. However, the two teams again traded blows throughout the second overtime. Indeed, despite losing Rodgers to fouls late in the second overtime, Temple again had the last possession, but Bill Kennedy's shot rimmed off, sending the game to a third overtime.

In the third overtime, the teams were tied at 81 after a Temple basket, with 1:53 remaining. Hatton took control, draining a basket thirteen seconds later and then, twelve seconds later, adding two free throws for an 85–81 UK advantage. Temple closed the gap to

Vernon Hatton shooting against Temple to tie the game and send it into a second overtime, December 7, 1957. Kentucky eventually won 85–83. Courtesy of the *Lexington Herald-Leader.*

85–83, but, finally, Kentucky ran out the clock and won the longest and probably most dramatic game in UK basketball history. The balanced Cats had been led by Johnny Cox's 22 points; Adrian Smith added 18, but Hatton's 17 points had been pivotal, and his shot to extend the game may be the most famous basket in UK history.

It would be logical for Rupp's squad to have capitalized on this victory by continuing to play well. Instead, UK lost three of the next four games, including a UKIT loss to West Virginia, which featured a sophomore guard named Jerry West. The Fiddlers had hit a few sour notes, but the season was young, and UK stepped up its consistency to new levels. Cox's scoring was a bit down from his spectacular sophomore season, but Hatton was having a superb scoring run, and Adrian Smith was hot more often than he was cold. Beck went on to be honored as the SEC Defensive Player of the Year, and Crigler added punch when needed.

Kentucky won eight in a row and posted a 12–2 mark in SEC play. In a pivotal late-season showdown with Mississippi State, UK wrapped up the league championship in a 72–62 win. Bailey Howell, Mississippi State's All-American forward, had 28 points, but Cox and Hatton combined for 40 in the win.

Nevertheless, UK entered the NCAA Tournament with a 19–6 record. The Cats were number 9 in the AP poll and number 14 in the United Press International rankings. Conventional wisdom had said that this would be another good, but not great, Rupp squad, which would probably be upset in March. But conventional wisdom didn't have to guard the Fiddlin' Five, nor did it figure on UK getting a bit of home cooking. UK was placed in the Mideast Region, which was played in Memorial Coliseum, and the Final Four was placed in Louisville's recently completed Freedom Hall. Now both Claude and the Wildcats could commute to the entire NCAA Tournament.

UK's first tournament foe was Miami of Ohio, with spectacular center Wayne Embry. Embry put up 26 points and fifteen boards despite Beck's steady defense, but UK led by 15 at the half and thumped Miami 94–70. Cox (23 points), Smith (18), and Hatton (14) led a balanced UK effort. Notre Dame was the opponent in the Mideast Regional Final. The number 8 Irish were expected to be equal or perhaps superior to Rupp's squad, as All-American forward Tom Hawkins was a player to be feared. Hawkins, however, was held to 15 points, and UK absolutely blistered Notre Dame, 89–56. Hatton had 26 points, but all five starters were in double figures for UK. For the first time since 1951, UK was bound for the Final Four—and it would be a short trip to Freedom Hall.

As a reward for winning the Mideast Region, UK was matched

up again with the Temple Owls. Vernon Hatton tells the story in his book *Adolph Rupp: From Both Ends of the Bench* of how Rupp was superstitious about a lot of things, including wearing his trademark brown suit. He also believed it good luck to find a bobby pin the day of a game. So before the 1958 NCAA the team planted bobby pins outside of Freedom Hall in Louisville and casually led Adolph to find them. He found a glob of pins and announced, "Don't worry about a thing tonight, boys. We don't even have to take the court: look what I have found!"

The day of the game a chippy Guy Rodgers told Rupp that Temple would win, and the 24–2 Temple squad fought the Cats bucket for bucket. The game was tied at halftime, 31–31. Kentucky went ahead by a few points, and Temple answered. Then Rodgers, playing like the All-American that he was, gave the Owls an advantage, but this time UK answered. The lead changed hands ten times over the course of the evening. Claude found himself having a strong sense of déjà vu as the game wound down. Rodgers gave Temple a 59–55 advantage, and Harry Litwack called for a stall. With 1:30 to go, Adrian Smith sank two free throws, halving the deficit. After a Temple free throw with fifty seconds remaining, Smith sank two more free throws, trimming the score to 60–59 with forty-three seconds to go. With the clock running down, reserve Lincoln Collinsworth fouled Rodgers, who then uncharacteristically missed the free throw. UK rebounded and called for time-out with twenty-three seconds remaining.

Rupp later said that assistant Harry Lancaster had suggested in the huddle that the floor should be cleared for Hatton to drive to the basket. Rupp assented, and Claude brought the pivotal possession to the Wildcat faithful with these words: "Odie Smith out of bounds, Hatton in backcourt, gets the pass, and here we go, twenty-two seconds as the clock moves, Hatton breaks to the right, goes for the basket, hooks it back AND IN! Vernon Hatton gets the field

goal, his fifth of the game. Temple has got time-out with twelve seconds to go."

With Coach Lancaster's play call (some have attributed the last
possession call to Ed Beck), Claude's audience was left to hold its
breath and hope for a defensive stop. In his later years, Rupp admitted, as recorded on a 1970 vinyl album called *Greatest Moments in
Kentucky Basketball,* that some said that Hatton had taken the shot a
little too soon. But Rupp quickly added that "when you are playing
for me, you can't take that shot soon enough!" Rupp had no need to
worry because Temple's Bill Kennedy lost the ball out of bounds on
the ensuing possession, and Kentucky ran out the clock. *"OH MY,
THEY DID IT!"* Claude shouted over the pandemonium following
the buzzer, *"LISTEN TO THIS!"*

From elation, Kentucky moved quickly back to earth. With
one day to strategize, Rupp had to prepare for Seattle University, led
by All-American Elgin Baylor. Baylor, a phenomenal athlete who
would fit in as well in today's game as in 1958's style of play, was not
only great—he was spectacular. Rupp knew that although defenders
such as Crigler and Beck would do their best, neither could run or
leap with Baylor, much less outrebound him. Rumors persist that an
opposing coach, Idaho State's John Grayson, who had faced Baylor
and Seattle in the regular season, paid a midnight visit to Rupp and
suggested the game plan that Rupp adopted. Regardless of whose
idea it was, it quickly became apparent to the Kentucky staff that the
one thing they didn't know if Baylor could do was defend. Accordingly, the Wildcats hoped to exploit the All-American at the defensive end of the floor.

Kentucky expected Baylor to be assigned to Ed Beck when
the game began. Beck, averaging around five points per game, was
certainly not an offensive threat. Fortunately, however, Seattle had
Elgin Baylor defend John Crigler, who had suffered an off night in
the victory over Temple. Rupp instructed Crigler to drive the ball

on Baylor and make him play defense. Although Seattle jumped out to an early lead, the strategy drew dividends. Baylor picked up two quick fouls and had a third by halftime. Seattle led by three points at the half, but the sagging defense that they played to protect Baylor was leaving scoring opportunities for Hatton and Cox.

UK reserve Don Mills found himself drawing major minutes when Beck was sidelined with foul trouble. After Seattle pushed its lead back to six early in the second half, UK began one more run. Mills dropped in a hook shot over Elgin Baylor, giving UK a 61–60 lead with 5:50 to play. From that point, Kentucky never surrendered the lead. Cox scored, Smith made a foul shot, and Hatton drained a free throw and a follow-up basket, for a UK lead 67–60. Although Seattle climbed to within 68–65, it came no closer.

Vernon Hatton was the top Cat, scoring 30 in his final game. Cox added 24 points with sixteen rebounds. Crigler had 14 himself and kept Baylor, who did score 25 points but connected only nine of thirty-two to do so, out of his comfort zone. The sophomore Mills had 9 points off the bench, which was nearly his best game of the season.

As the clock ticked, for the fourth time Claude found himself counting down to an NCAA Championship celebration. His call was as follows: "Kentucky is on top now 82–72, here it is to Don Mills, whips it over, Vernon Hatton jumps, lays it in. For Vernon Hatton, this is his eighth field goal. There are only five seconds to go, Kentucky has a 12-point lead. Elgin Baylor takes the last shot of the ballgame—no good. And . . . THE NATIONAL CHAMPION KENTUCKY WILDCATS!"

The Fiddlin' Five had done nothing less than make history. Six years after banning Kentucky from playing basketball, the president of the NCAA handed Adolph Rupp the championship trophy. History generally agrees with Claude, who, seconds after the buzzer, proclaimed, "This will absolutely, without a doubt, go down as THE coaching year for Adolph Rupp!"

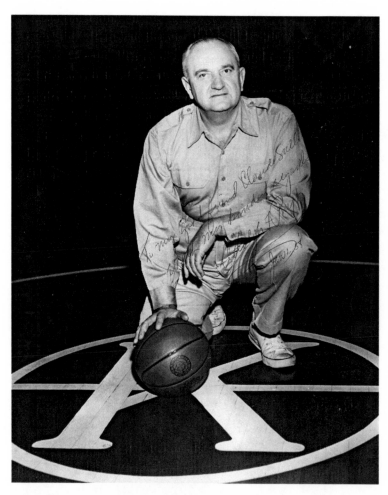

Adolph Rupp just before winning his fourth NCAA crown. The inscription reads, "To my good friend Claude Sullivan, with my kindest regards, Adolph Rupp, January 1, 1958." Courtesy of the UK Athletics Department.

Indeed, for Claude, Rupp, and the Big Blue Nation, several years of tumult and disappointment came to a triumphant end in Freedom Hall. The Kentucky Wildcats were back on top of the world. At thirty-three years old, Claude undoubtedly celebrated his

NCAA Tournament score card for the championship game between Kentucky and Seattle, March 22, 1958. From the Claude Sullivan Collection.

fourth NCAA title. He had no way of knowing that it would be his final NCAA Championship title as the Voice of the Wildcats.

Once the celebration died down, Claude prepared to renew his role as international journalist. WVLK sponsored another trip, this time to Israel and the Mediterranean. The twenty-four-day excursion, with flights on a newfangled Boeing 707, was advertised at $1,585. Claude no doubt expected that his days of international intrigue were over because he was not heading back into the Soviet Communist stronghold. The group began by traveling to Brussels on July 3, 1958, where it visited the World's Fair.

Once again Claude covered the trip for WVLK, with a lag of approximately a week and a half between his recorded reports and their playback in Kentucky. The tapes were flown to Bluegrass Field in Lexington by Piedmont Airlines and delivered to WVLK for broadcast. After Claude reported from Brussels, his trip wound onward through Egypt and into Israel. Although he was enjoying a nice summer vacation, things heated up quickly.

In mid-July 1958, Claude and his tour group walked straight into a governmental insurrection in Lebanon. With international news coverage then being less unified and timely than now, Claude found himself in rare position to report on the rebellion when he landed in Beirut. The rebellion came about when a group of Lebanese Muslims attempted to overthrow the government, with the goal of making Lebanon a part of the United Arab Republic. President Camille Chamoun requested international aid in upholding the established Lebanese government, and 5,000 US marines were briefly deployed. Ultimately, the government survived, and a popular general, Fuad Chehab, who was acceptable both to the United States and to the Muslim interests, became president of Lebanon.

Claude reported back to the United States that the standing Lebanese government had maintained control of the airport in Bei-

WVLK tour group in 1958, led by the Sullivans, on the Sabena Belgean World Airlines trip to the Middle East. *Left to right:* Miss Ruth Averitt, Miss Mildred Allen Moore, Mrs. D. L. Proctor, Mrs. J. R. Barker, Mrs. Alyce Sullivan, Mrs. Frank Christian, Mrs. A. N. Wiley, and Claude. This photo appeared on the front page of the *Lexington Leader* when the group encountered a United Nations action and the US Marines in Lebanon. Claude used his recorder (on shoulder strap) to document the event and called it in to WVLK by international phone. Courtesy of WVLK Radio.

rut and that United Nations airplanes were also in evidence when he landed. Although the rebellion had no real impact on Claude and his travel group, the situation was tense for a few hours, and Claude spoke to American media by international telephone calls from his next several stops. He gave one particularly thorough interview to Ray Holbrook and Ted Grizzard, who were home at WVLK. Meanwhile, a photo of Claude's tour group was featured prominently on the front page of the *Lexington Leader* with the latest international information.

WVLK tour group in 1958 at the Great Pyramid, Cairo. Alyce is second from right, and Claude is fourth from right. Courtesy of WVLK Radio.

With the threat of civil war no longer hanging over the trip, Claude and the travelers were glad to resume being mere tourists. Claude and Alyce, who not only joined him but featured prominently in one of the radio reports back to the United States, added an additional seven days to their trip, traveling through Italy and France on their way to England, where the journey ended in early August. Another exciting summer gave Claude a change of pace before Blanton Collier's Wildcats kicked off their 1958 football campaign.

The 1958 Wildcats faced down the annual gauntlet that was SEC competition. Blanton Collier no longer had Lou Michaels to count on, but his new main weapon was running back Calvin Bird, a whirling dervish of a player who could run, pass, and tackle. Kentucky continued to play physical football, which was heavy on fundamentals but light on scoring or any kind of offensive trickery.

Again, the oppressive SEC was a challenge. After UK opened
2–0 with wins over Hawaii and Georgia Tech, the next three weeks
featured SEC opponents who were in the nation's top ten in the
rankings, with two of the three games coming on the road. UK lost
handedly to Ole Miss and LSU and was edged out by Auburn at
home 8–0. After the three-game Murderer's Row, Kentucky headed
to Georgia and was drilled 28–0. The squad was 2–4, and the fan
base began getting rowdy in their demands for a new head coach.

Collier stayed the course, alternating Calvin Bird and Bobby
Cravens, who was named second-team All-SEC, in the running
game. Kentucky won three of its last four games, tying Vanderbilt in
a scoreless draw in the other contest. The season ended in the annual
battle with Tennessee. Collier continued his mastery of the Vols.
Following a third-quarter safety by Tennessee, on the next play from
scrimmage Kentucky's Jerry Eiseman literally took the ball out of
the hands of the Tennessee fullback. Eiseman then led a long drive,
and Kentucky finished by scoring a touchdown on a run by Glenn
Shaw. The 6–2 margin held up, and Kentucky finished the season
with a winning record at 5–4–1.

Although the mark did not earn a bowl bid, it did earn Collier a five-year contract extension. However, as Russell Rice relates
in *The Wildcats,* in a classic case of giving in one breath and taking away in another, the university simultaneously implemented an
academic policy that required all students to maintain a 2.0 grade-
point average, and out-of-state students had to be within the top 50
percent of their graduating classes even to enter UK. In February
1959, 37 percent of the UK freshman players were found ineligible.
Collier's job was destined to be difficult, but those difficulties were
increasing.

In the winter of 1958–1959, with his team now missing the four
senior starters from the Fiddlin' Five, Adolph Rupp's job seemed

likely to grow more difficult as well. Only Johnny Cox and pivotal reserve Don Mills were back, but the cupboard was actually far from empty. A talented sophomore class was now eligible, with Lexington Lafayette star Billy Ray Lickert leading the charge. Lickert, a six-foot-three wing player, would pick up some of the scoring slack caused by Vernon Hatton's graduation. Dicky Parsons, a guard from Harlan, and forward Bobby Slusher, another eastern Kentucky prospect who hailed from Four Mile, were also highly regarded sophomores. A pair of junior transfers, Bernie Coffman, a guard from Lindsey Wilson College, and Sid Cohen, from a Texas junior college, were also counted on to provide instant depth. Indeed, Rupp's team would again surprise with its quality.

New Year's Day of 1959 saw the Cats at 10–0 and ranked number 1 in the nation. Included in the December victories was another matchup with the Temple Owls. Calling his third Temple/UK game in twelve months, Claude probably could have switched teams and given a good insider's account of the Temple team. On this trip, a young Jim Host was traveling to the hotel in a cab with Rupp in the front and Jim sitting between Wah Jones on one side and Claude on the other. Playing a trick on the newcomer Host, the other three bailed out of the cab when it pulled up at their stop, quickly leaving a near-broke Jim scrambling to pay the cab bill. This was stage one of his initiation, the second coming when Claude and Wah "short-sheeted" his bed linens in his hotel room. Jim laughs today when recalling the story of getting initiated into an elite traveling team.

This time the game was in Philadelphia's Palestra, and the Owls acquitted themselves well in the first half, leading 41–34 at the intermission. Despite 27 points from Bill Kennedy, Kentucky rallied to an 11-point advantage and held on for a third straight win over the seemingly cursed Owls, 76–71. In the final seconds, Claude cautioned his audience, *"Don't think it [a comeback] can't be done. Temple had an apparently safe 2-point lead last year with only one sec-*

ond to go." However, after the clock finally ran down, Claude admitted, with great relief in his voice, *"Close ball games between the Cats and Temple are always true to form."*

Another close ball game that the Wildcats survived was a heart-stopping 58–56 overtime win over Maryland. Before the 3-point shot, Kentucky appeared to be hopeless as they trailed by 3 in the closing seconds. However, Coffman scored as a Maryland player inexplicably tried to block his shot and fouled him. The free throw sent the game to overtime, and Kentucky claimed the improbable victory.

On December 20, 1958, the Cats had hosted number 7 West Virginia in the finals of the UKIT. The Mountaineers' star guard, Jerry West, was absolutely unstoppable, dropping 36 points on fifteen of twenty-five shooting, and grabbing sixteen rebounds. Even so, the balanced Wildcats claimed a 97–91 win. Newcomers Cohen (23 points) and Slusher (19) combined with veterans Mills (17) and Cox (16) to ward off West Virginia. West and the Mountaineers ended up reaching the finals of the 1959 NCAA Tournament, losing that game by a single point.

Kentucky did prove to be mortal, losing a January game at Vanderbilt and a February game at Mississippi State, which cost them the SEC Championship. However, a number 2–ranked, 23–2 UK squad was awarded an NCAA berth after Mississippi State declined its own intended spot. Cox was an All-American, and Lickert was chosen first-team All-SEC by the conference's coaches. With Coffman and Mills averaging a little more than 10 points per game each, the team looked like a solid choice to repeat as champions.

However, the Mideast Region in Evanston, Illinois, pitted UK against the Louisville Cardinals in the Wildcats' first NCAA Tournament game. UK jumped out to a 27–12 advantage over its intrastate rival and looked to have matters well in hand. But Peck Hickman's Cardinals harassed the UK offense and turned an 8-point halftime deficit into a shocking 76–61 win. Both Cox and Coffman fouled out, and although Lickert scored 16, he could not carry the team. A win over Marquette in the consolation game did little to ease the sting of the difficult loss. Although this UK team had initially been expected to do very little, it had done much but had also run out of steam at the most important time of the year. Cox, who ended his three seasons with the fourth most points in UK history, thus saw his brilliant college career come to a close. The next few teams lacked an impact player of that caliber, and UK accordingly was consigned to play up-and-down basketball.

As the spring of 1959 turned into summer, Claude found himself again planning to set out on a WVLK summer excursion into new territory. This summer's trip began in Spain and moved through France, England, and Scotland, before moving north to Norway, Sweden, and Denmark. Claude continued to report back to WVLK on the sights and sounds of Europe that he encountered. With no international espionage or attempted coup on this trip, it was apparently a more leisurely affair than the previous visits had been.

In the course of all of his travel, Claude seriously entertained a major career move, far away from his old Kentucky home. Among the numerous documents he saved from his travels was a packet of information from the US Information Agency (USIA). These documents included a form labeled "Security Investigation Data for Sensitive Position."

The USIA was developed by President Eisenhower in 1953. It was, effectively, a reverse-propaganda agency established to improve the international community's view of America and to counter Russian propaganda efforts. There was a prestigious broadcasting wing within the agency—so prestigious that legendary broadcaster Edward R. Murrow left CBS in 1961 to run it.

It is unclear when or for how long Claude considered working for the government. A letter from Secretary of State Dean Rusk in March 1961 invited Claude to attend a foreign-policy briefing and expressed that Rusk and newly inaugurated President Kennedy hoped to meet with Claude. By all indications, Claude was very serious about the opportunity to join the USIA. However, he did not attend that seminar because he was being honored on the same date in Salisbury, North Carolina, as a finalist for the National Sportscaster of the Year award.

Frustratingly, little can be known regarding Claude's governmental ambitions. Like the photographs for the navy in 1957, the bits and pieces that are known have been pieced together after the fact from his private papers and from interviews with Alyce. Nonetheless, it seems plausible that he was weighing an opportunity to leave the Big Blue for the Red, White, and Blue as early as 1959. However, when the 1959 football season rolled around, Claude was still in Kentucky.

Kentucky football finished the 1950s relying mostly on the playmaking ability of Calvin Bird. Bird could run and catch and returned both a kickoff and a punt for touchdowns over the course of the 1959 season. The Kentucky offense still struggled with an uncertain passing game, and although the defense kept UK in many games, it could not win single-handedly.

The season began with a tough 14–12 loss to Georgia Tech. In the next four games, UK faced three top-fifteen SEC squads sandwiched around a nonconference tilt with Detroit. UK was shut out of all three SEC games, and although the squad did win decisively at Detroit, it was 1–4 after five games. A tough loss to Georgia followed. Kentucky beat Miami but then lost at Vanderbilt. However, a 2–6 UK team showed some surprising mettle late in the season.

A 41–0 win over Xavier was not entirely surprising, and number 20 Tennessee came to Lexington to finish the season. Kentucky had never led an SEC opponent all season, so Collier's winning streak against Tennessee was definitely on shaky ground. Lo and behold, Calvin Bird picked up a rushing touchdown in the middle of the first quarter and then made the ensuing extra point. Buoyed by an unexpected lead, the Kentucky players decided they liked playing from ahead.

A few minutes later UK found itself in unfamiliar territory, driving inside the Tennessee 5-yard line. Claude described the action to his audience:

> The ball is a shade inside the Tennessee 2, where it's third down and goal to go. The nose of it is about midway between. Sturgeon flanks right, Hughes to call, pitches to Bird, he's gonna try to sweep again, they're chasing him back at the ten, one man missed him, he's down the sidelines for a touchdown! HOW ABOUT IT? CALVIN BIRD AGAIN went all the way back to the 11-yard line, where Tennessee's Ken Waddell dived and hit him. He staggered loose and dug the shoulder loose to go down the sidelines for another touchdown. Calvin Bird has just scored 13 points, and Kentucky is ahead 13–0!

Bird wasn't finished, adding an 89-yard punt return for the Cats' third and final score. Tennessee had no answer, and once again Collier was a Volunteer killer, with a 20–0 win over the number 20 team in the country. That said, a 4–6 season mark ensured that this finale would be about the only memorable moment of the season. Collier knew he needed help, and with 1960 on the horizon he believed he had it on the way in the form of a pair of talented freshmen, quarterback Jerry Woolum and end Tom Hutchinson, ready to compete as sophomores. The 1960s held so much promise—for Collier, for Rupp, for Claude. Little could the men have realized that each of their futures would be very different and that their lives would change very suddenly.

8

When in Rome

The 1959–1960 season was the season that Kentucky's detractors had forecast for a long while. Johnny Cox had graduated, and the basketball team found itself relying on Billy Ray Lickert and a trio of seniors—Don Mills, Sid Cohen, and Bernie Coffman. The junior class was decimated as Bobby Slusher had transferred, and Dicky Parsons's shooting and scoring stats inexplicably dropped from his sophomore to his junior year (he repeated the pattern again the following season). Another talented player, Roger Newman, who had scored more than 16 points per game for the freshman team two years earlier, was expected to be eligible in 1959–1960 as a junior after missing his sophomore season due to academics. However, it was determined that Newman had played for the Lexington YMCA squad, and so the SEC ruled him ineligible. Rupp's recruiting pool had dried to the point where transfer players, by necessity, had become a central component of the team. The 1959–1960 squad featured only three players not from Kentucky, and two of them were transfers. The remaining in-state talent proved to be maddeningly inconsistent.

In all fairness to Rupp, there were other reasons for the difficulty. Longtime assistant Harry Lancaster told authors Bert Nelli and Steve Nelli, as recounted in *The Winning Tradition,* "[Rupp] was a sick man. He had back problems. He had had his spinal column fused and that bothered him. . . . Then he wound up as a diabetic and had a hole in one foot that wouldn't heal. Rupp suffered a lot of pain." Seasons such as the 1959–1960 one probably did little to make Rupp feel any better.

After winning the first two games, Kentucky lost to Southern California by 14 points and St. Louis by 12. Part of the team's skittishness was probably due to a horrifying road accident while it was traveling on the team bus. Kentucky had traveled west to play UCLA and Southern California, and on the day after the UCLA game Jim Host, then a young broadcaster who had made the trip with Claude, had turned around on the team bus to talk to Claude when the bus hit a car that had run a stop light. Host hit his head in the accident and recalled Rupp standing over him and saying, "My God, he is dead!" Host was not dead, but he believed that some of the people in the car were not as fortunate. Decades later, he still remembered the moans coming from the other vehicle. Claude emerged uninjured, but the brush with disaster doubtlessly reminded everyone involved that basketball was just a game.

A week after Kentucky returned from its road trip, for the second time in three years UK lost the UKIT—and, again, the upstart conqueror was West Virginia. Jerry West, exactly the sort of player who could have made UK a national favorite, fought through a broken nose to total 33 points and eighteen rebounds for the Mountaineers in their 79–70 win.

This isn't to say that Kentucky was horrible in 1959–1960. Indeed, in the last Kentucky game of the 1950s, on December 28, UK upset number 3 Ohio State 96–93 in Memorial Coliseum. That Ohio State squad, which Claude termed "the stoutest-looking team that we have seen," featured All-Americans Jerry Lucas and John Havlicek (as well as a benchwarming sophomore named Bob

Knight) and went on to win the NCAA Tournament. However, the duo was overshadowed by Billy Ray Lickert, who scored 29 points, and Bernie Coffman, who added 26 points despite having broken his nose in the West Virginia game. UK came back from 15 points down to pull the upset, but the win unfortunately ended up as the highlight of the season.

In SEC play, Kentucky was further slowed by a leg injury to Lickert, their best player, which caused him to miss five games entirely and affected the rest of his season. UK lost twice to Georgia Tech, who was then a member of the SEC, and dropped other conference matchups with Auburn and Tennessee. The squad finished 18–7 and did not earn postseason play. For Claude, however, the postseason proved much more memorable than the year itself.

In the spring of 1960, Claude was presented with an award through the National Broadcasters Convention as the outstanding broadcaster of 1959 in Kentucky. The award was the first such award presented through the Kentucky Broadcasters Association, and Claude won it in a field of highly respected newscasters and sportscasters. The award was part of the National Sportscasters and Sportswriters Association and was presented in Salisbury, North Carolina. Again, during this period, University of Kentucky sports did not use a single station or sportscaster to broadcast its games. Listeners could chose from among Claude, Cawood Ledford, or a host of others (including, eventually, Jim Host). The fact that Claude was chosen for this prestigious award by his colleagues shows the high regard for his broadcasts. He won the award annually for the first eight years of its existence, until his health limited his ability to complete his broadcasting duties.

One of the many attributes that gained prestige and respect from Claude's fellow broadcasters was his thorough preparation for broadcasts. He dubbed his technique the "Sullivan System." He often began by memorizing opposing players' names and numbers

Claude receiving one of eight Kentucky Sportscaster of the Year awards
in Salisbury, North Carolina. He missed a meeting with Dean Rusk
and President Kennedy to receive the 1960 state award when he was also
runner-up to Lindsey Nelson for the National Sportscaster of the Year award.
Courtesy of National Sportscasters and Sportswriters Association. From the
Claude Sullivan Collection.

the night before a game. He often practiced a mock "call" of the
game to be fluid with the names and information of the opposing
squad. At the game, Claude would watch the other team warm up
and continue to practice memorization while viewing the players.
He was careful to know of number changes, players who were not
dressing, or shifts in the starting lineups.

Jim Host recalled one of his first road trips with Claude and
his introduction to the Sullivan System. On the night before the
game, Claude allowed Host to join him as he sat and meticulously
filled out his score sheet with a mechanical four-color pencil. He
noted not only names and numbers, but heights, weights, home-

towns, high schools, and other relevant facts on the sheet. Claude advised that he found that writing helped him absorb the information. He would also review the information on the teams and draw out his own statistics. In an era before computer databases, checking a team's record in the previous ten games or its number of double-digit victories was a tedious process, but one that Claude relished. Host recalls that Claude always had yet another statistic to offer. Claude's preparation was an essential component in his success. Also in early 1960, the *Kentucky Kernel* (UK's student newspaper) published an article commemorating Claude's five hundredth consecutive broadcast of Kentucky football and basketball games. It referred to Claude as the "Dean of Kentucky Sportscasters." For his part, Jim Host had always called Claude "Dean," and he says he coined the name since Claude was older and wiser than the other announcers.

In addition to his personal triumph, Claude was prepared to enjoy athletic competition on a global level. The year 1960 was an Olympic year, and the Games of the Seventeenth Olympiad were slated to take place in Rome. Of course, in 1948 the entire UK basketball starting five had played in the Games in London, but Claude, due to the birth of son David and the relative expense of international travel, had not made the trip. Considering the season that the Wildcats had just completed, it seemed unfathomable that a Wildcat could compete for the 1960 Olympic basketball squad.

However, this time around the players were chosen on an individual basis after a trial tournament involving NCAA teams (not including UK), AAU teams such as the Phillips Oilers (also called the 66ers), which had also been represented within the 1948 US squad, and even the United States Armed Forces team. Adrian "Odie" Smith, who had started for the Fiddlin' Five, had chosen to join the army rather than enter the NBA in the fall of 1958. Accordingly, Smith found himself playing for Army All-Star teams and, to his delight, making Coach Pete Newell's final roster of twelve players who would play in the 1960 Olympics as the sole US Armed Forces representative.

Smith joined seven NCAA players and four AAU selections. Ten of the twelve players on the team ended up playing in the NBA. The biggest names of the group were Cincinnati's Oscar Robertson, West Virginia's great Jerry West, and Ohio State's Jerry Lucas. The squad seemed almost certain to continue the dominance of US basketball on the world stage.

But even better news for Claude was that via another station-sponsored international trip he would be able to attend the Olympics. Alyce was unable to join Claude due to recent back surgery, but in August 1960 he and a group of travelers from WVLK set out from New York for Amsterdam. Once on the ground, the group traveled back to London and spent several days there before meandering through mainland Europe toward the Olympics in Rome.

One of the highlights of the earlier part of the trip was a stop in Oberammergau, Germany, for a viewing of the town's famous Passion Play. The play had begun in the 1630s, when the residents of the village, which was ravaged by bubonic plague, swore to God that if they were spared, they would produce a great play depicting the life and death of Jesus Christ. After the plague indeed did not wipe away the village, the play began. Due to the extravagance of the performance (approximately seven hours' running time, with a meal break), it was too difficult and costly to produce annually, so it was put on in one year out of ten. It happens that the play is produced in years ending in zero, and so sometime in mid-August 1960 Claude viewed the famous play. He was greatly impressed with the splendor of the event.

The trip eventually wound to Rome in time to enjoy the Seventeenth Olympiad. Although the nature of the Olympics makes every edition of the Games special, 1960 stands out. David Maraniss's book *Rome 1960* provides an in-depth account of the Games. Among the more compelling stories (outside of US basketball) was that of Abebe Bikela, an Ethiopian marathoner, who won that race barefoot to provide Africa's first-ever medalist. Other highlights were provided by American Rafer Johnson, who won a dramatic decathlon; by the Tennessee State University Tiger Belles, led by Wilma Rudolph, who dominated women's running events with style and flair; and by eighteen-year-old Kentuckian and gold-medal-winning boxer Cassius Clay, who made a name for himself in Rome.

Before the Games themselves, the pageantry and pomp of the opening ceremonies are always impressive. Claude was front and center and recorded the action in his diary as follows: "August 24th at 3:45 PM—Hundreds already in line to see the Pope. I wedge forward and got close to the rail, hoping the sun would drop behind the Basilica. People jammed, with fathers and sisters pushing soldiers on guard at the barrier. Older women seem to stand it the best. Several younger ones fainted. . . . 5:30 PM—Ceremony began and the Pope was out quickly. He made mention of the 1905 games and his voice was extremely good, then translation began while the athletes came forward to him."

With the opening ceremonies completed at St. Peters Square and the pope receiving the athletes, Claude set out to enjoy the Olympics in a role somewhere between tourist and journalist. From his detailed diaries, it is clear that he witnessed as many of the Olympic events as time and the availability of tickets permitted.

His itinerary and programs indicate that the sports that he viewed in addition to basketball were women's swimming events, field hockey, and boxing. Claude saw Cassius Clay fight at least one of his early fights in the Olympics. Unfortunately, it does not appear that he was able to secure an interview with Clay.

Claude spent most of his time on basketball. On August 26, he watched the US team's opening game against Italy. He recounted

**1960 UNITED STATES
SPORTS TEAMS**

GAMES OF THE XVII OLYMPIAD
ROME, ITALY AUG. 25 - SEPT. 11

INFORMATION FOR

PRESS — RADIO — TELEVISION

Presented as a public service by Dairy Farmers across the nation through the
AMERICAN DAIRY ASSOCIATION
in cooperation with the United States Olympic Committee (Public Law 805)

Olympic press, radio, and television program featuring Cassius Clay and
Adrian Smith of Kentucky as well as Jerry West, Oscar Robertson, and Jerry
Lucus on the gold medal basketball team, 1960. From the Claude Sullivan
Collection.

that he had difficulty procuring a ticket, but with a soldier helping
him move up in line, he obtained a ticket for 4,000 lire (approximately US$6.40 in 1960). Once inside, what Claude encountered
was basketball unlike any he had seen before. He noted that the
floor was some type of linoleum and that the arena lighting was
poor. The foul line extended to about twenty feet wide from the basket, the clock had no second hand, and the ball was yellow and sewn
and looked more like a volleyball than a basketball. Apparently, the
facilities for the finals were improved, but the game did not resemble
American basketball very closely.

Nor, it is worth noting, did the 1960 Games much resemble the Olympic Games of today. Claude had spoken with Adrian

Smith on August 27, and since the team was off the following day, Smith asked Claude to meet him in the Olympic Village. Smith gave Claude passes and directions to his dormitory room in the village. In this pre–Munich 1972 era, Claude simply strolled right into the athletic dormitory. He knocked on the door and on Smith's command entered the room, where he visited with Smith and Oscar Robertson for some time. Later that evening, Claude returned and went to the lower levels of the Olympic dormitory with Adrian Smith and Jerry West for a soft drink. He recalled that the three of them passed the wrestling team on the way back upstairs. The wrestlers were practicing in their rooms, and one of them took a hard fall, injuring his neck. Again, this level of access is simply unimaginable now, but it was a pleasant treat for Claude.

The US basketball team won the gold medal at the 1960 Olympics. It was never really challenged, with the closest game in medal play being a 24-point win over the Soviet Union. It won the gold medal over Brazil, 90–63, and in 2010, on the fiftieth anniversary of its triumph, the team as a unit was inducted into the Naismith Basketball Hall of Fame.

As for Adrian Smith, he averaged 10.9 points per game, good for fifth best on the team. He also finished as the team's best free-throw shooter and eventually parlayed the performance into a successful career in the NBA.

Claude returned to the United States shortly after the Olympics. The international trips had become an important part of his life and career. He hoped to utilize the additional experience and information to obtain a national broadcasting job. Like Adrian Smith, he was taking a circuitous route to his goals but was getting closer every day. The waiting was the hardest part.

Claude had taken his sons to Stoll Field since at least 1958, especially on team picture day, and a photo of the boys with the squad's quar-

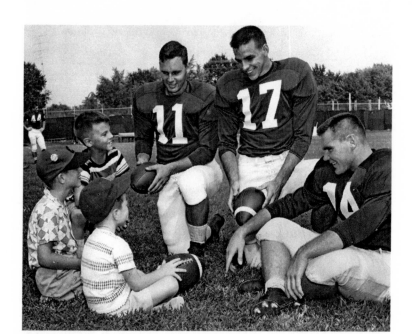

Football Media Day at UK, October 2, 1957. Alan Sullivan is in the foreground, wearing a cap, with David to his left, also wearing a cap. UK quarterbacks look on. Courtesy of the *Lexington Herald-Leader*.

terbacks, including Jerry Eisaman and Lowell Hughes, was published in a local newspaper in 1957.

By the mid-1960s, Claude's sons were established hands in the game-day routine. Meanwhile, Blanton Collier was looking to bounce back from two losing seasons in three years as the 1960 football season approached. Veteran quarterbacks Jerry Eisaman and sophomore sensation Jerry Woolum split snaps under center. Both spent much of their time throwing to sophomore end Tom Hutchinson, who hauled in more passes in 1960 than any Wildcat had since 1951. Hutchinson won All-SEC honors for his performances. Meanwhile, the UK defense was valiant, holding opponents to just 183.1 yards per game, the lowest total since Bryant's Sugar Bowl champions a decade earlier.

Despite the talent on hand, the 1960 UK football season began like a nightmare. UK dropped a 23–13 decision at Georgia Tech and then lost handedly to number 1 Ole Miss. The team dropped to 0–3 after a 10–7 heartbreaker to Auburn. From there, however, the team began to jell. A 55–0 win over Marshall ended the skid, and UK then beat LSU 3–0 on a field goal from Clarkie Mayfield. UK suffered a narrow loss to Georgia but then posted shutouts against Florida State (23–0), Vanderbilt (27–0), and Xavier (49–0). A 10–10 tie with Tennessee, topped by a minor brawl between the two squads, ended UK's winning streak over the Vols at three in a row but made the season a 5–4–1 slate. Claude had now broadcast six straight seasons in which the football Cats had failed to reach the seven-win plateau needed to have a shot at a bowl game.

On the one hand, with the young talent on board and a defense that forced five shutouts (equaling the total by Bryant's 1950 and 1951 teams), Blanton Collier's future at UK looked bright. On the other hand, promise did nothing to change the fact that Collier's UK coaching record stood at 36–31–3 and no bowl appearances. The 1961 season would be a pivotal one for UK's future.

Meanwhile, on the hardwood, things were not looking particularly brilliant for Adolph Rupp as the fall of 1960 rolled around. Billy Ray Lickert was a senior and was counted on to lead this group. Roger Newman was finally out of basketball exile, after last having played on the freshman team, and was eligible for his senior campaign. Larry Pursiful, a junior guard from Four Mile, Kentucky, also drew increasing minutes. Junior college big man Vinny Del Negro was expected to contribute substantially to the team.

The results were as inconsistent and uncertain as the previous campaign had been. By New Year's Day 1961, UK was 5–3, with another UKIT loss—this time to St. Louis and the third time in four years that UK had failed to win its own tournament. Things got worse in SEC play as UK opened 2–4 in the conference with three straight losses. Kentucky stood at 8–7 overall and looked to be no threat for postseason play. Del Negro had been a virtual nonfactor and left the team at this point in the season.

However, with their backs to the wall, the Wildcats responded by winning nine games in a row. Included in these wins was a gutty 68–62 win at Mississippi State in which Newman led UK with 24 pivotal points. This game would be recognized as the turning point of the season.

The atmosphere in Starkville was raucous, and Claude, straining to be heard, described the crowd chanting in cadence, "Ding-dong damn it, ding-dong damn it," in protest that the SEC had banned cowbells at games. With this background, Claude brought the final seconds home to the UK nation:

> Pursiful has the ball, 2-point lead, the shot, it's GOOD, IT'S GOOD, as Larry Pursiful drops it in, the Cats lead by 3, and he'll take a bonus shot. Four seconds to go, Kentucky, 65–62 over Mississippi State. Pursiful on the line for a bonus try. He got it. And as Pursiful drops 'em both in, Mississippi State, with four seconds to go, loses the ball out of bounds. They didn't touch it at all. So the ball goes to Kentucky right under their own basket. . . . So Kentucky has won the ball game. Kentucky has defeated Mississippi State on their home floor!

Mississippi State won the league championship but again refused an NCAA Tournament berth because of its racially segregationist policies.

After a one-point victory over UCLA, Kentucky played a revenge match against Vanderbilt in Lexington on February 21, 1961. Following a loss in Nashville, Kentucky was fighting for an SEC title and bid to the NCAA. According to Claude's broadcast, this was the first time he had witnessed Adolph being carried off the floor by his players. Vanderbilt had come from behind for a furious rally that fell short 60–59.

UK found itself playing Vanderbilt a third time in a one-game playoff in Knoxville on March 9 (the schools had split the season series, one win each), with an NCAA Tournament berth on the line.

Vandy was no match for UK this time, as the Cats stretched a 14-point first-half lead to an 88–67 victory. Five Wildcats scored in double figures, led by Larry Pursiful with 21 points. After the game, Claude witnessed another rare display of celebratory emotion when the Kentucky players gathered together once again to carry Coach Rupp from the court back into the locker room.

Kentucky was back in the NCAA Tournament.

After a tune-up game against Marquette, UK began the NCAA Mideast Regional in Louisville with a hard-fought 71–64 win over Morehead State. This win set up a showdown with the defending NCAA Tournament champions, top-ranked Ohio State. Despite 31 points from Roger Newman in his final game, Kentucky was outclassed. Jerry Lucas tallied 33 points and thirty rebounds as Ohio State crushed Kentucky on the backboards. John Havlicek added 8 points, and reserve forward Bob Knight managed 7 more.

Although a 19–9 record was Rupp's worst season to date, this Kentucky team had fought honorably to reach even those meager milestones. Simply put, for a few years Kentucky had not had the type of dominant, All-American talent that had made the program. But Claude and the insiders who followed the freshman team during 1960–1961 knew that was about to change. The 1961–1962 Wildcats would have a star to wish on. Again, the game was wrapped up in waiting.

Although Claude was still unsuccessful in landing a national broadcasting position, he continued to gain accolades in his current position. He still had his sights set on the national position, but he was very comfortable with Lexington and focusing on UK exploits for the time. Not only was he Kentucky Sportscaster of the Year for a second consecutive year, but he was also invited to the National Broadcasters Convention in North Carolina because he was a finalist for National Sportscaster of the Year. Claude ultimately finished as runner-up for the award, beaten out by Lindsey Nelson. He also attended the annual convention of the National Association of Broadcasters in Washington, where he heard speakers ranging from President Kennedy to Vice President Johnson and astronaut Alan Shephard.

As the national position that Claude sought continued to elude him, he instead worked on his business model, trying to spread his broadcasting net a bit wider. He moved to WINN in Louisville, where he served as station vice president and general manager and as executive vice president of Garvis Kincaid's Bluegrass Broadcasting Company, which owned WINN, WVLK, and several other stations at the time in Ashland, Frankfort, and Orlando, Florida. Claude had attained a portion of ownership in WINN and WVLK, and, according to Alyce, Garvis said that Claude was the only manager who was able to put WINN in the black.

WINN became the station of origin for Claude's broadcasts, but Standard Oil continued to serve as the corporate sponsor for the network, which would eventually extend to more than twenty stations in total. The Sullivan family eventually moved to Louisville for a short time. Claude seemed to be hedging his bets on the national position by entrenching himself in the business side at the local level. Either way his career went, he would win.

A man in a very different position in the fall of 1961 was Blanton Collier. With quarterback Jerry Woolum and All-SEC end Tom Hutchinson entering their junior campaigns and with a solid line

Claude was the general manger of WINN radio station in Louisville from 1962 until he took the position with the Reds in 1964. He hired local star Paul Hornung *(center)* to work on high school football with Charlie Ryle *(right)*. Courtesy of WINN Radio.

including All-American center Irv Goode, it was time for Kentucky to break the cycle of four- to six-win seasons and put together the sort of campaign that would serve as a mandate for Collier to move forward.

With a talented squad and a relatively light schedule, the UK camp had reason for optimism. That optimism didn't last very long, though, as UK dropped its home opener to Miami (Florida) by a 14–7 count. The following week was a 20–6 home loss to a highly regarded Ole Miss team. UK bounced back by winning at Auburn 14–12 (UK would not win at Auburn again until 2009) and then beating Kansas State 21–8. As the Auburn game clock wound down to less than two minutes, Claude described the entire stadium of Auburn fans standing in disbelief at what they were witnessing.

But the season intended to raise Collier above reproach didn't materialize. Tough losses at LSU and Georgia made a winning season a near impossibility. In a win against Florida State, Woolum, who was then one of the top passers in the nation, suffered a broken leg that ended his season.

Although the 3–4 Wildcats beat Vanderbilt and Xavier, both games were brutal fights against subpar foes. The season closer at home against Tennessee was a 26–16 loss, the first to the Volunteers in Lexington in a decade. Even Blanton Collier's vaunted run as Volunteer slayer had come to an end. His 5–5 mark left his future at UK in limbo. As 1961 ended, both Collier and Claude were approaching turning points in their professional careers. By February 1962, only one of the two was still employed in Lexington. The 1960s saw change, and there were ups and downs, and the decade's turbulence was mirrored in the fate of Claude and of the men on whom he spent the vast majority of his professional time.

9

Cotton, Bradshaw, and a "Dream Deferred"

Following the disappointing 1961 football campaign, there were some whispers that Blanton Collier's time in Lexington would not be long. However, in late November the University Athletic Board announced that his contract (with three years remaining) would be honored, and this statement appeared to put an end to the speculation. In reality, the university was simply biding its time.

On January 2, 1962, the university bought out Collier's contract, relieving him of his further coaching duties. His 41–36–3 mark had not equaled Bryant's, it was true. However, as Shannon Ragland writes in *The Thin Thirty*, the players "knew where they stood with Collier. They knew he loved them—that education came first and their development as people was Collier's fundamental purpose." Indeed, although Collier's accomplishments may lack luster in the shadow of Bryant's, time casts them in a very different light. No UK football coach since Collier has left the university sporting a winning record during his tenure. Collier went 5–2–1 versus Tennessee; since his departure, UK's record in the series features only seven wins in the ensuing half-century and more. Another of Collier's accomplishments as a coach was that he surrounded himself with outstanding young coaching talent. For instance, the 1959 UK squad, despite its humble 4–6 record, was coached not only by Collier, but by young assistants such as Howard Schellenberger, a UK alum who later won a national title at Miami and brought Louisville football respectability; Bill Arnsparger, who became a defensive guru and shone at the collegiate and NFL ranks; and Don Shula, who ended up with two Super Bowl victories and the most wins in NFL history.

As Kentucky's search for Collier's replacement moved along, two candidates quickly emerged—Jerry Claiborne, a UK alum and still holder of the single-season interception record for UK, and Charlie Bradshaw, a peer of Claiborne's who had also played under Bryant in Lexington. Claiborne was only thirty-three years old but had already assisted Bryant at Texas A&M and Alabama and had one season as a head coach at Virginia Polytechnic Institute (now Virginia Tech) under his belt. Bradshaw was thirty-eight years old and lacked head-coaching experience, but he had also assisted Bryant at Alabama and had spent five seasons on Collier's UK staff. Ironically, the student ultimately replaced the teacher as Charlie Bradshaw was named head coach of the Wildcats eight days later, on January 10, 1962.

On the day after the announcement, Claude interviewed Bear Bryant about his young prodigy. The Bear admitted, "We hated to lose Charlie [from Alabama], but we're certainly not that selfish. We're real happy for him. I think Kentucky made a wise decision. I think Charlie Bradshaw is one of the top young coaches in America. I have no doubt whatsoever that he'll get the job done." Although most Kentucky fans would have been glad to bring back the mentor rather than the student, Bryant's endorsement spoke well of the new coach.

Charlie Bradshaw being interviewed by Claude in the UK locker room after a ball game at Stoll Field, 1962. Courtesy of the *Lexington Herald-Leader.*

Bradshaw promised a system that he called "Total Football." Like most new head coaches, he preached a disciplined system that would produce physical football. Unlike most new coaches, though, not only was Bradshaw not exaggerating, but he was probably sell-

Claude with Ted Grizzard *(left)* in the Stoll Field press box. Courtesy of WVLK Radio.

ing himself short on how tough his team would be—indeed, how tough they would have to be. As for Claiborne, he went on to boost the fortunes of Virginia Polytechnic Institute and Maryland over the next two decades before he finally was named UK head coach in 1982. Claiborne was inducted into the College Football Hall of Fame. Bradshaw, however, proved to be a much more polarizing figure.

A few weeks later, in late January 1962, Claude found himself in unfamiliar territory. He took up his pen, writing a cover letter for a job audition—his first, as he wrote, in fourteen years. The recipient of the letter was J. F. "Bud" Koons Jr. of Midland Advertising Agency in Cincinnati, Ohio. Koons, on behalf of sponsor Burger

Beer, was tasked with hiring a new second announcer for the Cincinnati Reds. Claude saw his national opportunity at once.

Claude candidly admitted in the letter that he had been engaged in broadcasting basketball, football, and horse racing, but he recalled his work at WAVE with Don Hill calling Louisville Colonel baseball games. He mentioned broadcasting some UK baseball and recalled his old days of doing baseball re-creation via teletype.

Baseball was certainly not a stranger to Claude. He had kept his ticket stub from game seven of the 1940 World Series, when the Reds, in front of Claude and his father, had defeated the Detroit Tigers. In the days before professional basketball had any sort of national following, and before NFL football had gained the marketing frenzy that pushed it into position as the most financially lucrative professional sport, baseball was the national game. The American athletic pantheon consisted mainly of stars such as Cobb, Ruth, Gehrig, Robinson, and Mantle.

Accordingly, Claude had long since recognized that baseball was the best choice for a national sportscasting endeavor. Claude had kept up with Mel Allen since their meeting in 1950, and Lindsey Nelson, who had been the voice of the Tennessee Volunteers and had just been announced as the voice of the New York Mets in their inaugural 1962 campaign, was among the references that he mentioned in his application letter.

Claude's application letter is intriguing in several other areas. He expressed his admiration for Waite Hoyt, the Reds' primary announcer. Hoyt, a veteran of the great New York Yankee squads of the 1920s, had been the voice of the Reds since 1942. He was, simply put, a fixture, as beloved in Cincinnati as four-way chili. Hoyt had broadcast the 1961 World Series for NBC, and his stories during rain delays, particularly those about his friend and teammate Babe Ruth, were so legendary that after his retirement, two record albums of the stories were released for sale. Per the arrangement of the time,

Hoyt, as the primary announcer, would broadcast the first three and last three innings, and the second announcer would broadcast the middle three innings.

Claude was eager to get on Hoyt's good side. He wrote, "For many years, I've followed Waite Hoyt, who to me is one of the truly great announcers, and I would deem it a pleasure to work with such a man. I've met Waite on several occasions and have the greatest admiration for him, which in part is a reason for my desired association with the Cincinnati Baseball club."

Another interesting aspect of the letter is that unlike many of the other applicants, who doubtlessly aimed to obtain the Reds job as sole employment, Claude was honest about his vision of his broadcasting future. "For over a year now I've been a Vice President of Bluegrass Broadcasting Company. This ended my travels abroad, and has made me realize more than ever that play-by-play sports announcing is my great love," he wrote to Koons. "As I see the job with Burger, it would still leave me free to work Kentucky football and basketball for the Standard Oil Network in the fall and winter."

Years later Alyce Sullivan said that she believed that Claude would have left the Kentucky position for a national baseball or football post. However, Claude was confident enough in his credentials that he was honest—given his choice, he wanted to broadcast baseball, football, *and* basketball. However, after only a brief interval, a form letter arrived from Koons. The Reds had decided to go in a different direction—Gene Kelly, a veteran of a decade of baseball broadcasting, was being hired for the position.

Very much a man of his times, Claude did not let his true feelings show through. His sons were unaware not only of Claude's disappointment, but even of his application for the position until the correspondence regarding the matter was found some time after his death. Alyce Sullivan knew better—she remembered that Claude was very hurt by the rejection. He had been honored time and again for his broadcasting work. He had broadcast great moments in college football and basketball history and had traveled extensively. But was this all there would be? Was Claude doomed to get inches from his dream of a national position but never attain it? These were the questions that undoubtedly occupied his mind much of the late winter and early spring of 1962. For the time being, Claude was again consigned to wait and wonder.

During all of the public turmoil over the direction of the Wildcat football program and the private turmoil of Claude's rejection for the Reds job, there was one constant that gave Claude an outlet—Wildcat basketball. The temporary struggles of mediocrity had been banished in Lexington—mostly courtesy of one young man, nineteen-year-old Charles "Cotton" Nash. Nash was the bona fide star that Kentucky basketball had been missing at least since the days of Johnny Cox. In fact, Nash, with his movie-star good looks, soft perimeter jump shot, and ability to slash to the basket, was probably better than Cox. Although he is sometimes forgotten in the discussion of the best Wildcat basketball players ever, the omission is not a product of his play.

Nash had played high school basketball under Fabulous Five member Cliff Barker for two years in Indiana. Although Nash had moved to Texas (and attended high school in Lake Charles, Louisiana, so that he would not have to sit out a year), Rupp had the young man on his radar. As for Nash, the first question was what would he want to play. Cotton was also an all-state football talent, and the locals wanted him to stay home and star for LSU or Tulane on the gridiron. Meanwhile, others believed that baseball was where the young man's talents were best emphasized, given his smooth power stroke and boundless athleticism. But basketball had his heart, and Lexington was his destination.

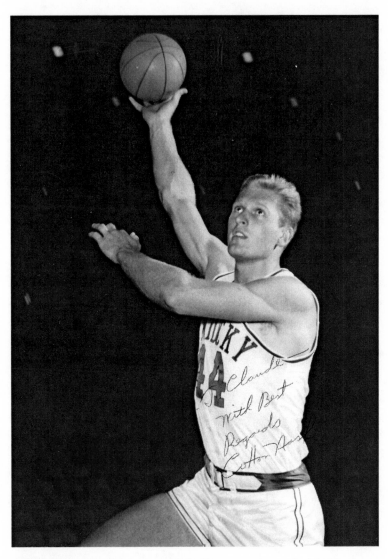

Cotton Nash, UK All-American, 1962. The inscription reads, "To Claude—
With Best Regards Cotton Nash." Courtesy of the UK Athletics
Department.

Media basketball game at Memorial Coliseum. Five of the eight players are shown here. *Top left to right:* Jim Host, Earl Boardman; *lower left to right:* Claude, Hugh Jones; *center:* Jack Lorri. Absent from the picture are Wah Wah Jones, Buzz Riggins, and Dick Roy. Courtesy of the *Lexington Herald-Leader.*

While Nash was setting high scoring marks as a freshman, Claude participated in a Press versus Radio–TV matchup on New Year's Eve at halftime of the Missouri game. Claude, Jim Host, Jack Lorri, Earl Boardman, and Claude's good friend Wah Wah Jones were among those who were included on the Radio–TV team. The Press team delivered a 36–18 drubbing, and the Radio–TV team wished they had entreated Nash to do some broadcasting work, which might have landed him on their pickup squad. Claude had not played in the public spotlight since his injury at Winchester High launched his broadcasting career. This game was rewarding for him to experience at Memorial Coliseum alongside his contemporaries.

Meanwhile, after this brief diversion for Claude, in the midst of the difficult 1960–1961 season, those who watched the freshman squad play knew that help was coming for the varsity. Nash averaged 26.4 points per game and set a host of records.

In the 1961–1962 varsity campaign, he joined forces with Larry Pursiful, now a senior and the owner of a sweet shooting touch as well, and other wily veterans such as Carroll Burchett and Scotty Baesler, a competent role player who went on to gain fame as a member of the US Congress in the 1990s.

Kentucky was a national power once again. UK opened the season with a 93–61 win over Miami (Ohio). In his first varsity outing, Nash put up 25 points and seventeen rebounds—eye-popping numbers that he made routine. After a tough 2-point loss to number 4 Southern California in their second game, UK won sixteen games in a row. Kentucky won each of those games by at least 9 points and beat number 4 Kansas State by 13 points in the UKIT Championship. Against Temple, the six-foot-five Nash, who spent most of his UK career playing out of position at center, grabbed thirty rebounds in addition to scoring 20 points. He broke the 30-point mark five times during the winning streak, and UK rose as high as number 2 in the national polls.

Mississippi State and Babe McCarthy ended the streak, playing a slow-down game and beating UK 49–44. By playing at the slow pace, Mississippi held Nash to 23 of UK's 44 points. The game was probably less remembered for the outcome than the bizarre postgame proceedings. Claude brought the odd scene, punctuated with loud boos from the Memorial Coliseum crowd, to his audience: "Mississippi State will not put it in play. They let the clock run out and upset Kentucky on their home floor, 49–44. . . . And the Mississippi State bench comes off with a wreath and places it on top of the Kentucky basket. A wreath draped in white ribbon has been placed on top of the basket down at Kentucky's bench, and the net is being cut with scissors from the basket itself as Babe McCarthy is being hoisted to the shoulders of his players."

The wreath that Mississippi State placed on Kentucky's goal was the same one that Kentucky players had placed on the Mississippi State locker room the year before in Starkville. The point of the wreath had been that Rupp did not like the "stall ball" brand of basketball being played by Mississippi State, Georgia, and others. Rupp was not alone in his dislike for the delay game. A few years later during a broadcast, Claude commented, "Is there another sport in which the offense can so completely dominate? In football you've got to have one fine offense to stall . . . say like the 3 yards and a cloud of dust like Woody Hayes at Ohio State. It's not possible in hockey, golf, tennis, soccer, or any other sport, team or individual . . . but in basketball a team can look great on defense by merely refusing to play."

UK shared the regular season conference title with Mississippi State and won the last five games of the season, setting itself up for NCAA Tournament play. UK began the Mideast Regional in 1961 by beating Butler 81–60 in the first round. Pursiful's 26 points added to Nash's 23 to subdue the Bulldogs. Somehow, this win placed number 3 UK in a matchup with number 1 Ohio State in the Mideast Regional final. With the six-foot-five Nash jumping center, size again proved to be UK's Achilles heel. Ohio State assigned John Havlicek to Nash, and Nash could manage only 14 points on five-of-nineteen shooting. Pursiful, who won All-SEC honors for the season, countered with 21 points of his own for the Cats, but Jerry Lucas was the difference. The big man totaled 33 points and fifteen rebounds and had 25 of his points in the first half. The Buckeyes won 74–64 and advanced to the NCAA title game, where they lost to Cincinnati. Kentucky once again went home unhappy from a regional final.

Nash's season, however, had to take some of the pain out of the tough loss. Nash totaled 608 points in twenty-six games played. This was the fourth most points in a season in Wildcat history. His 345 rebounds were the ninth most rebounds ever grabbed in a single season at UK. Although much of the supporting cast would be graduating, including Pursiful, who averaged more than 19 points per game while shooting greater than 50 percent, Nash had two more seasons in blue and white. The future looked bright, but, of course, it is always uncertain.

Charlie Bradshaw had inherited a roster of eighty-eight players when he took the UK football head-coaching position in January 1962. By the fall, the roster had been trimmed to a young-and-tumble group of thirty survivors. The team, which came to be known as the "Thin Thirty," had been through a grueling conditioning program in the spring and another stringent workout before the 1962 season. In the days before the NCAA carefully mandated practice hours and conditions, Bradshaw put his team through full scrimmages and intense practices, with players working to and sometimes beyond the point of physical injury. In *The Thin Thirty,* Shannon Ragland depicts Bradshaw's training methods as being brutal and almost sadistic. Whether this is accurate or not, the simple fact remains that Bradshaw trimmed his roster by almost two-thirds. Among the defections was Dale Lindsey, who transferred to Western Kentucky and ended up playing nine seasons for the NFL's Cleveland Browns. Star sophomore halfback Darrell Cox initially left the team, along with eighteen other players, after a particularly brutal scrimmage but convinced a reluctant Bradshaw to let him back on the team. Claude later indicated that he believed Bradshaw had been trying to mimic Bear Bryant's unyielding squads but did not always understand when to bear down on players and when to let up. Fortunately, Bradshaw was apparently easier on sportscasters than players—his family and the Sullivans were neighbors in Lexington's Landsdowne Estates community. Despite the transition, Claude continued to enjoy a very pleasant relationship with Kentucky's head coach.

Of the group that survived Bradshaw's purge, quarterback Jerry Woolum, end Tom Hutchinson, and Cox were expected to be among the stars. Of course, on a team that utilized only twenty to twenty-five players, playing meant spending virtually the entire game on the field in many cases. Star lineman Herschel Turner logged 523 minutes in the team's ten games, meaning that he was on the field roughly 87 percent of the time. In an era of increasing specialization, Tom Hutchinson and Junior Hawthorne joined Turner in averaging more than 50 minutes of playing time per game, and tiny Darrell Cox nearly did so. As a result of their dedication and endurance, the Thin Thirty stand as tall in Kentucky lore as many of the more tangibly successful Wildcat squads.

The group began the season by playing Florida State to a scoreless tie. After a loss to top-ranked Ole Miss and a home defeat to Auburn, Kentucky picked up a win over Detroit, 27–8. The team suffered a tough 7–0 loss to LSU and tied Georgia 7–7. With the season record at 1–3–2, UK traveled to Miami, and a 17–6 third-quarter lead evaporated in the crushing heat and humidity of the Florida environment. Miami won 25–17. Kentucky won Bradshaw's first SEC game with a 7–0 triumph over Vanderbilt. Darrell Cox scored the winning touchdown. After a puzzling 14–9 defeat to Xavier, UK entered Neyland Stadium to play Tennessee.

UK was 2–5–2 at that point, and Tennessee's season had scarcely been better, sporting a 3–5 mark. However, with the Beer Barrell trophy on the line, both schools saw the game as a chance at redemption. For Claude, the game was especially meaningful because both of his sons traveled to assist him in the broadcast—

fourteen-year-old David as engineer and eleven-year-old Alan as spotter. From the press box high atop Neyland Stadium, young Alan earned his keep in trying to discern the glaring white numbers on the Tennessee jerseys.

Tennessee took a 10–3 lead on the strength of a long interception return that set up their only touchdown. In the fourth quarter, Kentucky answered as Darrell Cox snagged a Woolum pass and took it 58 yards for a touchdown. Bradshaw elected to go for a 2-point conversion for a shot at the lead, but Woolum's pass misfired, and UK trailed 10–9.

On the Wildcats' final possession, Kentucky drove the ball downfield before stalling out on a fourth down at the 3-yard line with mere seconds on the clock. Claude broadcast the game's pivotal play to his audience:

> Now here it is, it's last down, the clock is stopped, just twenty seconds left, and coming in is Clarkie Mayfield. This is your field-goal attempt. It is for a less distance than the extra point try would be. In other words, it is just a 19-yard attempt. Kicking from the 9, right where he would be kicking if he was trying to convert after a touchdown. Tennessee juggling the defense, HERE IT IS, the kick's in the air, AND IT'S GOOD! AND KENTUCKY GOES AHEAD OF TENNESSEE, but fifteen seconds remain.

A few plays later, a Tennessee Hail Mary fell incomplete, and the Thin Thirty had upset the Volunteers, 12–10. It had been a difficult season, but the finale provided redemption for the hearty band of survivors who won. It also bolstered hopes that Bradshaw's extreme discipline could produce the results UK football fans craved. With a few seasons to clean up the program, Bradshaw hoped to put a Bear Bryant–like streak of success in place. Unfortunately, the triumphant afternoon in Knoxville proved to be the exception rather than the rule.

A few weeks after Clarkie Mayfield played the hero, Adolph Rupp's latest squad took to the hardwood. Cotton Nash was returning from perhaps the best debut campaign in the history of Wildcat basketball, so expectations were high for the 1962–1963 squad. Nash could do it all, but as it turned out, he couldn't do it all by himself. Scottie Baesler was back for his senior campaign, but the rest of Nash's supporting cast consisted of players such as Charles Ishmael and Ted Deeken, both of whom had been benchwarmers the previous year, but as juniors found themselves shouldering more of the load. Opponents double-teamed Nash from the moment he stepped into the gym, and his game suffered. Even the injury bug bit the Cats when a foot injury slowed the heretofore unstoppable Nash.

Kentucky opened the season ranked third in the nation, but after an opening 80–77 loss to Virginia Tech, the team was exposed. Nash had 34 points and eleven rebounds, but the next highest scorer for UK was a reserve guard named Sam Harper, who scored 12 of his career 48 points in the game. On a good night, Nash's teammates would carry part of the load, and Kentucky could resemble a good college basketball team. The season's highlight was a UKIT championship win over number 7 West Virginia. That night, Nash's 30 points and fifteen rebounds were complemented by a 19-point, fourteen-rebound effort from senior forward Roy Roberts and 14 points from Baesler, among other contributions.

However, nine days later UK lost by 24 to unranked St. Louis. This Kentucky team simply was not very good. They were swept by both Tennessee and Georgia Tech and lost again to Babe McCarthy's Mississippi State Bulldogs. UK finished the year 16–9, far out of the race for postseason play. Nash was All-SEC and was chosen for many All-American squads, but his 20.6 points and twelve rebounds per game had not salvaged the season. The season's highlight came in a win over Florida on February 3, when Claude broadcast Nash's joining of UK's prestigious 1,000-point club in his forty-fifth game, a mark that still makes him the fastest Wildcat to reach this milestone. The season had been tough for Nash, however—tough enough that some suggested he bypass his senior year in order to play baseball. However, Nash looked forward to another season—trusting that a group of intense freshmen known as the "Katzenjammer Kids" would make for a memorable final campaign.

"Harvey Kuenn, lead-off batter for the Giants, will lead off the fourth inning. He grounded out, Coleman-to-Maloney to start the ball game. Only one base runner so far. The pitch is on the outside edge at the knees by Maloney, for a called strike. Top of the fourth with no score. Vada Pinson, an infield single in the first, has been the only base runner." With those words, Claude Sullivan found himself announcing an August 13, 1963, game between the Cincinnati Reds and San Francisco Giants. However, Claude's broadcasting audience on this occasion, rather than thousands, was exactly one. Claude, seated inside Crosley Field, was broadcasting the game into a tape recorder for the benefit of J. F. "Bud" Koons Jr., who had found himself searching for a new baseball broadcaster once again. Gene Kelly had not proven to be a hit in Cincinnati. Cincinnati fans were slow to warm to him, and he apparently had not gotten along terribly well with Waite Hoyt. Kelly had indicated that he would not return for the 1964 campaign, and so Claude found himself auditioning in a rather unusual way.

The surviving recording, which picks up with Claude explaining to Koons that he had missed the third inning because he was rewinding the reel-to-reel tape player, is the only known evidence of this second audition. Intriguingly, also within the recordings in Claude's audio archive is a partial September 1963 broadcast of a game between the Cardinals and Dodgers. This may have been another broadcast for Koons, or Claude could have been trying to practice up on his baseball. What is known is that in the later part of the 1963 baseball season the Reds second announcer spot was again vacant and that Claude Sullivan was once again seeking to fill it.

After an auspicious debut season, Charlie Bradshaw did not find himself trimming players leading into the 1963 season. He had a talented sophomore class that he turned loose during the season. Quarterback Rick Norton was perhaps the best athlete that UK had ever placed under center. Running back Rodger Bird was so talented that he assumed the starting mantle over Darrell Cox. End Rick Kestner competed for time alongside Tom Hutchinson. The offense was young but talented. Unfortunately, Bradshaw's defense had dropped off a bit, and thus the improvement in the program was apparent mostly in still-unfulfilled promise.

The season began well enough, with Rodger Bird returning the opening kickoff against Virginia Polytechnic 92 yards for a touchdown. UK rolled 33–14 in that game. However, the impenetrable competition of the SEC soon made clear that UK had some growing up to do. Ole Miss and LSU steamrolled the Cats, while Auburn sneaked past by a single point, and Georgia won by only three. However, by season's end, the UK team had added only two more wins—over Detroit and Baylor—to its résumé. It ended the year 3–6–1, with a bizarre and numb 19–0 loss to Tennessee on November 23, 1963—the day after Lee Harvey Oswald shocked the world by assassinating President John F. Kennedy in Dallas, Texas.

Although the team's record was essentially unchanged from the previous campaign, Bradshaw's second Kentucky squad, with its potent offensive attack by young stars, gave fans a reason to look to the future. As for Claude Sullivan, spending the weeks after the end of the football season awaiting word from Cincinnati, his future was about to get much more interesting.

10

Moving on Up

As Claude Sullivan spent the winter of 1963 wondering if his big break was coming around the corner, he had plenty to occupy the cold winter weeks. Cotton Nash was back for his senior campaign, and the 1963–1964 basketball season was poised to be special. Rupp's sophomore class, the "Katzenjammer Kids," promised to bring depth to the team again. Forward Mickey Gibson, from Hazard, showed plenty of promise. A tall guard, six-foot-five Tommy Kron, provided some much needed size and toughness. But the biggest name of the group was six-foot-four guard Larry Conley. Conley was one of the most well-rounded players ever to wear the Kentucky uniform, and, among his many skills, perhaps the most remarkable was his superb passing. He was exactly the sort of player whom Nash needed in order to succeed. His ability to score, defend, rebound, and pass also allowed role players such as Ted Deeken to step up their productivity.

Kentucky began the season by winning its first ten games, with seven of the wins coming by 20 or more points. Nash had picked up where he left off, scoring 30 points five times during the streak and never dipping below 23 points in a single game. Deeken added 15 or more points in each of the ten games. Kentucky's good fortune and solid play were especially notable in the tenth game, a Sugar Bowl Championship matchup with Duke in New Orleans. The Wildcats and Blue Devils found themselves tied at 79 in the closing seconds, after UK had rallied from a 12-point deficit. UK held possession for the last shot, and the prevailing expectation was that the last shot would go to Nash. The All-American had 30 points in the game, after all. If Nash couldn't get the shot, Deeken had 18 points and would be a viable second option. Reserve guard Terry Mobley, who had just 18 points in the two Sugar Bowl games combined, was an unlikely choice for a hero. Claude brought the action from the Big Easy back to the Big Blue Nation:

> Kentucky's trying to freeze for that closing shot. Here's Embry, moving to the right against Ferguson. Incidentally, Duke is not in the bonus. Fifteen seconds remaining, the clock running. Kentucky is going to set it up now and go for it. Eleven seconds to go as Embry moves to the left. Ten seconds—it's down to Deeken and out to Mobley. Mobley breaks to the left, seven seconds to go. Mobley is shooting—IT'S GOOD. IT'S GOOD. Mobley hits. What can Duke do? One second left, and it's all over. IT'S ALL OVER, AND KENTUCKY HAS DONE IT!

On the strength of that basket, Mobley, a hometown Wildcat, hailing from Harrodsburg, Kentucky, achieved a measure of instant fame. To this day, Mobley is still known in some circles as the Sugar Bowl hero who downed Duke. The victory was especially significant for Mobley because of his roots close to the Lexington community. So deep were those roots that Mobley recalled in a recent interview that he had followed Claude's career even before his time at UK. "What I enjoyed from listening to him, when he did high school games, before UK . . . Claude would get animated. I mean, he got excited." Mobley went on to say that in all of his interactions with Claude outside the intense moments of a live broadcast, "I don't really recall [Claude] not having a smile on his face." Mobley's shot undoubtedly produced such a smile.

After the dramatic victory, UK was ranked first in the nation in both major college basketball polls. The ranking did not last long because Kentucky then lost consecutive games at Georgia Tech and Vanderbilt. But Rupp's squad next won ten in a row for a second time and reached a mark of 20–2. Included in that span was a 103–83 win at Georgia on February 3, 1964, which marked Rupp's seven hundredth career victory. After the game, Rupp was honored by the Georgia officials for the milestone victory. Terry Mobley recalled, "With about two minutes to go, the Georgia public-address announcer asked everyone to remain seated after the game. . . . And they rolled out, on a table, this cake . . . it had [seven] hundred candles. . . . We're the visiting team, and Coach Rupp is being honored. I mean, you just don't do stuff like that." Claude commemorated the odd occasion in his broadcast and was photographed in a group with Rupp and his cake.

Unfortunately, the atmosphere of celebration did not remain. Rupp's 20–2 team was ranked number 4 in the nation on February 24 when it played at Alabama. That game was Mickey Gibson's final playing appearance as a Wildcat. The speedy guard was kicked off the team a few weeks later. And at the end of Cotton Nash's brilliant three-year career, as he was closing in on Alex Groza's school scoring record, King Cotton proved to be very much a mere mortal. After a season in which he had not been held to under 13 points, Nash scored only 9 in a loss to Alabama. Five days later he managed only five free throws in a hard-fought win over Tennessee. In a final pre-tournament tune-up, UK was upset by St. Louis, and Nash could add only 15 points in that game.

Rupp's seven hundredth victory celebration in Athens, Georgia. *From left to right:* Claude, UK publicity director Ken Kuhn, and Adolph Rupp. Courtesy of the *Lexington Herald-Leader.*

A 21–4 Wildcat team was still number 4 in the nation, but the squad was the walking wounded. UK was matched up with Ohio University in the NCAA Tournament's Mideast Region. The Wildcats never had a chance. They trailed 40–24 at the half and lost 85–69. Nash again was subpar, totaling only 10 points, although even in the loss he did move past Groza to become UK's all-time leading scorer. The team lost to Loyola of Chicago in the consolation game on the following day, marking four losses in the last five games.

Nash, on everyone's All-American squad, not only was denied a championship but never played in a Final Four. If a player like Nash couldn't lead UK back to basketball glory, could Rupp be counted on to win a national championship again? Rupp was sixty-two years old when the season ended, and many believed that the game had passed him by. Claude and a few other insiders recognized, however, that between the two-thirds of the Katzenjammers who remained and another superb freshman class, the Baron of the Bluegrass still had some noise to make on the college basketball scene.

On January 27, 1964, a mere week prior to the Georgia celebration, Claude had another more personal celebration that added the largest spoke yet to his professional wheel when he finally received word that he would be part of the Cincinnati Reds 1964 broadcasting crew. As planned, he was successful in his bid to become the second announcer alongside Waite Hoyt and broadcast three innings a game. Also as planned, he would be allowed to continue his broadcasting of UK football and basketball over the Standard Oil Network. To make this work would be a feat very few broadcasters have ever accomplished with the overlap of schedules between baseball, basketball, and football. Claude also was determined to keep his string of high school Sweet Sixteen tournaments going.

Claude hastily called a family meeting. The Sullivans were residing in Louisville at the time due to Claude's management position with WINN. He wondered if the family would prefer to stay in Louisville, move to Cincinnati, or move back to Lexington. The latter option was the family's choice, and thus it went. With both David and Alan now teenagers, Claude accepted his additional duties but also planned, personally and professionally, to make sure that his family was a part of his new world.

In the spring and summer of 1964, Claude commuted from Lexington to Cincinnati on the newly finished Interstate 75, driving a Pontiac Bonneville provided by one of the Reds' sponsors. Whenever possible, he brought David or Alan or both along with him. Crosley Field, the home of the Reds, had opened in 1912 and was truly one of the great old-time stadiums. Its seating capacity was a relatively small 29,604, and its unusual setup was part of the park's charm.

Claude and crew parked in the press lot and passed by the vendors setting up for the day's game. The boys often enjoyed fried-fish sandwiches or bratwurst outside the park, but Claude preferred the press box's ham-and-cheese sandwiches, and so he would wait to eat. The Crosley Field clubhouse was separate from the rest of the stadium. Near the clubhouse was an elevator that took Claude and his visitors up to the press area, where a small bridge led to the actual press box. The box was above and directly behind home plate and afforded a wonderful view of baseball.

Once Claude made his way to the press area, he would grab a sandwich and engage in banter with his broadcasting partner, Waite Hoyt. Unlike Gene Kelly, Claude had no problems getting along with Hoyt. For his part, Claude had procured some kind words from A. B. "Happy" Chandler, governor and former Major League Baseball commissioner, who first commended Claude to Waite, writing, "I am very much pleased that you now have young Claude Sullivan to assist you. Under your tutelage, and if he takes advantage and learns the wisdom of a 'pro,' he too will be a great sportscaster. I believe he has the qualities to achieve his goal, and the advantage that can be gained from associating with you will certainly lead him to the top in this field."

Chandler, working both sides of the connection, then wrote to Claude, saying, "I think you are going to make a wonderful baseball broadcaster and the time you spend with Waite Hoyt will help

Claude and Waite Hoyt at the Crosley Field radio booth for the Cincinnati Reds, 1964. Courtesy of the Cincinnati Reds.

you immeasurably. He admires and respects you and can be of tremendous value to you. I am pleased and delighted to know that you are willing to sit at his feet and learn from him." With the assistance from Chandler, the connection between the two was quite smooth. Given the difference in their ages and backgrounds, Hoyt, who was two years older than Adolph Rupp and had grown up in Brooklyn, enjoyed teasing Claude about his Irish heritage and genially picking at his Kentucky background.

Banter aside, Claude and Waite would discuss the day's game for a few minutes, and Claude would then head down to the field, often with his young charges in tow, for batting practice. He used this time to speak with players, coaches, and managers, checking for fresh information to use during the broadcast. Claude recorded

Left to right: Claude, Waite Hoyt, and Reds television announcer Ed Kennedy along the left field foul line at Crosley Field, 1964. Courtesy of the Cincinnati Reds.

a pregame interview segment, *Diamond Dope,* in which he featured an opposing star or a Reds player. Before game time, David or Alan were dispatched back into the stands to sit with Alyce.

Weekend series were a true family affair, with all three other Sullivans joining Claude and staying at the Sheraton Hotel. During the summer weekday games, David or Alan would bring a friend along when possible.

Once all of the preparation was over, there was baseball—162 games of it, and 20 spring-training games per year. Claude had to learn an entirely new set of skills—filling time in rain delays, bridging the vast gaps between meaningful action, and trying to blend in smoothly with a veteran announcer for the oldest professional baseball team.

The year 1964 was an exciting time for Major League Baseball, and Cincinnati was very much a part of that excitement. The
Reds had played in the World Series just two seasons earlier, in 1961,
when they lost to the Mantle- and Maris-led New York Yankees
in five games. Alan and David had experienced their first major
league game with their grandfather Grubbs and father in that 1961
series. Fred Hutchinson had become the Reds' manager in 1959 and
remained very popular with Reds fans. The 1964 squad was a youthful bunch. None of the regular starters was out of his twenties, and
most of the pitching staff were relative newcomers as well.

Frank Robinson, a talented outfielder and the 1961 National
League Most Valuable Player, was a fan favorite. He had missed
some games in 1963, and his production had dipped to twenty-one
home runs and ninety-one runs batted in (RBI), but Robinson was
always a threat to opposing pitchers. Twenty-five-year-old outfielder
Vada Pinson, in contrast, had thrived in 1963, hitting .313 and leading the league in hits and triples. The pitching staff was led by Jim
Maloney, who won twenty-three games in 1963, including a shutout
of the Giants on Claude's audition tape from August of that year.

But the player who captured Cincinnati's heart more than
any other was a scrappy middle infielder who had won the 1963
Rookie of the Year award. Peter Edward Rose was twenty-four years
old when Claude began broadcasting his games. He had hit .273
as a rookie, but what endeared him to Reds fans was his absolute
refusal to play at anything less than full intensity. With Rose's grit
and determination, Pinson and Robinson slugging the ball all over
the National League, and Maloney and Jim O'Toole anchoring the
pitching staff, Cincinnati was as good as any team in the league. Perhaps a World Series would be in the cards for Claude and his excited
sons.

With its grueling season, baseball is a game of the routine.
Being part of this exciting new world was quickly incorporated into

Claude's own routine—and those of his sons. Alyce recalled sitting in the family section near Carolyn Rose and seeing Pete Rose Jr. at the games with his mother, playing in his child-size uniform and watching his father. Pete's flashy Stingray Corvette drew mention from the crowd and perhaps from many of his teammates.

For the boys, the daily interaction with baseball legends was the stuff of dreams. One evening, during batting practice, Alan and a friend stood by as Claude conducted a pregame interview. Meanwhile, Pete Rose ambled over and, noticing that his bat had cracked, handed the bat off to Alan. Alan, taken with benevolence because he had previously received such a bat from veteran Reds first baseman Gordy Coleman, gave the bat from young Pete Rose to his friend—a move he has regretted a time or two over the ensuing decades.

On a more substantial level, Claude arranged for both of his sons to join him on a road trip during the summer when school was out. David and Alan now received insider treatment in Pittsburgh, where they met the great Roberto Clemente and took in Forbes Field, with its old, stained grandstand, of which Claude noted, "You can almost see the layers of beer on the concrete." They traveled on to Philadelphia, where they watched games at Connie Mack Stadium and visited Independence Hall. Finally, in New York the boys saw the brand-new Shea Stadium, where the Beatles would play a famous concert a year later. Although the Mets were terrible at the time, Claude took advantage of the opportunity to introduce his sons not only to Lindsey Nelson, the voice of the Mets, but also to another local reporter who was much less famous at the time, Howard Cosell. Of course, Cosell and Louisville's Muhammad Ali (formerly Cassius Clay) went on to become part of boxing and broadcasting history within the next few years.

Baseball aside, the World's Fair was the major attraction of the trip for the Sullivan boys. They viewed numerous attractions, such as a major Disney feature that was so successful that Walt Disney World began as an attempt to incorporate and house some of these exhibits in a permanent structure. The Carousel of Progress, which depicted the advances that electricity would make possible, was also very memorable. Finally, the exhibits put up by other countries were interesting to the boys because of Claude's extensive travels to Europe and the Middle East.

Family benefits aside, Claude enjoyed his new position. Hoyt proved to be wonderful to work with—a friend not only to Claude, but to the rest of the family. A letter survives from after the 1964 season, when Claude had written Hoyt and mentioned that David had broadcast a youth All-Star game. Waite's joking rejoinder, "Give a guy an inch and he'll move in a whole family," and comparison of the Sullivans to the Beverly Hillbillies were belied by his friendly tone and his final comment: "Well, I'll be waiting for you." Hoyt's attitude spilled over into the broadcasts. On June 16, 1964, a note from Billy Thompson in the *Lexington Herald* noted, "More and more folks we bump into heap praise on Lexington's Claude Sullivan and the way he broadcasts Cincy Redleg games. Claude will be one of the best 'casters in the majors, but we're not surprised—we knew from the very beginning he was tops. . . . So keep up the good work, 'voice.'"

Claude's triumph and the excellence of the Reds team were marred by the illness of manager Hutchinson, who before the season began had been diagnosed with malignant tumors in his lungs, chest, and neck. Hutchinson managed the team through July 27, when he was hospitalized. He returned for another nine days in August but eventually had to turn day-to-day management of the team over to first-base coach Dick Sisler. Hutchinson died of cancer on November 12, about five weeks after the season ended.

Meanwhile, Hutchinson's team was almost as good as he could have hoped. Frank Robinson rebounded with a superb season, hitting .306 with twenty-nine home runs and ninety-six RBI. Pinson's

Left to right: Cincinnati Reds manager Fred Hutchinson, Claude, and Reds owner William O. Dewitt, 1964. Courtesy of the Cincinnati Reds.

batting average dropped, but he managed twenty-three home runs and eighty-four RBI as well. Jim O'Toole won seventeen games, and Maloney added fifteen more. Of the team's top performers, only Rose struggled—missing some time with injuries and thus hitting only a decent but unspectacular .269.

The Reds hung around the playoff race, although by mid-August, after Hutchinson's final departure, they had fallen eight and a half games back of first place in the pennant race. The team then caught fire, winning twenty-nine of their final forty-seven games. At the same time, the Philadelphia Phillies, who had led the league for most of the season, began an epic collapse that is still discussed among baseball historians.

For a horse-racing broadcaster, it was an appropriate end to his first pennant race. The Phillies were fading fast, and the Reds were among a pack of teams hustling in from the outside and trying to catch up. The Reds reached a tie with four games to go but lost three of their last four, including a 10–0 shutout in the season's last game that left them tied with the Phillies—but one game behind the St. Louis Cardinals, who went on to win the World Series that year.

Still, the chase had come close enough that the Reds had printed up World Series tickets in case they were needed. When they didn't have occasion to be used, Claude was given a few sheets of the tickets for a souvenir.

It had been an exciting season for Claude and for all of the Sullivan family. A few days after Christmas, Claude turned forty years old. He had reached all of his professional goals. He was enjoying his work, his family, and his life. If this season hadn't ended in a World Series, well, there would be next year. There would always, it seemed, be a next year.

It was a short transition from Cincinnati's Crosley Field to Lexington's Stoll Field for Claude in the fall of 1964. The offensive stars from the previous gridiron season—Rick Norton, Rodger Bird, and Rick Kestner—were juniors, and fellow junior tackle Sam Ball was just as talented. After Bradshaw's Wildcats opened with an uninspired 13–6 win, in their second game the squad went to top-ranked Ole Miss and shocked the Rebels with a 27–21 upset. The win was UK's first over a top-ranked team since Bryant's 1951 Sugar Bowl win. Rebel coach Johnny Vaught was effusive in his praise of the Wildcats. Kentucky had opened the game with Rodger Bird running an end sweep and improvising a 79-yard scoring pass, which was called back because of an ineligible receiver downfield. In the second half, Bird ran the same play, and this time his 32-yard scoring pass to Rick Kestner stood. Although no recording of the game survives, eyewitness accounts from the WVLK booth indicate that Claude found himself exhorting, "Run, Rick, run!" Kestner, who caught two more touchdowns from Norton, received national honors for his play and his nine catches and 185 receiving yards. After the game, Claude gave young Jim Host a ride home, and Host recalled Claude telling him it was the greatest football game he had ever called.

When Kentucky followed this game by thumping number 7 Auburn 20–0, many wondered if Bradshaw could be growing into the position of successor to Bryant's legacy at UK. Claude opened the Florida State game by stating that it was Kentucky's fourth straight undefeated opponent: "This one [Florida State] is unbeaten, untied, and unscored upon . . . and dangerous. . . . Now, we see something really strange for a Kentucky team. Protecting a national reputation. Not for many years has a Kentucky team been in the wonderful position of being among the nation's elite." Kentucky had a letdown, however, and was handed a 48–6 beating by Florida State, featuring star receiver and future NFL Hall of Fame inductee Fred Biletnikoff. This loss brought the then number 5 Wildcats back to earth.

The Florida State game was no fluke, as Florida State finished 9–1–1 with a Gator Bowl win over Oklahoma. Although UK's Rick Norton led the SEC in passing and total offense, UK could not break through the tough SEC. Road losses at LSU and Georgia humbled the Wildcats. Before the Georgia game, Claude had reminded his listeners, "Remember 1951? Kentucky lost four games, including a 28–0 lacing by Tennessee . . . but wound up in the Cotton Bowl because of an exciting quarterback named Babe Parilli. Certainly Rick Norton is every bit as exciting." The road loss at Georgia prompted an unusual comment from Claude about a Georgia team that beat defending national champion Alabama and Rose Bowl champion Michigan. He stated that "the stadium here now seats 43,000 and is surrounded by a hedge that seems to always reach its peak of beauty when Kentucky comes down every other year!"

Kentucky did defeat Vanderbilt and Tennessee in order to secure a break-even 5–5 mark—the first nonlosing season since Collier's identical mark in 1961. Bird and Kestner were All-SEC, and although this year's Kentucky team had shown promise, many thought that the following season's senior-laden team would lead the Wildcats back to the postseason bowl picture. Claude observed before the loss to West Virginia, "The survivor [of today's game] has hopes, and the loser has an acute problem for a winning season." Once again, there would always be a next year.

The best component of the new season for Adolph Rupp and his 1964–1965 Wildcats was the trio of talented sophomores who were moving up from the freshman team. A great raw talent was six-foot-six Wayne Chapman. Playing much like his son Rex would two decades later, Chapman lit up scoreboards from the inside and outside. The Owensboro product was joined by an even better shooter, Louie Dampier, a slim and small Indiana schoolboy who didn't look like much until he unleashed his textbook jump shot. The third member of the trio was a New Yorker with decent size, excellent athleticism, and tremendous toughness. Before Pat Riley began building championship basketball teams, he was no mean hand on the hardwood himself. Each of the three had averaged more than 20 points per game for the UK freshman team, and the combination of the three seemed like enough firepower to keep Kentucky competitive.

Kron and Conley returned, and so Rupp was cautiously optimistic. With only one player in the normal rotation being taller than the six-foot-five Kron, however, Rupp's team was short on height—and on depth. A crushing blow was laid before the season began when Chapman decided that he would transfer to Western Kentucky University. Just like that, the bubble burst on this particular Kentucky basketball team.

Kentucky's troubles came to the forefront as early as the annual UKIT, the eleventh edition of the annual matchup. Claude always enjoyed the tournament and introduced his broadcast by revisiting the history behind the tournament's beginning the year after the probation scandal. He proudly told his audience that "our invitational tournament is the richest in the nation. During the past eleven tournaments, the teams have divided the net gate receipts and taken home anywhere from $8,200 dollars by LaSalle, UCLA, and Duke in the first meet back in 1953 . . . to the $15,400 checks [taken] by West Virginia, St. Louis, and North Carolina in 1959." These numbers pale in comparison to the huge numbers in television and athletic budgets of today, but in that era they represented an incredible amount of money for playing in a holiday tournament.

The UKIT was popular with Claude and others, remaining an annual tournament until 1990 when second-year UK coach Rick Pitino bypassed it to play in his East Coast stomping grounds. Meanwhile, Claude's enthusiasm was thumped as Kentucky lost that opening round of its tournament 102–78 to West Virginia and then reached New Year's Day 1965 with a 4–4 record and a three-game losing streak, including this UKIT defeat. The team fared somewhat better in SEC play, posting a 10–5 mark and losing only one conference game at home. On a given night, Kentucky could be a fine team, or it could be a poor one, depending mostly on whether the sophomores were hitting their shots.

Dampier was sensational. In his third varsity game, he dropped 37 points on Iowa State. He added 31 more in the next outing against Syracuse. For the year, Dampier averaged a little more than 17 points per game in earning All-SEC selection. His range and touch were superb, and his high scoring was perhaps less impressive than his careful shot selection. Despite being a long-distance ace whose game would have been even more deadly with the 3-point shot, Dampier connected on 51.2 percent of his shots from the field, leading the team.

Riley was less explosive, but still impressive. He scored 15 points per game and was also second in rebounding for the under-size squad. Riley broke the 20-point barrier five times during the season. Juniors Kron and Conley were also impressive, each averaging double-figure scoring. In fact, including senior center John Adams, Kentucky had five players who averaged double-figure scoring. The problem was defense. Rupp's squad was actually outrebounded for the season, and although the team averaged 84 points per game, it also allowed 77 per game.

The 15–10 Wildcats found themselves on the outside of the postseason again. Popular opinion was that if Rupp would recruit a capable big man or two, the rest of the squad might be redeemable. There was some offensive punch, but with the six-foot-seven Adams graduating, there looked to be even less height on hand for the following season. Again, there was grumbling against Rupp. He was too old, people claimed, and the game was passing him by. However, Rupp had one more basketball magic act left, and although few would have dreamed it possible, the next year would be golden. Claude had broken through into the major leagues, and Kentucky basketball was about to return to form. All, it seemed, was right with the world.

11

The View from on Top

As soon as basketball was finished, Claude hurried off to the warmer climates of spring training, where the Reds were busy preparing for the 1965 season. With the team faring so well in the 1964 pennant race under Dick Sisler's guidance, Sisler returned for a full season as manager of the team. The Reds' personnel was much the same as in 1964. The team again fielded a squad with no starters older than thirty—only first baseman Gordy Coleman had attained that mark, although right fielder Frank Robinson was infamously noted as being "an old twenty-nine" by owner Bill DeWitt. One of the freshest faces was a young first baseman who made the roster out of spring training. Tony Perez had gone just two for twenty-five in a brief 1964 big-league stint, but his promise was undeniable, and he became a full-time big leaguer, where he remained until 1986.

Claude was fortunate to be a part of Major League Baseball in an era of great transition—a transition that became apparent when the Houston Astros opened the Astrodome during the 1965 season. The first domed stadium and first artificial turf field (indeed, the con-cretelike surface was initially dubbed "Astroturf"), the Astrodome was often considered to be the eighth wonder of the modern world.

Claude and the Reds made their first trip into the Dome on May 24. The Reds were 21–14 at the time, one game out of the lead for the National League pennant. The team won two of three games in the cavernous new stadium. So significant was the Dome that Kentucky sportswriter Billy Reed asked Claude for his impressions. Claude's letter on the subject stated:

The Astrodome is like the Grand Canyon. You cannot tell a person what it's like because there is nothing to compare it with. Like the Canyon, a picture of the Dome doesn't really give you the idea of size. It's amazingly clear and clean inside. A habit I've developed over the years is to always anchor any piece of paper around a ball park, football stadium, or race track. But here . . . no wind.

Dick Sisler said he was reminded of a large circus tent before it was filled with people. Most of the players said they had an artificial feeling about everything. You're afraid to trust your judgment. This seems to show up on the field. The outfielders "rivet" their attention on a fly ball and never leave it. Just as soon as they step into foul territory following a foul fly, they're looking for a wall. Generally, they like the conditions, but Houston players say that night ball is easy compared to the afternoon games. . . .

Walter Bond of the Astros offered Vada Pinson of the Reds $20 if he could catch 15 or 20 balls hit to the outfield in daytime. Batting practice is taken during daylight hours, and the instant the ball enters the lights, you lose it. There have been only 15 home runs in 19 games.

The Reds went 5–3 in the Dome during the 1965 season, so the abundance of talent on the team apparently overcame the bizarre conditions Claude described.

From the unusual to the sublime, 1965 was a very memorable season for the Reds and for Claude. On August 19 in Wrigley Field, Claude fulfilled one of every baseball announcer's dreams when he broadcast a no-hitter. Jim Maloney of the Reds blanked the Cubs in the first game of a doubleheader on this date, scattering ten walks over the course of the game and hitting a batter, but allowing no base hits. Unfortunately for Maloney, the Reds couldn't bring across any runs on his behalf. Finally, in the top of the tenth inning, Cincinnati shortstop Leo Cardenas homered off hard-luck Cubs pitcher Larry Jackson. With one out and a runner on first in the bottom of the frame, Maloney induced Ernie Banks to ground into a double play and complete the no-hitter.

The Reds were 66–52 after the no-hitter and were still within striking distance of the pennant, at three and a half games out of first place. The team struggled even closer, tying for first on September 1 and remaining a mere half-game out of first place as late as September 9. However, the Reds finished 9–12 from that date and ended up in fourth place, eight games back of the league champion Dodgers.

In failing to win, the Reds spoiled a superb season by Frank Robinson, who hit .296, with 33 home runs and 113 RBI. Second-year third baseman Deron Johnson had a career year, almost matching Robinson with a .287 average, 32 home runs, and 130 RBI. Pinson hit .305 and played a majestic center field, and Pete Rose made his first All-Star team, hitting .312 and leading the league in hits for the first of seven times. The pitching staff was uneven, but Sammy Ellis was 22–10 at age twenty-four, and Jim Maloney also won twenty games.

Down the stretch, even as the Reds faded, another story kept fans following the team closely. Waite Hoyt announced that he would retire following the season. On October 3, at San Francisco's Candlestick Park, Waite and Claude broadcast their final game together. Claude asked the venerable Hoyt about his greatest thrills in baseball. Among the memories that Hoyt recalled was making his first start, a 2–1 win over the Tigers in 1919, five years before Claude was born. Hoyt talked about his first World Series appearance, in 1921, again before Claude was born. When he made his retirement speech, Hoyt broke down in tears. He later handed out a mimeograph sheet with his statement, which included the following: "My wish and that of Burger [the sponsor] is for my associate at the present, Claude Sullivan, to announce as broadcaster for the Cincinnati Reds, if possible. My affiliation with Claude has provided two of the happiest years of my radio life."

Hoyt's support was significant. It was not a sure thing that the Reds would retain Claude as their primary broadcaster in spite of the success of the past two seasons. Pat Harmon wrote in the *Cincinnati Post and Times Star* that "unless those that are picking his successor are blind and deaf," Hoyt would be replaced by Claude. The new sponsor of the Reds, Wiedemann Brewing Company, called a press conference for October 22 to announce the new broadcaster at Cincinnati's Queen City Club. Sportswriter John McGill wrote years later in the *Lexington Herald-Leader* of his relief at seeing Claude enter the room that night to a loud round of applause. "The man deserved the job and I was thankful he got it," wrote McGill.

Claude prepared to begin 1966 as the primary broadcaster for Cincinnati Reds baseball. He was on top of his game, and everything seemed to be going along smoothly. It had taken two decades for Claude to build his career, but it would take much less time for the entire endeavor, indeed the entire wheel and spokes of his life, to be jeopardized.

Such negative thoughts were far away for Claude as he prepared to broadcast the 1965 Kentucky football season. His voice, oddly, was sounding a bit rough. Vin Scully, the young Los Angeles Dodgers broadcaster, had mentioned this to him during one of the Reds' final road trips of the 1965 season. Claude probably suspected that the wear and tear of the long baseball season was grinding on him a bit. Football, with only one game per week, would be easier. Football also looked to be, for the first time in a long while, very exciting.

Bradshaw, in his fourth season, was now being judged solely on the strength of a group of players he recruited. Those players—Norton, Rodger Bird, Rick Kestner, Sam Ball, and junior Larry Seiple—gave him the makings of a fine football team. Expectations were high—and, perhaps, UK's thirteen-year bowl drought would come to an end.

In the opener, Kentucky beat a tough Missouri squad, 7–0. UK's only score came on a long pass from Norton to Seiple, and the Kentucky defense had a gutsy goal-line stand in the fourth quarter to protect the lead. Kentucky's win moved them into the AP poll's national rankings at number 10. Kentucky had not reached the top ten since 1951.

The following week's game with Ole Miss was a barn burner. Kentucky was clinging to a 9–7 lead in the final seconds, with Seiple, who was not only a fine receiver and runner but the team's punter, preparing to kick the ball away on fourth down and 41 yards to go. He took the snap and, seeing no rush, hesitated. He prepared to kick and again saw no oncoming players, so he pulled the ball down and ran 70 yards for a touchdown and a 16–7 victory. UK moved up to sixth in the AP poll with the victory.

From there, the team became somewhat inconsistent. A 23–18 loss at Auburn dropped Kentucky back out of the national rankings. The team pulled out a 26–24 squeaker over Florida State but lost at LSU 31–21. Kentucky then played Georgia, with the Bulldogs having taken over the number 10 spot in the AP poll. Kentucky slaughtered them 28–10 as Norton dissected the Georgia defense. He continued this pattern in a 28–8 thumping of West Virginia the following week. Kentucky assumed the number 10 spot in the national rankings again. With Kentucky at 5–2, an end to the bowl drought seemed certain. On his weekly *Football Predictions* show, Claude spoke for much of the Big Blue Nation when he noted, "We've said ourselves that Kentucky now is in the second half of the season, and the second half of the season is not nearly so tough as the first half. But you always make these statements on the assumption that the team will play as well against the lesser lights in the second half as they did the brighter lights in the first half. If Kentucky plays that type of football, they certainly can beat Vanderbilt and Houston, and probably Tennessee. But this is all ahead, and it's all probables." Claude predicted a 14–7 UK win over Vanderbilt and was looking ahead to what might come next.

Kentucky outplayed Claude's prediction, shutting out Vanderbilt 34–0. Kentucky was then 6–2, with a road game at Houston and the home contest with Tennessee left on the schedule. After the Vanderbilt win, the Gator Bowl's representative approached Coach Bradshaw, offering a bid in its game. The coach, thinking that Kentucky could climb higher in the bowl pecking order, spoke with his team. The team decided to turn down the bowl. Another, better bowl would come calling—especially after they thumped Houston.

Claude was in his element in Houston: Houston played its games in the Astrodome, and in 1965 he had already made two trips to cover the Reds and Astros. Admittedly, on the gridiron, there was no danger of losing a fly ball, but the environment was still unusual. By November, the Lucite dome no longer let in the light that was to let the grass grow. The natural grass in the Astrodome was gone, and the field was reduced to a sandlot-type "dirt bowl," as Claude referred to it. Since he had given his detailed description of the Astrodome to Billy Reed for his newspaper column, Claude did his opening to the Houston game without mention of the eighth wonder of the world. He did mention that Ole Miss had lost here the previous weekend by 17–3. Claude calmly ended his introduction and game setup with, "No need to give you a weather report. . . . We're inside!"

Kentucky, fueled by Norton, moved the ball at will in the first half. He hit a 75-yard pass to Seiple and connected on another score, giving UK a 21–16 halftime advantage. For the game, Norton was nineteen of twenty-three for 373 yards passing. He had reached 1,823 yards passing for the season—besting Babe Parilli's school record and being just a yard shy of the SEC single-season yardage mark, then held by Georgia's Zeke Bratkowski. However, in the second half Houston denied the Wildcats any scores, added three of its own, and knocked Norton from the game and the season with a knee injury. Houston's 38–21 victory was painful on several levels. Jim Host recalled Claude saying to him after that game, "We have screwed up this program forever."

Indeed, Bradshaw's career never recovered, and it was another eleven years before Kentucky appeared in a bowl game.

Without Norton, Kentucky's offense was a shell of itself the following week. Tennessee won 19–3, and the 6–4 Wildcats were out of the bowl picture. Ball, Bird, and Norton received All-American honors from *Time* magazine. NBC also chose Bird and Norton for its squad, and Ball was named to no less than six other All-American teams. Each of the three was a first-round draft choice in the following spring—Norton by the American Football League's (AFL) Miami Dolphins, Ball by the NFL's Baltimore Colts, and Bird by the AFL's Oakland Raiders. As for Bradshaw, he made history in the winter of 1965, integrating SEC football when he signed Nat Northington and Greg Page, two African Americans from Kentucky, to scholarships. The coach received a contract extension after Thanksgiving, although everyone who remembered Blanton Collier wondered about exactly how firm the vote of confidence from the Athletic Department was.

Claude's comment to Jim Host showed that he understood what a missed opportunity the 1965 season had become; however, he wasn't aware that it would be the last meaningful chance he would have to see Kentucky football achieve success. His voice was still a bit off as the 1965 season ended. Only those who knew exactly what to listen for, such as Vin Scully, caught it. To the rest of the world, he was still a great broadcaster, staying active in his trade, strengthening that professional wheel that he had built up over the past two decades.

Given Claude's love of broadcasting and his family, it is hardly surprising that he sought out ways that he could involve the latter with the former. He had established Sullivan Enterprises in 1962 as a means of helping to manage his growing business interests in radio.

Claude was managing the Kentucky Central Network as well as the Standard Oil Network. Jim Host eventually became the main broadcaster for the Kentucky Central Network because Dee Huddleston was getting older and did not wish to continue with large amounts of travel for small amounts of money. With Claude's multi-sport and multinetwork schedule, he needed to utilize other broadcasters to help him fulfill multiple engagements at the same time. He hired Charlie Maston and Paul Hornung to broadcast high school games in Louisville. He also hired Jim Host and Ralph Hacker to announce Lexington's high school sports action. His role as general manager of WINN and simultaneous manager of two networks created a legitimate need for Sullivan Enterprises. In addition, such a business would be helpful when and if Kentucky ever gave in to the growing trend toward a single authorized radio broadcast.

Claude conducted the business formally—holding an annual meeting at which a board of directors for the next year was elected. David and Alan soon gained additional responsibilities, aside from their titles as officers in the company. By 1962, both sons, at ages fourteen and eleven, routinely worked at the press table, flanking Claude. They enjoyed football, with its pageantry and pomp, but also appreciated basketball, which was played in smaller and warmer confines, and the boys were close enough to see the players sweat and to hear the squeaks of their Chuck Taylor All-Star sneakers. A quick review of the typical game-day routine for football and basketball illustrates the inner workings of Sullivan Enterprises—and the working camaraderie between Claude and his sons.

The trip to the broadcasting booth at Stoll Field was made by slowly walking up the thirty-stair steps to the approach to the press box level. Claude carried a briefcase full of equipment. The boys carried additional equipment, and once the trek was complete, they set up the station banner, a small amplifier, a crowd microphone, and a reel-to-reel tape deck to be used for commercials.

The station booth was just wide enough for four chairs. There was room for Claude, David as engineer, Alan as UK's spotter, and a visiting team's spotter. While David assisted with the technical side of the broadcast, Alan assisted by indicating the players that made key tackles and plays by watching the action with binoculars and referencing the players by a depth chart. Claude invented several examples of spotting equipment, looking for the most efficient model and constantly inventing and revising several methods to track the players, including a wood case that folded out to have a lighted display with a push button to light the name of the players who were in the game. He also designed a box with square pegs that rotated with up to four players' names at each position to be displayed on each of the four sides. Claude saved two of these contraptions and the spotting charts for the games. A simple depth chart showing positions on the field was his favorite for its simplicity and portable format.

The booth at Stoll Field was not a luxury box, nor was it enclosed. It was not heated and had concrete floors and walls, with no glass to protect its occupants from the wind or cold from the field side of the stadium. The back side was enclosed with a window and door to the walkway, so the booth was always cold, and the hard concrete floor wreaked havoc on the broadcasting team's feet.

In addition to getting paid by Sullivan Enterprises for spotting and keeping scores of other games, Alan received $10 a game from Cawood Ledford, whose WHAS booth was adjacent to Claude's booth, to post the scores for him. This was great money at the time because Alan could essentially double-dip and collect $20 or $25 for an afternoon's work. The work was disciplined and serious, with no real room for mistakes. At the conclusion of an exciting play, Claude often gave David the signal to turn up the crowd microphone while he muted his own mic and whispered the next instructions to Alan. The time spent with family was precious to Claude, and he enjoyed working side by side with his two boys, who were rapidly becoming young men.

Before a typical basketball game, Alan and David hung the WVLK/ Standard Oil Network banner on the midcourt press table at Memorial Coliseum. David then set up the broadcasting equipment, prepared a transformer and tape deck for commercials and promos, and checked the phone line to make sure that it was suitable for broadcasting purposes.

Claude would prepare for the broadcast and visit the UK locker room, sometimes taking one or the other of his sons if all was well in their nightly setup. Claude often touched base with the opposing team's media relations director for a player status, number change, or roster status or for information on players who did not make the travel squad at the last minute. Claude inserted these references and notations into his broadcast.

Finally, Claude and the boys visited the pressroom. The boys often grabbed hot dogs and Coca-Colas and supplied Claude with a Coke to soothe his throat during the broadcast. Alan made sure

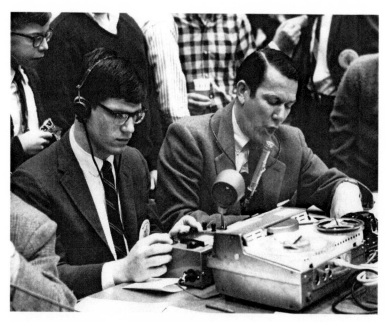

Eighteen-year-old David Sullivan engineering for Claude at the Memorial Coliseum press table, 1966. Courtesy of the *Lexington Herald-Leader*.

to keep an ice-cold Coke at the ready at all times during the game. Once the game began, it was nonstop work for the broadcast team. It was the family business in action, with David acting as the engineer and Alan keeping statistics, including the running play by play of the action. When asked why he hired his sons for these important positions, Claude said that since he had to pay someone to do it, it might as well be his sons. "Besides," he noted, "I don't have to pay them union scale." Incidentally, Claude did hire union employees on road trips and would readily tell others that he did not receive the high quality of work from them that he did from David and Alan.

Although Alyce was exempted from production responsibility, she still usually sat with several of the players' parents, across the aisle from A. B. "Happy" Chandler at midcourt. The coach's wife,

Esther Rupp, was a few rows behind her, and actor William Shatner, who had a horse farm in Versailles, sat just across the aisle. It was a happy time for the Sullivan family because Sullivan Enterprises was keeping everyone involved in Claude's work.

Claude had one more business goal in mind at this time. Over the years, the process of admitting as many broadcasters as wished to carry the game was going out of favor. Meanwhile, collegiate athletics, having always been a business, was becoming a much more lucrative one. Claude figured that it was only a matter of time until UK went to a single official feed of the games, and he wanted to be the broadcaster at the head of that network. Both Dee Huddleston and Ray Holbrook, two fellow broadcasters of the era, recalled the topic being a heated one.

The contest for such a network, again relevant only if UK ever decided to allow it, stood to be between WVLK, which was Claude's largest station, and WHAS, where Cawood Ledford called the UK games. Dee Huddleston recalled a meeting at the university in which WHAS was pushing to create a single network and to head that network. However, there was resistance—in large part because of Claude's popularity and infiltration of Kentucky's radio markets. Within Claude's correspondence was a letter from athletic director Bernie Shively dated June 1, 1965, advising that a committee had decided to keep the existing policy in place and that WHAS and WVLK would alternately have the designation as the "official" UK station in terms of the right to a free outlet for home-game broadcasts. That is to say, the status quo would remain in effect—for the time being.

Claude continued to discuss this single-network plan with Shively. Many believed that if a single network obtained UK's rights, Claude would be the primary broadcaster. Among them was Cawood Ledford himself. Ralph Hacker, then a young broadcaster who worked with Ledford for years, commented in an interview that he recalled Ledford telling him that if there were a single network, he expected Claude Sullivan would be UK's choice as the broadcaster of preference. For the time being, however, Shively made no changes, and Claude and Cawood remained friendly competitors, both preparing to broadcast one of the greatest seasons in UK history.

The 1965–1966 Kentucky basketball campaign had a new lineup for WINN and WVLK. The new pregame interview show *Warm-Up* was aired. The first guest was Adolph Rupp, followed by his longtime assistant Harry Lancaster. On the way to Champaign, Illinois, for the Illinois game, Claude stopped off to interview his Reds broadcast partner, Jim McIntyre, in Indianapolis. It seems that Indy racers Mario Andretti and A. J. Foyt were at the 500 doing tire-testing trials, with Foyt being clocked at 190 miles per hour before the third turn. Claude explained on the pregame show that "we took our recorder to the track Thursday morning, went to the gasoline alley, and talked with Foyt before he went out on the track. After the interview, Foyt let 'er wind up and did 145 miles per hour warming up and running right at us along the pits." Claude then played the interview and soundtrack for the pregame *Warm-Up* show audience.

The 1965–1966 team seemed to have little "high-octane" performance ahead of them, coming off a disappointing previous 15–10 season. There was little reason to expect much from the team. Although Dampier and Riley returned, and seniors Kron and Conley promised to be solid, these same players had had a disappointing year in 1964–1965 simply by missing the NCAA Tournament. Lexington's own Thad Jaracz, a sophomore, was the team's fifth starter. Jaracz, at six foot five, was undersized for the post position that he filled and seemed unlikely to effect a great change in the nature of the Kentucky team.

Claude interviewing Adolph Rupp after a rare loss for the Cats 49–40 at Georgia in the 1966–1967 season. Courtesy of University of Georgia Sports Communications.

But it turned out that this group—"Rupp's Runts," as they became known—ran and passed and scored with an ease that almost defied common sense. Rupp was in his element coaching a team of scorers, as he had long disdained defensive tactics that slowed down games. He marveled at growing ticket prices and the lessening amount of action that a fan would see with that ticket. The Runts provided nonstop action. The team shot almost 50 percent for the season as a team, with Conley's total of just under 47 percent being the lowest mark of the starters. The team passed brilliantly, led by Conley and Kron, as they totaled almost two and a half times as many assists as their opponents. Again, the squad was small, with only the six-foot-four Riley and six-foot-five Jaracz to protect the backboard. But with a little help from a new assistant coach, Joe B. Hall, and his devilish conditioning program, the team adapted to outrun the squads that they couldn't outjump.

Kentucky was unranked at the beginning of the season, but it proceeded to win its first ten games by 28, 26, 18, 11, 20, 35, 16, 34, 10, and 14 points, respectively. The 10–0 Wildcats, now up to number 2 in the AP poll, had a struggle at Georgia, where it took two overtimes to defeat the Bulldogs 69–65 on free throws by Cliff Berger. Besides Berger, Dampier was the difference in that game, scoring 23 points on his perimeter jumpers, with Riley and Jaracz each adding 14 points in the win. Before that close game, Claude had been outside the coliseum at Athens, and he later told his audience that "Rupp found a bobby pin on the sidewalk in the shade. Of all good omens, Adolph considers this one perhaps paramount. . . . Ask him sometime to show you his collection, especially on the day of a game." Kentucky then won the next twelve games as well, topping 100 points four times during the streak.

With the team at 23–0, it finally lost a game, 69–62 at Knoxville against Tennessee. To open the last game of the season and the last game against Tulane as an SEC member, Claude had this to say: "This is Claude Sullivan from Lexington. The bubble burst! . . . After the defeat in Knoxville last Saturday, thousands of fans gathered at the Lexington airport to welcome the team. This spirit from the fans has an untold effect on the players and coaches. This reminds them, this is Kentucky, where a broken twenty-five-game winning streak is used only as the starting point for another one."

The Wildcats, by then number 1 in the nation, rebounded and won by 29 points against Tulane in their regular season finale and so moved into the NCAA Tournament. After the Tulane game wrap-up, Claude explained to his audience the complicated travel schedule he had with the NCAA regional and the Reds' spring training starting up. He was leaving that night for Tampa.

In NCAA play, Kentucky dispatched Dayton and seven-footer Henry Finkle 86–79. Finkle had 36 points for the Flyers, but Dampier nearly matched him with 34, and Riley added 29 of his own. In the regional final, Michigan's Cazzie Russell scored 29 points to try to upset Kentucky, but each of the five starting Runts reached double figures, led by Riley's 29 points, and Kentucky won 84–77.

After an eight-year hiatus, Kentucky was back in the Final Four. The semifinal matchup with number 2 Duke was expected to be the de facto championship by most knowledgeable observers. Kentucky struggled past the Blue Devils, 83–79. Dampier led the way with 23 points as Larry Conley fought the flu throughout the game. Ignored by most, Texas Western sneaked past Utah in the later semifinal matchup.

Accordingly, Kentucky took on the Miners in the NCAA Championship game in College Park, Maryland. On the microphone for the Standard Oil Network was a road-weary Claude, having flown from Tampa, where he was broadcasting spring-training games for the Reds, up to College Park. Claude had a frantic schedule to make the Mideast Regional in Iowa City, then to spring training in Sarasota, then back for the regional final. He had to go back and forth between games to College Park and Sarasota after the Duke game, and he returned to Sarasota for the remaining couple of weeks of spring training before the opening day in Cincinnati. A standby announcer had been kept available for the NCAA final

Claude's interview with Adolph Rupp after the final regular-season game against Tulane at the WVLK press table in Memorial Coliseum, 1966. From the Claude Sullivan Collection, donated by Jim Host.

broadcast in case the flight ran slow, but the listeners who tuned in heard this: "Good evening, basketball fans! Here in College Park, Maryland, tonight, University of Kentucky takes on Texas Western in the NCAA Tournament. This is the fifteenth consecutive year Standard Oil Company and Standard Oil Dealers throughout Kentucky have had the opportunity—and pleasure—of bringing you all of UK's basketball games over the Standard Oil Sports Network of fourteen Kentucky stations, with Claude Sullivan at the mic."

In the opening minutes, Claude and the college basketball establishment were surprised as five-foot-ten Miner Bobby Joe Hill stole the ball from Kentucky players twice and raced to easy layups. Texas Western led 31–28 at the half, and although Kentucky stayed close, pulling as close as 54–51, Texas Western had all the momentum. The Miners won 72–65, with the diminutive Hill scoring 20 points to lead the way. Kentucky was paced by Dampier and Riley, each of whom had 19 points. The Cats, however, shot just 39 percent for the game, were outrebounded, and took twenty-one fewer free throws than their Texas opponents.

Rupp was devastated. The coach was not getting any younger; he would be sixty-five years old when the next season began. He had also a lengthy history of injuries and illnesses over the past decade, all of which had combined to slow him greatly. Indeed, Claude had made arrangements for a telephone line on the floor so that Rupp would not have to climb stairs to reach Claude's broadcasting position for his postgame interview. Poor David, working the Final Four with his father, had arrived at the gymnasium to find the setup completely wrong and nervously arranged the correct placement. This was only part of a very lively time for the elder Sullivan son. Charlie Ryle from WINN was scheduled to be the replacement announcer if Claude did not arrive in time, but David recalled that Ryle disappeared and left him to set up for the championship game and wrangle with the telephone company. Overall, it is difficult to say who

Rupp's Runts on the UK campus during the 1966 season. *Left to right:* Tommy Kron, Louie Dampier, Thad Jaracz, Pat Riley, and Larry Conley. Courtesy of the *Louisville Courier-Journal.*

had a tougher night—David Sullivan or Adolph Rupp. Rupp was gracious in defeat, giving a healthy dose of credit to the victors and exchanging pleasantries with Claude. Rupp noted that he hoped to get up to Cincinnati to watch the "Redlegs," as he called them, play some baseball.

Conspicuously absent from the recording in the historical aftermath of this game is Rupp's alleged racism. The matchup between the white Wildcats and the mostly African American Miners is one that Disney deigned to moralize in its 2006 film *Glory Road,* which was only very, very loosely based on the truth. Revisionist history certainly has its flaws. If Kentucky had lost the semifinal to an all-white Duke team, would the Blue Devils have been branded scheming racists as the movie brands Rupp?

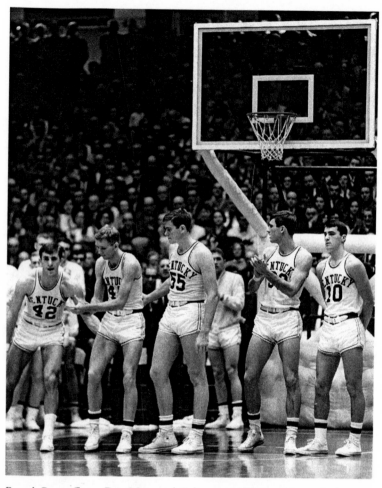

Rupp's Runts Game Day, Memorial Coliseum, 1966. Pat Riley is the last one out to complete the starting five. *Left to right:* Riley, Conley, Jaracz, Kron, and Dampier. Courtesy of the UK Athletics Department.

Neither Alyce Sullivan, reflecting over her husband's friendship and business dealings with Rupp, nor David Sullivan, present at center court at the game in question, recalls any racist remarks or tendencies from Rupp—or, according to David, any unusual ten-

Texas Western versus UK score card for the NCAA Tournament final at College Park, Maryland, March 19, 1966. From the Claude Sullivan Collection.

sion in the air at the game, not to mention any Rebel flags being waved at the game, which Disney added in a particularly heavy-handed dose of inaccuracy. Claude was used to players of various races and nationalities, thanks to his work with the Reds. Had he believed Rupp to be the type of man later characterized by *Glory Road* and other would-be historians, their friendship would most likely not have held up.

Unlike in Hollywood, in the real world time moves on, and even beautiful things march toward an end. Kron and Conley graduated. Although their loss was not immediately appreciated, and many believed that Kentucky would be back in the Final Four sooner rather than later, the next Final Four trip would be under a different coach in a different decade, and Claude would not be there to participate in it. The next year would bring challenges unlike any that had come before.

12

Tragedy

The 1966 season for the Cincinnati Reds was Claude's first as the number one announcer following Waite Hoyt's retirement in 1965. The sponsorship changed from the longtime Burger Beer to the Wiedemann Brewing Company. Waite had been very loyal to Burger and could not think of aligning himself with another competing sponsor, but Wiedemann had sponsored Claude's show *Wiedemann Sports Eye* for ten years on WVLK, and he was a known entity to the company. Jim McIntyre of Indianapolis was added as the number two announcer and had known Claude from Kentucky sports, having worked in Louisville at WAVE. The new broadcast team prepared for the 1966 season with excitement; however, Claude's first opening day for the Reds was a rainout. This was Waite Hoyt's specialty, but Claude had to ad-lib and get interviews together because he did not have the bevy of baseball stories to equal Waite's repertoire.

Although the Reds had remained in contention in 1965, after the season owner Bill DeWitt began rebuilding the team. Never mind that the Reds were far from old or that the team had hung in the pennant race over the past two seasons. DeWitt, allegedly

Claude in a 1966 Wiedemann Brewing Company–sponsored hospitality event in Tampa to open spring training for the Reds. Claude is with new assistant at the mic Jim McIntyre. Courtesy of the Cincinnati Reds.

fueled by rumors that the team might be relocated to another locale, wanted to remake the franchise. He hired a new manager, Don Heffner. On December 9, 1965, he traded Frank Robinson to the Baltimore Orioles for pitcher Milt Pappas and two other players. Pappas was a solid right hander and went 30–29 for the Reds in two and a half seasons. The other two players acquired with Pappas would barely play for the Reds—or for anyone else in the major leagues, for that matter. Robinson, who had hit 324 home runs for the Reds, promptly won the American League's triple crown in 1966 for the Orioles, hitting .316 with 49 home runs and 122 RBI. The Robinson trade later came to be known as one of the most lopsided deals in Major League Baseball history.

Nevertheless, there was still plenty of talent in Cincinnati. Now the Reds' oldest everyday player was twenty-eight-year-old catcher Johnny Edwards. Tony Perez continued gaining additional playing time, and Pete Rose was rapidly on his way to becoming the best second baseman in baseball. Vada Pinson and shortstop Leo Cardenas were also among the league's best players at their positions. Jim Maloney anchored the pitching staff, and with Sammy Ellis and Milt Pappas the Reds had enough quality at the front of their rotation to contend in the National League.

It did not work out that way on the field, however. After the opening-day rainout, the Reds started 1–7 and never held the lead for the pennant for a single day. The Reds offense had plenty of singles hitters and base stealers, but without Robinson the team lacked a real power threat. Deron Johnson's twenty-four home runs led the squad, and part-time outfielder Art Shamsky was next with twenty-one. Meanwhile, Jim Maloney was as good as advertised, with sixteen wins and a 2.80 earned run average (ERA). However, Ellis, a year removed from winning twenty-two games, staggered to a 12–19 mark, with a horrible 5.29 ERA. Pappas, with a 12–11 record, was decent, but all he seemed to do was remind the fans how much Frank Robinson was missed.

On July 10, the Reds were 37–46, and the team fired Don Heffner and replaced him with Dave Bristol. It made little difference. The Reds finished at 76–84, seventh place in the ten-team National

League. The squad ranked ninth in the league in paid attendance, and the city was being pressured to replace Crosley Field with a new, modern ballpark. According to Waite Hoyt, the bigger issue was not Crosley's capacity, but the available parking and access of traffic to the park. The new interstate did not allow easy access to the ballpark, which irritated Waite.

For the broadcasters, the biggest problem they face is that a 162-game season following twenty spring-training games can seem like an eternity when your team is out of contention. Claude was working through these patches and again found himself having some struggles with his voice. After a July 4 game with the Dodgers, he eventually remembered Vin Scully's words of concern and had himself checked by the Dodgers' team physician, Dr. Kurlin. Dr. Kurlin referred Claude to an ear, nose, and throat doctor in Los Angeles. That doctor noted that Claude's right vocal cord was paralyzed, but he was more concerned by something else—an odd growth in Claude's chest. It might be cancer, the doctor told him.

The Los Angeles ear, nose, and throat doctor referred Claude to the Mayo Clinic in Rochester, Minnesota, already a leader in the move to fight cancer. After three days of testing at the Mayo, he was again told that he *might* have cancer—or a deep chest inflammation or fungal growth. Only exploratory surgery would reveal the truth.

On July 19, 1966, Claude underwent the surgery. Doctors found aggressive cancer in his right shoulder next to his lung. They removed part of the right lung immediately and scheduled Claude for fourteen linear accelerator radiation treatments. The treatment was brutal, and Claude was sick and worried. After the first set of treatments, Claude received a thirty-day break, essentially to give his body a chance to recover from the invasive and painful radiation treatments—before he was plunged into an additional set of fourteen more treatments.

During the break between treatment sessions, Claude returned to the microphone, broadcasting Reds games during August and early September. Claude's first game back came on August 10, against the Giants at Crosley Field. Before the game, Claude was reintroduced by Jim McIntyre, his broadcasting partner. His voice shaking a bit, whether from poor health or the emotion of the moment, Claude told his audience:

> Jim, thank you so very much. It's overwhelming to me to see and greet everybody again. I hope I'm a pleasant surprise for everybody to be back—and an opportunity for me right at this moment to just offer my personal greetings to what I consider to be the greatest folks on earth anyway. But, as a man who stood on Crosley Field last year [Waite Hoyt] and preceded me with these very same words—there are no words at the bottom of my heart to express the esteem which I hold for the folks here in Cincinnati. And when I say that, I take in Cincinnati fans everywhere. Your cards and your letters, but, I think most of all, your prayers, have certainly given me very great hope for the future.

Claude recounted a story of a young boy who had written him to advise him that not only he but his cat and dog were all rooting for him. Buoyed by the strong support from the Cincinnati fan base, Claude enjoyed a few weeks of relative normalcy before his return to the Mayo. However, as a good patient, he put in his fourteen additional treatments. As the 1966 season came to an end, the Reds limped through the final stages of a hopeless season, and Claude found himself in a fight not only for his future, but possibly for his life.

Despite his ongoing health problems, Claude broadcast the 1966 Kentucky football season. That 1966 squad was probably a poor

Claude clowns with Reds star Pete Rose in a Cancer Crusade campaign that
Claude spearheaded in 1967. Courtesy of the Cincinnati Reds.

distraction because the professional ranks had claimed the talented
playmakers who had made the 1965 team entertaining. In 1966,
much of the load was shouldered by Larry Seiple and a new all-
purpose player, sophomore Dicky Lyons. Lyons, whose son became
a star receiver at Kentucky in the late 2000s, was a threat as a runner,
receiver, passer, defensive back, and kick returner. Although Bradshaw did not return to iron-man football as he had with the Thin
Thirty in 1962, Lyons often saw double or triple duty. However,
Terry Beadles as quarterback simply could not equal Norton in passing, and the offense often bogged down.

Kentucky won its opener 10–0 over North Carolina. Lyons
brought about both scores with big plays, returning a punt to set
up UK's lone touchdown and returning an interception to put Ken-

tucky in position for the team's field goal. After a loss at Ole Miss, UK beat Auburn 17–7 when Lyons again made a big play with a blocked field goal that prevented three Auburn points and, after a long return, set up seven Kentucky points instead.

Claude was experiencing some health issues after his surgery, and he completed the baseball season but had to miss UK's football games against North Carolina and Mississippi. On October 1, 1966, he began his broadcast by thanking Jim Host for a great job with the two games he had missed: "It is wonderful to be back behind the Standard Oil mic. For me personally . . . I would like to thank each of you for the cards and letters you have sent during my illness, but most important—your prayers." Claude continued by describing his treatments at the Mayo Clinic and noting that the progress was very satisfactory. "Although I must return every three months for a checkup . . . I will not be missing any more action by the Wildcats!" Those were the only two games Claude had missed in the past eighteen years.

Although the current team showed promise with a 2–1 record, the offensive shortcomings caught up with it. Kentucky was shut out three times in the first five games and made only 27 total points in that span. When the offense came alive, as in the last two of those five games, finally scoring 18 and 19 points, the defense could not turn in the stops to capitalize on this productivity. Kentucky tied West Virginia in late October and beat Vanderbilt on the first weekend in November. The team finished 3–6–1. Lyons had been exciting, netting two punt-return touchdowns on the way to setting UK's single-season punt-return yardage mark. Seiple had been a credit to the squad and was chosen in the following season's NFL draft. But after a couple of competitive seasons, the squad had fallen back, and Bradshaw's days in Lexington were numbered.

For Claude, the highlight of the season came after the season ended, when Bradshaw extended a scholarship offer to high school linebacker David Sullivan. David was a bit undersized and rail thin, but Bradshaw thought that with enough strength work he could become a solid SEC linebacker. Claude was thrilled and hoped that he would be able to broadcast his son's games.

Shortly after football wrapped up, Claude returned to the Mayo Clinic for a checkup. His strength had been holding steadily once the radiation treatment was over, and he felt optimistic. Indeed, the doctors, after performing another battery of tests, joined in the optimism. The X-rays showed no trace of the tumor. The remaining matter on the right lung was apparently scar tissue. Claude was elated. After receiving the good news, Ted Grizzard, Claude's old radio mentor, called and spoke with Alyce. He noticed a loud noise in the room, and when he asked about it, Alyce jokingly told him, "That's just Claude bouncing off the walls."

A few days later, in January 1967, Claude was featured on Ted Grizzard's *Man on the Street* radio segment on WVLK. He told Grizzard that the doctors were as pleased as he was. He described their reaction on conveying the good news to him, saying, "It was like looking into a mirror, looking at your own emotions." Claude was thrilled and very thankful for the support from his listening audience. He was, however, cautious—noting that the tumor would have to be gone for five years before the Mayo Clinic doctors would pronounce him to be cured. Claude admitted, "Although the tumor is not there, you have to keep a watch over it." With his health officially on the mend, he dived back into UK basketball with renewed enthusiasm.

Claude's enthusiasm might have been one of the few things the 1966–1967 Wildcats had going for them. Claude told Ted Grizzard in January that when he had called Waite Hoyt with his good medical news, Hoyt told him, "I guess you're the first winner they've had this year in Lexington." The retired baseball announcer was just joking, but he was too close for comfort in his assessment.

Both Riley and Dampier had returned for their senior campaigns, but Riley had sustained a significant back injury before the season began. As Riley went, so went the Kentucky team for the most part. Although the Wildcats began the year at number 3 in the AP poll rankings, without Kron and Conley the passing was not as crisp, the defense was not as dogged, and the results went from outstanding to abysmal. Guard Bob Tallent, a Parade All-American out of high school, was a solid third player on the team, but he and Rupp butted heads near the end of the season, and he was kicked off the team.

Kentucky began the year 5–4 in nonconference play and then opened the SEC schedule by losing its first three games. Dampier averaged 20 points a game, and had he been surrounded by a group equal to the previous year's team, he might have broken Cotton Nash's school scoring record. Riley fought doggedly through the pain, although both his scoring and rebounding took a downturn due to his injury. Kentucky finished the year with a 110–78 win over Alabama, which drew the team to an even 13–13 mark. The season was by far Rupp's worst and, on top of that, the university's worst record since 1926–1927.

That said, even in a down season Claude found plenty to enjoy. The third game of the season was a 118–116 win (in regulation) over Northwestern that kept him hopping. The two teams combined to shoot 56 percent from the floor and 82 percent from the foul line. Riley had 33 points, Dampier added 32, and Jaracz and Tallent chipped in with 23 and 20, respectively. A fan recorded Claude's broadcast on cassette, and it is the last full Kentucky recorded basketball game in the Sullivan Collection in the UK Archives. The quality is not good, but the cassette tape of the broadcast was sent to Alyce by the fan who recorded the game.

Claude shared the tense final few seconds as Northwestern missed two shots to send the game to overtime. His call: "The ball is tipped up by Gambier, no good, tipped up again, NO GOOD, and . . . the ball game is over! The ball game is over! . . . And Kentucky has won an incredible game over Northwestern 118–116 here tonight in Evanston!"

Rupp was in particularly fine form after the game, telling Claude, "In the first half, I looked at [assistant coach] Harry [Lancaster] and said, 'I don't think both teams can keep up the pace. Someone is going to collapse.'" He admitted, "I have never witnessed a shooting contest like that!"

The following week Kentucky played North Carolina at home in Dean Smith's sixth season at the helm. At the end of his game introduction, Claude remarked that ever since he had returned from Evanston, "the only comment we've heard has been, 'Did you ever see a game like that?!'" Responding to his own question, he said to his Standard Oil audience, "The answer is NO . . . neither had Adolph Rupp. Adolph still finds it hard to believe that the Cats have scored 215 points in the last two games and have only one win. On the other hand, Rupp finds it hard to believe there have been 214 points surrendered by the Kentucky defense."

Claude also reported to his audience in the introduction to a January 28 game that the LSU coach, Press Maravich, was visiting Memorial Coliseum for the first time. Claude went on to explain that Adolph Rupp could be one reason why freshman standout Pete Maravich was part of a great LSU freshman team. "The Baron wrote the boy [Pete Jr.] a personal letter advising him to play for his father. . . . He is a tremendous boy with plenty of hustle, desire, and determination. . . . Things look up at Baton Rouge."

Rupp discussed with Claude that the difference between the 1966 team and the 1967 team was defense was superior in 1966. In 1967, the opposing teams averaged 10 points more a game, from 75 up to 85. The only player lost from the 1965 team was John Adams, but one change can cause a great reversal. In 1966, Thad Jaracz came in, and that made the difference between a 15–10 season the previous season and a 27–2 one. Now two changes were made in 1967, Larry Conley went to law school, and Tommy Kron went to the pros.

Claude did reflect on the team's recent seven games, in which it showed flashes of the previous year's team. One such game was at Starkville, where the hostile Mississippi State crowd had been experienced by the Runts, when number 1 Kentucky squeaked out a 73–69 win. Larry Conley, who played in Starkville in 1966, told Claude that he had not seen anything like it before: "You can't hear yourself think . . . and if you've never been through it, you can't imagine what it's like." Despite Claude's warnings, the 1967 team was not affected, winning easily 103–74.

Unfortunately, there were few games like the Mississipi State win in 1966–1967. The break-even win over Alabama was Adolph Rupp's 762nd win, and the team's 444th win since Claude began broadcasting the Wildcats on a full-time basis in 1947. Claude summed up the disappointing season with a comparison to baseball. The last game deciding whether a .500 season or the first losing season ever for Adolph was like the slump pitcher Milt Pappas, who never had a losing season in the majors. "He [Pappas] started the final game of the season with a record of 11–11 last October, and although he pitched well, he was not involved in the decision. He was given that assignment because the Giants might come to town for an extra game, and manager Dave Bristol wanted Jim Maloney ready. As we watched Pappas battle for position last October, tonight we watched Adolph Rupp."

It was, although no one knew it, the end of an era.

Claude reported to spring training in 1967 ready for his fourth season of Reds baseball and his second season as the featured broadcaster. However, he was noticing some weakness in his voice at the end of basketball season, and he began growing hoarse during spring training. A quick check at the Mayo Clinic failed to detect any change in his condition.

Claude was in the broadcasting booth on April 10 when the Dodgers came to Crosley Field for Opening Day. The Reds continued to feature a group of exciting young stars. In 1967, Tony Perez was the everyday third baseman. Pete Rose shifted mostly to the outfield but continued to play like a whirling dervish. Young Gary Nolan, at nineteen, was one of the best young pitchers in baseball, and late in the season a nineteen-year-old catcher named Johnny Bench made his major league debut.

For Claude, however, it was a difficult season. He did broadcast the opener and the first few games, but on April 18, when the Reds left for a West Coast road trip, Claude stayed behind. He saw a local throat doctor, who ordered him to remain silent until the Reds returned to town eleven days later. Although the rest made little difference in his voice, Claude returned to try to broadcast after his enforced rest break.

This pattern was repeated several times. Claude managed to work a few games but would ultimately give up and take a few games off in the hopes that rest might provide relief. When the rest either did not improve the situation or improved it only minimally, he would lose patience and then try to power through with additional broadcasting work. By midseason, he decided to give up baseball and try to focus his energies on basketball and football. However, his frustration was mounting.

In August, he wrote George Webb of WVLK, advising him, "George, my voice is acting up, and I'm afraid that'll force me to talk with you through Alyce and by notes. After meeting with Ted [Grizzard], my voice steadily went down[,] until last Monday, it was gone. I called Rochester, and they thought it best I return. I entered the Clinic last Tuesday."

Claude advised that the doctors saw no change but told him that his vocal cords were simply not meeting. His condition was termed "hysteria euphonia," apparently a stress-induced loss of voice. All of the doctors agreed that his voice would return, but that there was nothing to be done to make it return. Claude talked about pressure from Wiedemann Brewing Company, the Reds' sponsor, to return to the air and admitted that he himself was frustrated, saying he was losing everything that it had taken him twenty-five years to build.

Claude arranged a meeting with Standard Oil. Again, Alyce was needed to help with conversation, but the oil company's conclusion was that they wanted Claude's name to remain affiliated with the broadcast, whether he could call the games or not. If his voice did not recover, he could utilize another announcer of his choice and would be named as producer. The substitute announcer would be encouraged to invoke Claude's name extensively—for example, "Claude Sullivan tells us that UK has outgained the Tigers by 23 yards in this quarter." The arrangement was encouraging, at least to the extent that Standard Oil wanted to keep up the affiliation regardless of the difficulties Claude was having with his voice.

Claude used the down time to be with his family. His sons were becoming young men. One Friday, despite the fact that he was feeling particularly poorly, he and Alyce traveled to Clark County to see Alan play football for Tates Creek High School against the squad from Claude's old stomping grounds. Alan had earned his first starting assignment after an injury to the usual center in the previous game. It was the only time that Claude saw Alan play, and after a rough first half the boy sprung the key block on the game-winning touchdown in the closing moments of the game. Alan recalled getting up in the end zone after the play and looking up into the stands, seeing both of his parents applauding the play. In some ways, that night represented Claude's life coming full circle: he had been a standout in Clark County himself two and a half decades earlier, until an injury had changed his life forever.

Not all of Claude's domestic life was quite as pleasant as Alan's triumph. Claude broadcast a few baseball games into a tape recorder at home in the latter part of the season in order to assess his voice and see how a broadcast would go. The recordings, included in the Sullivan archives, are painful to hear. Claude's insight is as keen as ever, but his smooth, clear voice sounds jagged and cracked. David Sullivan recalls Claude asking him to check the tapes and see what he thought. David, now entering UK and preparing to play football for Charlie Bradshaw, didn't have the courage to say how bad the situation was getting. He simply couldn't hurt Claude's feelings by telling him what he heard on the tapes.

It was not only Claude's audience who were distraught over the situation. Claude was much beloved within the media because of his down-to-earth nature and ability to help his fellow broadcasters and media members. Billy Reed, a young sportswriter at the end of Claude's career, recalled their meetings and said that Claude was "even better than you thought he might have been" in light of his celebrity status in Kentucky.

Jim Host, a broadcasting colleague, recalled Claude taking the time to sit down and critique Host's tapes with him. He specifically recalled Claude teaching him about diction. Host, in a recent interview, praised Claude and specifically his voice—"one of the most distinct, recognizable voices that you could hear."

Ralph Hacker was another young broadcaster who has fond memories of Claude to this day. In addition to his memories of the spoke-and-wheel advice that an ailing Claude delivered to him, he fondly recalled Claude's intricate preparation. Hacker appreciated the Sullivan System and its impact. He recalled Claude always having an extra fact—he joked about Claude knowing that a player liked butter on his mashed potatoes, but his point was that Claude's meticulous preparation extended to his audience. Hacker remembered Adolph Rupp telling him that, particularly in the lean years of Rupp's later career, if Claude Sullivan had not passed away, Memorial Coliseum might not have sold out because "people would have stayed home and listened to [Claude] rather than come to the game."

Ray Holbrook was another broadcaster who held Claude in particularly high esteem. He once complemented Claude on his ability to ad-lib witty lines during his broadcast. He was surprised when Claude told him, "I have found that the best ad-libs are the ones that are written in advance." He watched Claude carefully thereafter, and Holbrook realized that he was always making notes and taking down information—and that he used this information to craft the "ad-libs" that seemed so spontaneous and natural.

Claude was beloved by workers in all levels of media. In the *Kentucky Kernel,* the university's paper, shortly after Claude's death, an anonymous collegiate writer recalled an athletic banquet at which he had asked Claude about his broadcasting preparation. While they talked, several of the major luminaries of the athletic program called to Claude as he stood in line, telling him to come on to the main table. Claude thanked them but said, "I must talk to my young friend here about broadcasting." Claude sat at a lower table and answered every question. That writer went on to say that he had implemented the Sullivan System for personal assistance with organization and that Claude periodically dropped him tips throughout the season when they would see each other at the Coliseum—for instance, if a player was wearing a different uniform number or there was a change in the lineups. The unnamed reporter did not believe that Claude ever knew his name but noted that "the way he treated this near stranger indicates the style of the man. He certainly was that sort of rare, superlative being, which those who knew him as Claude say he was."

The poet John Donne famously wrote that no man is an island. Claude Sullivan was living proof. His connections extended far and deep, and his struggles in the summer of 1967 saddened and concerned not only his listening audience, but virtually the entire Kentucky media—from Cawood Ledford to the unnamed student newspaper reporter. The concern, unfortunately, was well founded.

Charlie Bradshaw's 1967 Wildcats were the final team that Claude covered. It was an odd swan song for the man who had covered so many legendary squads. The team started 0–6, and a winless season looked possible before a pair of wins over West Virginia and Vanderbilt broke the string. David Sullivan was on the team but was redshirting. Bradshaw later said that if he had realized how ill Claude was, he would have played David so that Claude could have announced his son's UK debut.

On November 25, Claude broadcast the season finale against number 2 Tennessee. It was his final broadcast. His voice remained ragged, and he pushed through the last game, hoping for the sudden improvement that the doctors had forecast back in the spring. Although Claude probably didn't realize how sick he was, he likely did realize that he could not complete a season of anything until his voice repaired itself. Kentucky fought doggedly against the Volunteers but, despite fine play again from Dicky Lyons, came up on the short end of a 17–7 score, ending the season at 2–8. Alan was present with Claude in the press box for the game, engineering the broadcast because David was on the sidelines. It was the last game in which all three Sullivan men were in the same place.

The 1967–1968 Wildcat basketball team was full of phenomenal talent—sophomores Dan Issel, Mike Casey, and Mike Pratt had the makings of a championship team. Unfortunately, Claude never broadcast their games.

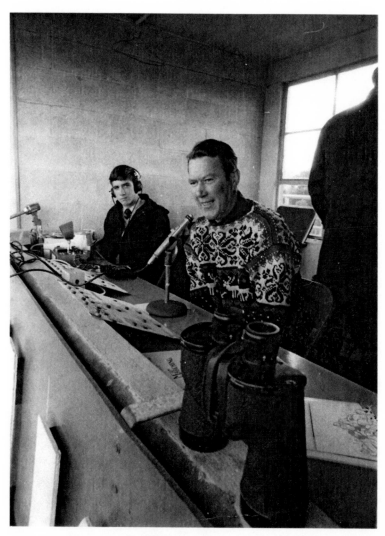

Claude broadcasts the Kentucky versus West Virginia game at Stoll Field,
November 4, 1967, with sixteen-year-old Alan engineering in the
background, while brother David dressed for the UK squad. This picture
was taken just a month before Claude passed away. Courtesy of the *Louisville
Courier-Journal*.

The team opened at Michigan on December 2. David and Alan Sullivan made the trip to Ann Arbor with broadcaster Earl Boardman to call the game. Claude's condition had worsened after the Tennessee football finale, and for the first time in two decades he was not behind the microphone for a Kentucky basketball game. Even so, Kentucky won 96–79, with Casey scoring 28 points in his first varsity game, and Issel adding 18 points and fifteen rebounds.

Claude's condition continued to worsen. For months, he had struggled to draw quality breaths. He had taken to sleeping at night on a large wedge because he was simply unable to breath while lying flat. Alyce eventually drove him to the Mayo Clinic, and Claude nearly passed away in the car on the trip. He was connected to a breathing machine, which helped sustain him for the remainder of the trip. However, on his arrival the doctors were deeply concerned by the deterioration of not only his vocal passages, but his breathing pathway.

Claude was scheduled for emergency surgery, the surgeons hoping to be able to open up the restricted passages. Claude told his wife that he was proud of her, that she had really grown up on the horrifying trip to the clinic. He was ultimately saying good-bye to the love of his life.

On December 6, 1967, Claude was in surgery at Methodist Hospital in Rochester, Minnesota. His physicians labored in vain to open his once-active air passages and keep him alive. Kentucky was in action that night against Xavier at Memorial Coliseum. Neither Alan nor David nor Claude Sullivan was in the building. Substitute announcer Jim Host was calling the game over the Standard Oil Network when someone handed him a slip of paper. Host remembers freezing up before telling his audience, "One of the greatest announcers of all time, Claude Sullivan, has just died."

13

Aftermath of a Tragedy

Claude's life ended suddenly in December 1967, but his peers, contemporaries, and family eventually had to move on, trying to cope with the deep void his loss left in their lives.

David and Alan had just returned home from Ann Arbor, Michigan on December 3. Shortly thereafter, on December 6, they heard the news that their father had died on the operating table in Rochester, Minnesota.

Claude's death was a huge emotional loss to his family, but Alyce, David, and Alan also had to meet Claude's broadcasting commitments to UK, already two games into the 1967 contract for the UK basketball season.

Claude had prepared Alyce as best as he could for what she needed to do to fulfill Sullivan Enterprises' contractual obligations to the university and the Standard Oil Network. With his health failing, he had to confide in her. Alyce fulfilled her husband's business obligations and completed the 1967–1968 basketball season as the head of Sullivan Enterprises, surrounded by those whom Claude trusted to advise her, including attorney and NFL referee Tommy Bell. Alyce worked with replacement announcers Earl Boardman

241

and Jim Host, and the productions moved ahead, even through the 1968 NCAA regional games played at Memorial Coliseum. She made all the arrangements for the NCAA games in Memorial Coliseum and at the end of the season received a letter from Adolph Rupp noting her hard work. With the 1967–1968 basketball season complete, Alyce did not pursue Sullivan Enterprises any further. She never remarried, although she did maintain a close friendship for many years with a friend, Ace Parker, who had lost his wife to cancer. Ace had his own UK connection: his daughter had married Jim Lemaster of Rupp's Runts.

Dr. Peter Bosomworth, Alyce's next-door neighbor and the chancellor of the UK Medical Center, urged Alyce to get involved in helping to establish the UK Medical Alumni Association around 1970. She then worked in the Continuing Education and Medical Illustrations Departments at the University Medical Center. After seventeen years of service, she retired from the Medical Center and enjoyed her retirement for twenty years.

Alyce saw Claude honored by induction into the Kentucky Athletic Hall of Fame (a state award) in 1975 and the Kentucky Journalism Hall of Fame in 2006, followed by the UK Athletics Hall of Fame later that year, as portrayed in the introduction to this book. She passed away after her third bout with cancer two days after her eighty-fifth birthday in August 2007. She had survived her husband by nearly forty years.

David played football at Kentucky over four years and two injuries. He had a stress-fracture injury to his leg similar to the one later suffered by UK basketball star Sam Bowie, and it hampered his return to the game. After redshirting his fourth year, he elected not to stay and play under John Ray in his fifth year of eligibility. Instead, he decided to follow in his father's footsteps, starting out in the news department at WVLK, where he quickly became news director.

David soon left Lexington to spend most of his professional

career outside of Kentucky, determined to stand on his own merits rather than on his father's legacy. He quickly moved into television in Virginia Beach and continued to move to larger markets that Claude had attempted to reach early in his career. He was in Atlanta and Pittsburgh before moving on to a bigger opportunity. Eternally his father's son, he saw the promise inherent in a new cable network called ESPN and spent approximately five years working for the station in its infancy as a Sports Center anchor with Chris Burnam and Greg Gumble. He moved along as ESPN anchor to Los Angeles in time to cover the 1984 Olympics, twenty-four years after his father had covered the Games in Rome.

David eventually returned to Lexington and worked briefly for Jim Host before becoming the voice of the Louisville Cardinals for eight years on WDRB Fox television, a run that included "Game One" in 1994, the game that marked the beginning of the annual UK/University of Louisville football series. As in the old days, David utilized Alan as his spotter for that broadcast, marking the first time they had worked together on a game since 1966.

In an interesting moment while at WDRB, David was covering the NCAA Tournament when Paul Rogers, the radio voice of the Cardinals, suddenly lost his voice. David, cornered by the Louisville athletic director, filled in for Paul in the second half. It was a difficult job because although David was familiar with the Louisville team, he was unfamiliar with Tubby Smith's opposing Tulsa squad. After all, without preparation time, he could hardly incorporate the Sullivan System. David had been doing television work and had done little radio play by play. Inspired by recalling Claude at Memorial Coliseum, he concentrated on giving the score and time left in the game often and describing the action in more detail, just as Claude had painted word pictures for his audiences years earlier.

A brief story may best sum up Claude's influence on his eldest son. In the late 1970s, David was contemplating obtaining a sailboat for the family. He found himself uncertain about the purchase and wondered what his father would do. He recalled Claude telling him that if you were going to do something that brought pleasure to you, "plan for it and do it right." He bought the boat and named it *Claude's Advice.* Today, David is semiretired and lives in St. Petersburg, Florida, with his wife, Mary. They have an adult son, Luke. *Claude's Advice* number 4 is in the planning stages.

Unlike David, Alan did not choose to follow in Claude's footsteps. While studying at UK, he became interested in architecture and pursued a career in that field. He studied not only at UK, but for two years at Southern Tech, a division of Georgia Tech located in Atlanta. Remembering his father's ire at the ill treatment he had suffered at Tech back in 1950, Alan thought it was probably best that Claude didn't know about this part of his son's life.

Alan studied internationally for a year, drawing inspiration in Florence, Venice, and Athens, just as Claude had two decades earlier. Alan was owner of his own architectural firm before age thirty. In 2006, looking for a change in his work, he considered a position with a national firm in Cincinnati. Alyce encouraged her son, reminding him, "Go for it! Your dad did the same thing—he would say 'Go for it!'"

Although Alan has benefitted from his father's legacy in less overt ways than David may have, he still sees the effects of his father's teaching in his life. He cites his father's eternal insistence on preparation as being something that he has incorporated into his own life. That preparation has been key to this book—his research of his father's career began in 1998 with the discovery of boxes of old materials and tapes when Alyce moved away from the family homestead.

Alan is currently a health-care architect doing consulting work in Nashville, Tennessee. He and his wife, Jan, have two children, son

Blake and daughter Alycia. Unfortunately, his children know their grandfather only through the recordings and stories they have heard.

Claude's premonition was correct—the days of multiple concurrent broadcasts of UK basketball and football were indeed numbered. When athletic director Bernie Shively passed away six days after Claude, plans for a UK network were placed on hold for the short term. Harry Lancaster moved from his assistant basketball coaching position into the vacant athletic director's position. The longtime coach was not especially interested in the business end of athletics, and, with Claude's spot now vacant, before the end of the 1960s the university decided to go with a single-network feed.

The effects of competition had already thinned out the crowd somewhat. J. B. Faulconer had dedicated his time to horse racing since the mid-1950s, when he became the first full-time director of publicity at Keeneland. J. B. and Claude had often gone fishing with Phil Sutterfield of WHAS. The two had even done a joint interview with Bear Bryant in 1952. Best remembered for his work with the horse-racing industry, J. B. passed away in 2000 at his home in Vero Beach, Florida.

Claude's mentor, Ted Grizzard, had long since moved the majority of his time into nonsports programming. His *Man on the Street* show was a favorite at WVLK for years. Ted's last broadcast was in 1968, when with Ralph Hacker he broadcast Alan Sullivan's last high school football game at Tates Creek against Frank Lemaster and Doug Flynn's Bryan Station High team. He paid tribute to his career with Claude and said hello to Alyce as she left the game that evening. Ted had retired from radio altogether by the time the station celebrated its fiftieth anniversary in 1979. In 1981, Grizzard published a book, *#1 Is Chicken*. He passed away in Lexington in 1985.

Claude's successor at WVLK for his sports show *Wiedemann Sports Eye* was a young talent from Lexington, Tom Hammond. Tom had worked at WVLK while Claude was there and knew of

Claude's reputation at the station but had never worked directly with him. Tom was influenced equally by Claude and Cawood Ledford, having worked with Cawood and Mike Battaglia at Keeneland. Tom was let go at WVLK and so moved on to television, channel 18, the NBC affiliate in Lexington. From there he became involved with the first Breeder's Cup held at Keeneland in 1984 and worked initially as a contract employee with NBC. That catapulted him into a career with NBC that included the Olympics four years later in Barcelona, and he has broadcast each Summer and Winter Games since. Tom recalls Claude in his convertible with the "whiplash" antenna on the trunk driving down Reed Lane near Lafayette High School in his neighborhood. He also reminisces that while he was playing basketball at Lafayette High, it was a big deal to the players when Claude came to broadcast their games.

Dee Huddleston had decided to have Claude as his mentor back in 1949 when he was a graduate of the first broadcasting class at UK. He eventually began to tire of the road life and spent more time on station ownership in central Kentucky. He also began calling more Western Kentucky University and University of Louisville games by the end of Claude's career. The move was born of necessity in part— Huddleston was elected to the Kentucky state Senate in 1964. Huddleston went on to win two terms as a US senator in the 1970s. He was finally edged out by 0.4 percent of the vote in the 1984 race by Mitch McConnell. After he left the US Senate, Huddleston returned to Elizabethtown, Kentucky. In 2012, he retired from his position as CEO of First Financial in Elizabethtown. In 2009, Alan Sullivan had the opportunity to work alongside Dee and UK Library dean Terry Birdwhistell on the UK National Library board.

After Claude's death, Cawood Ledford became the single-network "Voice of the Wildcats." He parlayed that fame into also calling games for the NCAA Network on CBS Radio. After Claude won the Kentucky Sportscaster of the Year award for his last eight years as an active broadcaster, Cawood went on to win the award twenty-two times before he retired in 1992. His final game was Kentucky's heart-breaking loss to Duke in the 1992 NCAA Tournament, and he was honored with a banner in Rupp Arena. He passed away on September 5, 2001. He was born less than a year and a half after Claude, and their careers overlapped for fourteen years, yet Cawood survived Claude by more than thirty-three years.

As a result of the changes in coverage of UK sports, many of the young broadcasters whom Claude had mentored shifted their career plans. Jim Host is now in his seventies and has made his greatest mark in business. He went on to found Host Communications in 1974, which controlled the rights to UK's radio and television networks. At the company's peak, it totaled more than $140 million in annual revenue. In more recent days, Host invested a large portion of his time in bringing the Yum! Center to Louisville. In 2012, he was inducted into the National Collegiate Basketball Hall of Fame.

Ralph Hacker joined the UK Radio Network team in 1972–1973. He became the color commentator to Cawood Ledford on the network. After Ledford's retirement in 1992, Hacker had his own turn as the "Voice of the Wildcats." He called five seasons of Wildcat football and nine of UK basketball, including the 1996 and 1998 NCAA Championship games, before he retired to Florida in 2001. He still spends time in Lexington and Richmond, Kentucky, with the latter his hometown. Hacker was also very successful on the financial side of radio—demonstrating the lessons he had learned from Claude about the wheel and spokes many years earlier.

Waite Hoyt, who along with Ted Grizzard was one of the great mentors of Claude's career, had already retired before Claude became ill. He made occasional guest appearances after his retirement, doing some television color commentary for the Reds as late as 1972. In 1969, he was inducted into the Baseball Hall of Fame. Hoyt maintained a friendship with the Sullivan family after Claude's death. One of his hidden talents was painting, and he sent Alyce a watercolor that she treasured. Waite and his wife, Betty, visited the Sullivans in Lexington in 1979, and Jan and Alan spent all Sunday in his room at the Campbell House Hotel listening to stories of Babe Ruth and other Yankee stars whom Hoyt had played with. Waite remained active until he suffered a heart attack in 1984 and passed away a few weeks later. He was survived by his wife, Betty, and three children.

Claude did not spend enough time covering the Cincinnati Reds to get attached to any manager other than the unfortunate Fred Hutchinson, who died in 1964, after Claude's first season with the team. The Reds built a minidynasty, the Big Red Machine, beginning with parts assembled during Claude's time in the press box. Rose, Perez, and Bench were crucial parts of the squad. Those Reds won the 1975 and 1976 World Series. Since that time, the Reds' only additional title has come in 1990. The team has been competitive intermittently but has not appeared in a World Series in almost two and a half decades.

In mid-1970, the Reds moved from Crosley Field to the new Riverfront Stadium. The new stadium had artificial turf and an upper deck all the way around the playing surface. Seating capacity increased from approximately 29,000 to around 53,000. The old field sat vacant for a year and a half before it was demolished in April 1972. Before his death, Claude was asked to contribute his ideas to the design of the new press box for Riverfront Stadium.

Ironically, Riverfront Stadium was a multipurpose, cookie-cutter stadium that was used for baseball and football and rapidly went out of fashion. In 2003, the Reds moved to Great American Ballpark, which is adjacent to where Riverfront stood.

Claude started his career as the voice of the basketball Wildcats at Alumni Gym on Euclid Avenue, the Avenue of Champions, in

1947, and the gym still stands today. It was opened in 1924, the year Claude was born, as UK's new palace of basketball. The first game there against Cincinnati was the first time Kentucky played a game before New Year's Day. It was December 13, and Kentucky won 28–23. Claude once reminisced to his audience, "I remember the later Professor Gillis at the university telling me the State High School basketball tournament was held there [at Alumni] before all the windows had been installed. It was a wind-blown championship in March 1924." Adolph arrived six years later, and Claude arrived in 1947 for his first full season. He covered championship teams there in 1948 and 1949 and never saw the Cats lose there.

Claude's next two NCAA squads made their homes in Memorial Coliseum in 1951 and 1958. He was the only sportscaster to follow the Cats 129-game winning streak from Alumni Gym to Memorial Coliseum. He finished his career there with Rupp's Runts in 1966–1967.

In 1976, the basketball Wildcats moved out of Memorial Coliseum and into an off-campus arena. The behemoth 22,000-seat arena, again derided as a white elephant, as every new Kentucky gym apparently has been, was christened "Rupp Arena." The Coliseum hosted one more Kentucky game in 2009, when the Cats were in the NIT and Rupp Arena was occupied with the state tournament. Kentucky won.

Memorial Coliseum is still used by the university's women's basketball team. It was utilized as a practice facility and office space before the addition of the Joe Craft Center in 2007. At last notice, the ticket office is still in the Coliseum. However, the glory days of Kentucky basketball in the raucous gymnasium are as gone as Claude's WVLK banner is from the press table.

Adolph Rupp did not make another Final Four after the Runts in 1966. The Issel/Casey/Pratt class was denied that achievement when

Casey missed a season due to injuries from an auto accident, and the team ran into Artis Gilmore and Jacksonville in the 1970 NCAA Regional Finals. Two years later, the university forced Rupp into retirement because of the mandatory retirement age in place at that time. He finished his career with an 876–190 record. His record for most Division I coaching victories stood for twenty-five years until Dean Smith broke it in 1997. Only John Wooden has won more NCAA championships than Rupp. Rupp was enshrined in the Basketball Hall of Fame in 1969, when he was still an active coach.

After his university coaching career, Rupp held positions with the Memphis Tams and later the Kentucky Colonels of the American Basketball Association. The titles were essentially for publicity because Rupp did no more coaching after his work at Kentucky. He had always suffered from poor health, and he died of cancer in Lexington on December 10, 1977. He was seventy-six years old and was survived by his wife, Esther, and their son, Herky.

Since Rupp, Kentucky has gone through six head coaches. Four of the six have won national titles—Joe B. Hall, who played on the 1949 squad, for which Claude broadcast, as well as Rick Pitino, Tubby Smith, and John Calipari. In between, there have been some difficult moments, including when the program was placed on probation late in the ill-fated Eddie Sutton era in the 1980s. However, the University of Kentucky still holds the record for most victories in the history of college basketball.

Paul "Bear" Bryant left UK after the 1953 football season. He went on to Texas A&M, then ended up at Alabama, his alma mater. He won 232 games at Alabama, making his career record 323–85–17. Only Bobby Bowden has eclipsed Bryant's record win total in Division I FBS football. Bryant won six national championships and thirteen SEC titles at Alabama. He won eleven SEC Coach of the Year awards with the Tide. Bryant reached his three hundredth win when Alabama played against UK in Lexington in 1980, delivering a 45–0 shellacking to the Wildcats on national television. He retired at the end of the 1982 season and died a month later of a massive heart attack. Kentucky football has never been the same since he left. Claude remained friends with Bryant and interviewed him in 1962 about the hiring of Charlie Bradshaw as UK head coach.

Blanton Collier returned to the Cleveland Browns after leaving Kentucky. After a year as an assistant coach, Collier was the head coach of the Browns for eight seasons, posting a 76–34–2 record and winning the 1964 NFL championship. He retired in 1970 because a hearing loss made it difficult for him to communicate with his players. Collier passed away from prostate cancer in 1983.

Charlie Bradshaw was fired after the 1968 season. His career record was 25–41–4. Nine football coaches have followed Bradshaw, and none has finished his time at UK with a winning record. Fran Curci won an SEC title and a bowl game at UK in 1976 and had a 10–1 squad in 1977 but could not sustain that momentum. Jerry Claiborne, an outstanding defensive back under Bear Bryant at Kentucky in 1949, had some success in the 1980s but ended his career much like Blanton Collier—he never won quite enough. Rich Brooks had some bursts of success in the 2000s, and Mark Stoops's tenure is off to an energetic beginning.

McLean Stadium at Stoll Field was demolished in 1973. The football Wildcats moved into Commonwealth Stadium, which marked an increase in seating capacity from 37,000 to 58,000. Expansions have subsequently driven capacity of the new stadium to nearly 68,000. Current plans are to upgrade the stadium while downsizing the capacity to 61,000. Bernie Shively had asked Claude to write down his comments on the new press box design for the original Commonwealth Stadium. Alan Sullivan was studying at UK when the old McLean Stadium was demolished. He had prepared a senior thesis proposing to incorporate a portion of the old

Stoll Field being razed in 1974. Alan Sullivan took the picture as part of an architectural project at UK College of Architecture. The entrance that Claude used to get to the press box for twenty years is being razed. Photograph by Alan Sullivan.

Flag Pole Dedication before the Kentucky versus Indiana football game in 1969. Alyce Sullivan is presented the dedication scroll from Kentucky Broadcasters Association president Ray Holbrook as UK athletic director Harry Lancaster looks on. Courtesy of UK Public Relations.

ivy-covered concrete structure and the botanical garden wall into a combined Art and Architecture building.

Today, the Otis Singletary Center for the Arts stands on a portion of the site where the old stadium stood. Part of the field is still used as a practice field for the marching band and for intramural games. It was at that site, Stoll Field, that the flag pole was dedicated in Claude's memory in 1969 before the Kentucky/Indiana football game.

Before the game, Alyce, David in his UK uniform, and Alan stood with Kentucky Broadcasters Association president Ray Holbrook and UK athletic director Harry Lancaster to dedicate the new flagpole. Claude had repeatedly noted that UK was the only SEC school that did not have a permanent flag pole. After the team moved to Commonwealth Stadium, the plaque bearing the flag pole's inscription was re-created and placed in Commonwealth Stadium in a ceremony with President Todd, Alan, and David just after Alyce passed away in 2007. The plaque reads: "Claude Howard Sullivan 1924–1967. An uncommon man who retained the common touch; whose excellence in his profession and whose qualities of humanity continue to guide and challenge all broadcasters."

After this first honor for Claude in 1969, others would come. In 1975, he was inducted into the Kentucky Athletic Hall of Fame with Cliff Hagan, Frank Ramsey, and Lou Tsioropoulos from the 1951 NCAA Championship team he covered. Adolph Rupp's longtime assistant and athletic director Harry Lancaster was also in the 1975 class as well as posthumous inductees Blanton Collier and Bernie Shively.

Claude's next major honor would not come for more than thirty years after that, in April 2006, when it was realized that the Kentucky Journalism Award had not been awarded until after Claude passed away. It was then unanimously decided in 2006 that he definitely belonged with this select group of journalists that included his old colleague Cawood Ledford.

Finally, in August 2006 Claude was inducted into the UK Athletics Hall of Fame with Adrian Smith of the 1958 NCAA Championship basketball team and the 1960 US Olympic team. Other members of the 2006 class included Gay Brewer, who won the Masters Golf Tournament in May 1967, the year Claude died. Claude had interviewed Brewer in 1949 when the seventeen-year-old won the National Amateur Golf Championship. Brewer passed away in 2007, just a week before Alyce—both from lung cancer.

Epilogue: The Big Blue Sports Archives, Claude's Final Gift

In 1978, the Claude Sullivan Collection was created when Alyce made the first donations of tapes and recordings of Claude's work to the University of Kentucky Archives. Twenty years later, volumes of new material were discovered and a few years later restored by the Sullivan family. They made a huge addition to the collection and to the UK Archives and prompted an interest in restoring the original 1978 donation, which had been degrading in this period. Donations from Alyce's estate made possible the restoration of the recordings with Alan's supervision. The university wanted to come up with a way to honor both the Big Blue Sports Archives (which had been created when the UK Library Archives and the Athletic Department joined together to house the entire UK sports collection in the Library Archives—the Athletic Department hadn't been maintaining its own archives very well) and its largest digital sports collection—and the Claude Sullivan Collection.

In 2009, promoting the upcoming event to celebrate the sports collection, Terry Birdwhistell, dean of UK Libraries, wrote, "I never met Claude Sullivan, but I spent a lot of time with him. Growing up in Hopkinsville, Kentucky, I only saw the Wildcats play basketball in person one time. . . . I faithfully followed the team whether [it was] playing on the UK campus or in some exotic place like New Orleans or Starkville. At the beginning of the games, Claude Sullivan often said on the Standard Oil Network that 'the Wildcats, wearing their blue travel uniforms, will be going from the left to the right of the radio dial in the first half.'" Birdwhistell advised that he never missed a play and had "the best seat that was not in the house." "It is," he stated, "singularly appropriate that Claude Sullivan represent the national and even international scope of UK sports history."

These words provided a preview of the newly restored Claude Sullivan Collection, the largest digital collection in the university's

Big Blue Sports Archives. The university held a $115 per plate dinner to honor Claude's career, with Coach John Calipari serving as keynote speaker at the dinner.

That night at the Marriott Griffin Gate in Lexington, broadcasters from Jim Host to Ralph Hacker to Tom Leach spoke about Claude and his influence on their careers. Ralph Hacker began his presentation with the introduction that Claude prepared for the last game Bear Bryant coached at UK against Tennessee in 1953. Afterward, Ralph told the audience of the advice Claude gave him in 1967 at the Phoenix Hotel in Lexington—build yourself a wheel, with a hub and spokes. Ralph related the significance of the lesson in his own life.

Next Jim Host, who started his career with Claude, recognized Claude's influence by saying, "Without Claude Sullivan, I wouldn't be here . . . without him believing in an eighteen-year-old from Ashland who was at the university doing games for WBKY. . . . He heard me . . . and he called and said, 'Would you come see me?' . . . and he introduced me to Ted Grizzard, and I started doing high school sports." Jim continued on to say that Claude gave him the advice that "everything in life is based on preparation, because if you prepare, you will succeed."

Tom Leach is the current UK Radio Network broadcaster. He was too young to remember Claude's broadcasts, but he borrowed a few tapes from the family prior to the Outback Bowl in 1999. He told Alan, "Jim Host told me to get tapes of Claude Sullivan's football broadcasts from you because he was the best to ever broadcast football." On returning some of the broadcasts, Leach wrote, "Now I am getting a feel for what I missed." He indicated that he wanted to hear more of the recordings and planned to utilize the university's archives to do just that.

Wah Wah Jones, Vernon Hatton, and Kyle Macy, among other Wildcat basketball legends, were in attendance at the Marriott event.

A montage of interviews and highlights was played on a large screen for the guests to enjoy. David Sullivan, narrating the video presentation, summed up his father's career neatly, saying, "He could paint a picture with words, transport you to the center of the action. When you listened to Claude Sullivan call a game, it was as if you had the best seat in the house."

The keynote speaker, John Calipari, had just been hired by UK only a few months prior to the event and was not aware of the Sullivan legacy. After viewing the presentation and witnessing the photo of a packed Stoll Field for the Olympic trials in 1948, Calipari quipped, "You know, one thing I took away from that presentation is that they were playing basketball on a football field! So we can get that done."

Kentucky athletic director Mitch Barnhart spoke last on this evening and reminded the crowd of the importance of keeping the heritage of UK athletics preserved for generations to come. Players will come and go, Barnhart noted, "but the fans will only remember the players of today if they do not have the archives."

The university's Big Blue Sports Archives house not only all of Claude's restored tapes, but pictures, magazines, videos, and other assorted memorabilia. Some items have been restored and cataloged, but the work of preserving UK's athletic history remains constant and ongoing.

Although Claude passed away in 1967, memories of him have remained behind with his family and his work. Claude will never truly be gone until the last fan who heard his calls, the last broadcaster who picked up a tip from him, and the last recordings of him are gone—which all those who knew him hope will not be for a long, long time.

Hundreds of Claude's restored broadcasts are available for free listening at the Kentucky Digital Library, located on the Web at http://kdl.kyvl.org. At that main page, type "Claude Sullivan" in the search box and prepare to be amazed at all of the recordings that the university and the Sullivan family have restored. Treasure the memories or learn, as Tom Leach did, what you missed.

This collection is Claude's final gift to the Big Blue Nation.

Afterword

To this day you can find old-timers such as yours truly who will insist that Claude Sullivan was such a superb radio play-by-play announcer that he could hold his own with anybody who excelled at calling a game. Yes, I'm including the likes of such golden-throated icons as Graham McNamee, Ted Husing, Red Barber, Mel Allen, Vin Scully, and Jack Buck. Trust me, Claude was that good.

I doubt seriously that he would like the way that the craft has been commercialized. It's tough for today's play-by-play announcers to paint lovely word pictures when they're required to relentlessly plug this product or that one. But Claude would have adapted because he was a pro's pro. Heck, he had much to do with inventing an unwritten code of conduct in sports broadcasting.

For example, nobody ever told Claude that he wasn't supposed to be a "homer." That's because back in the 1940s and 1950s sports broadcasting was still such a relatively new occupation that its practitioners made up the rules as they went along. Some, such as Harry Caray of the St. Louis Cardinals (long before he went to the Chicago Cubs), did indeed become unabashed rooters for the home team. But Claude instinctively determined that his broadcasts would be better if he served his audience more as a reporter than as a cheerleader.

I've always regretted not taking the opportunity to sit down with Claude and talk about how he became interested in radio.

Back in the 1930s, when Claude was growing up, the most promi-nent members of the sports media were newspaper columnists. On a national level, syndicated New York writers such as Grantland Rice, Damon Runyan, and Jimmy Cannon were every bit as prominent as today's ESPN stars. On a local level, Earl Ruby of the *Louisville Courier-Journal* had a following in all 120 Kentucky counties. The *Courier*'s main rivals in central Kentucky were Lexington's morn-ing *Herald* and afternoon *Leader*, which featured such sports colum-nists as Babe Kimbrough, Ed Ashford, Larry Shropshire, and Billy Thompson.

Considering that the era of commercial radio didn't begin until 1920, when Detroit station WWJ broadcast the Jack Dempsey–Billy Miske heavyweight boxing bout, it's incredible that any young boy in America would focus on sportscasting as a career. Newspapers, yes. But radio? In 1924, the year Claude was born, the Indianapo-lis 500 was broadcast for the first time. It also was the first year the Cincinnati Reds began broadcasting their games on station WMH, Gene Mittendorf doing the play by play.

The 1930s and 1940s were arguably the golden era of sports radio. With television still very much in its embryonic stage, fami-lies got in the habit of gathering around the radio to hear the news, sports, concerts, soap operas, and popular comedy shows. During the Great Depression, radio provided escape and diversion for citi-zens desperate for work. And, of course, baseball became the back-ground soundtrack for American summers in the big cities and small towns from Boston to St. Louis. (In those days, none of the sixteen big-league teams was located west of the Mississippi River or south of Cincinnati.)

Just as the sound of a railroad engine's whistle was a siren call of adventure, romance, and mystery for American youngsters, so radio—and its announcers—brought new and exciting places into our homes. Through radio, youngsters developed vivid imaginations about games, the places they were played, and the people who played them. Indeed, the players and parks took on such a larger-than-life quality that sometimes the real thing would prove to be disappointing. But, my, there was no better way to spend a hot, lazy summer afternoon than sitting by the radio, imagining what it was like to be in Crosley Field while Frank McCormick and Paul Derringer and Ernie Lombardi were trying to win another one for the Reds.

Claude and I come from the same neck of the woods. He was born in Winchester in 1924, me in Mount Sterling some nineteen years later. Both of us were sixteen when we began our professional careers. But by the time I began covering high school sports for the *Lexington Herald* in 1959, Claude already was a statewide icon, the most popular of the five or six radio play-by-play announcers who called UK football and basketball.

Claude called the games for WVLK in Lexington and the statewide Standard Oil Network. His main rivals were Cawood Ledford of 50,000-watt WHAS in Louisville and J. B. Faulconer of the Ashland Oil Network. When Faulconer got out of broadcasting to become publicity director at Keeneland—and later commanding general of the One Hundredth Division, US Army Reserves—Claude and Cawood were left as friendly rivals in the field, vying for the hearts, minds, and ears of Wildcat fans from Ashland to Paducah.

Ledford had an aura of sophistication that belied his roots in Harlan. A graduate of Centre College, he was a much sharper dresser than Claude. Nevertheless, they liked and admired each other until they got behind their microphones. Then they turned into competitors every bit as fierce and determined to win as Paul "Bear" Bryant and Adolph Rupp, the legendary UK coaches who wanted themselves and their sport to be number 1 in the Commonwealth.

"The first time I met Bryant," recalled Ledford in the 1991 autobiography I did with him, "he told me how good he thought

Claude Sullivan and J. B. Faulconer were. I was more familiar with J. B. because his radio network, the Ashland Oil Network, was bigger than Claude's, the Standard Oil Network. . . . Even though I was the new guy on the block and the one at the bottom of the totem pole, both Claude and J. B. were so damned nice to me. It would have been natural for them to resent me, but they couldn't have been nicer."

All three treated me the same way. I met Claude at a high school basketball game—yes, he also did high school games when he wasn't busy with the Wildcats—and it might even have been at Clark County. I didn't know what to expect when I introduced myself to him because, heck, he was a star, and I was just a high school kid. But, perhaps remembering his own youthful start with WCMI in Ashland in 1940, Claude greeted me warmly, treated me seriously, and told me to let him know if he could ever do anything for me.

Although Claude was best known for his work in football, basketball, and baseball, he also was an accomplished caller of horse races, as were Cawood Ledford and J. B. Faulconer. All agreed that calling the races was more difficult than calling games because the action was so far away, and the only way to identify the horses was by memorizing the colors of the jockeys' silks. Yet all three mastered the art to the point that the Kentucky Derby became part of their résumés.

However, Claude had more of an entrepreneurial spirit than either of his friendly rivals. Beginning in 1949 with Bryant and shortly thereafter with Rupp, he pioneered the concept of the coach's radio show. He also formed his own company, Sullivan Enterprises, so he could talk eighteen stations around Kentucky into forming the Standard Oil Network in 1951.

I'm delighted that Claude's son Alan has worked so diligently to preserve his dad's legacy. To this day, a team's radio announcers have a special bond with their listeners that TV announcers have never been able to equal. Maybe it has something to do with the fact that radio is available almost everywhere, even when you're riding in an automobile. Maybe it's because we still like to have something left to the imagination—and listening to a game, enjoying it through someone else's eyes, is infinitely more romantic than watching TV. Whatever, it still means something special to be the radio voice of the Cats or the Reds or whomever.

In Claude's case, the fact that he was one of us—a small-town Kentuckian, born and reared—was important. We love to see our own succeed, especially when they come from the humble roots that Claude did. So whenever he would broadcast an NCAA Championship game or an Olympics, whenever he would do interviews with the most famous names in sport, we vicariously shared in his success.

When he joined Waite Hoyt on the Cincinnati Reds' broadcast team in 1963, it certified his ability to perform on the big stage of professional sports. Of course, to those of us who knew him and had followed him, this was no surprise. We always knew that our Claude was as good as they come, just as we always knew he would remain humble and ever mindful of his Clark County roots.

I would urge today's aspiring announcers to study Claude's life and listen to his tapes. Other than the intrusion of commercial plugs, broadcasting has remained more or less the same game over the years—and Claude would be as much of a star today as he was back then. The best ones still are pros. The best ones still paint word pictures. The best ones still remind us of Claude Sullivan.

Billy Reed

Acknowledgments

My brother David and I dedicate this book to the loving memory of our parents and the untiring love they had for our family, which was always at the forefront no matter how involved our father was in his career. This book is his legacy told from the collection of his personal memorabilia and recordings.

The only problem with this book is that Claude was not here to put his pen to it. He collected and gathered information for twenty years, and in 1998 more than thirty boxes of photos, programs, and letters were removed from the Sullivan house that we had built in 1962 on Brookhill Drive in Lexington and sent to the University of Kentucky to expand the Claude Sullivan Collection that had been in its archives since 1978. At this point, I embarked on a journey of discovery, deciding that there was a book in all of it that needed to be written. The first of five research and writing retreats was at Pine Mountain in 2003. Since then, information has slowly marinated until this book was complete.

The University Press of Kentucky and especially Ashley Runyon have been great to work with and have allowed me to stay close to the book I have lived with so long! I thank friend and colleague Florence Huffman for introducing me to Joe Cox at the Kentucky Book Fair in 2012. After that introduction, Joe and I decided to collaborate, and Joe (assisted by his wife, Julie) has provided a fresh look at the volume of material submitted to the University Press of Kentucky for its initial comments. Joe has condensed the information into a cohesive work, feeling, however, that there is two books worth of material and possibly a second project in the Sullivan Collection. Florence, an attorney and publisher herself, has given continued guidance and support throughout this long journey.

My wife of thirty-five years and counting, Jan, along with son Blake and daughter Alycia, has been my inspiration and encouragement. They never met Claude but must feel as if he has come alive with the years of reviewing the photos and memorabilia and listening to the tapes in the car on road trips. Jan and I spent many weekends together editing and developing material for the manuscript.

The UK Archives have been a partner in this effort since the Claude Sullivan Collection was created in 1978 when Alyce made the first donations of tapes and recordings. Terry Birdwhistell came to the house to pick up the first batch of information as an archives assistant and is now dean of the University Library and remains dedicated to this endeavor. He also opened the newsletter announcing the event honoring the Big Blue Sports Archives and the Claude Sullivan Collection in 2009 with "I never knew Claude Sullivan, but I spent a lot of time with him." A great way to introduce himself as a fan and follower.

Terry and Jim Host spearheaded the October 13, 2009, Big Blue Archives event that honored Claude and developed *The Best Seat in the House with Claude Sullivan*, the award-winning video by my high school friend and neighbor Arthur Rouse of Video Editing Services, which utilized many of the recordings digitized in 1998 for the UK Basketball Museum. Rouse's donation of his services for the effort shows the respect for Claude that remains today.

Ernest Holdredge of Lexington was contacted and started the restoration of the more than four hundred tapes and records in the Sullivan Collection, some of which had been stored in the UK Archives since 1978 and were nearly ruined. This four-year project was finished in 2010 when the last of the European tapes were restored. All of us involved with the restoration project and generations of fans to come greatly appreciate Ernest and his dedication to detail. Director of the Archives Deidre Scaggs, Director of Oral History Doug Boyd, and Sarah Price have been instrumental in making this collection available to the public online. Deirdre says Claude's call of the Vernon Hatton shot against Temple in December 1957 still gives her goose bumps.

I also want to thank the many friends, players, and announcers who knew Claude for the extensive time they allowed for me to interview them. Longtime friends Wah Jones and Humzey Yessin were especially helpful. Having lunch with Herky Rupp, Adolph Rupp's son, and reminiscing about our families growing up together recalled the professional and personal relationship our fathers had for more than twenty years.

I thank longtime colleagues Jim Host and Billy Reed for their relentless help and encouragement in addition to their interviews. Jim approved my access to his oral history at UK, and I am especially grateful that Billy wrote the afterword, lending his knowledge of Claude as a friend and contemporary. Ralph Hacker contributed the hub-and-spoke concept through his interview and has been very supportive.

I would be remiss if I didn't thank all those who encouraged me along the way with their direct or indirect help.

Ric McGee encouraged me to submit the book to the university press and Edie Maddox gave me my first lessons on writing and developing a voice for the book. Leslie Lyons, sister of Dicky Lyons Jr., guided me in the formal organizational process, giving the book an overall concept. Carol Cornell of the Northern Kentucky Small Business Development Center consulted and then volunteered to lend her time to go through the first full edit. I am grateful for her interest and friendship.

I also thank Dana Cox for her encouragement. I have known Dana through the College of Design, and her background as a former employee of Jim Host's and the University Press of Kentucky's was beneficial. Dana always offered good judgment, advice, and encouragement at times when it seemed nothing would ever be finished!

In 2013, Joe Cox pulled it all together. Thank you, Joe! Joe added some material from his vast experience as a Kentucky sports enthusiast, having published a previous book on UK basketball in addition to this one.

Finally, I am truly grateful to my mom, Alyce, Claude's true inspiration in all he accomplished in life, for her support, time, patience, and most of all love, without which this book would not have been possible. Casting a light on areas I would never have researched, she knew Claude the best and was most influential in making him the man David and I called "Dad." Although Alyce knew I was writing the book and was both interviewed and included in many discussions about it, I only wish she could have made it long enough to see Claude recognized. I'm glad she was able at least to accept three hall of fame awards for him.

Alan Sullivan

There are a few folks on my end whom I'd like to thank for helping to bring this project to fruition. Ryan Clark has always been a wonderful friend and has brought me into this writing world. Without him, I wouldn't have been a part of this book, and I appreciate his help and friendship. I echo Alan's thanks to Florence Huffman for connecting this new writer looking for a project with Alan and his years of research and compilation. The good folks at the University Press of Kentucky have been delightful to work with, especially Ashley Runyon, who helped to meld Alan's vision and mine into this book. And I certainly want to thank Alan Sullivan. I was born more than a decade after Claude Sullivan passed away, but getting to know his youngest son has spoken volumes to me about his high character and the influence he had on those who knew him. As Alan notes, he had worked on this material for years—this book is essentially his baby, and he trusted me with it. Some bumps and bruises undoubtedly followed, but at the end of the process I consider Alan not only my colleague, but my friend. I trust that Claude would be proud.

Finally, I thank my own family. Much love always to my children, Natalie and Ryan, who are two special little people I enjoy more every day. My wife, Julie, is not only a great editor, but my compass, always guiding me away from error and in the right direction. This book is the story of a great man and recounts the adventures of a number of other great men. But don't kid yourself—you wouldn't be holding this book without Alyce Sullivan, Jan Sullivan, or Julie Cox. I hold both Claude and Alan in the highest regard, but I also say with certainty that one thing all three of us have in common is that we outclassed ourselves greatly on the day that we walked down the wedding aisle.

Joe Cox

Appendix

The Claude Sullivan Collection in the University of Kentucky Archives

The research for this book included looking through volumes of collected media guides, programs, letters, and scorecards of games that Claude Sullivan had collected beginning in 1948 (still privately held by the Sullivan family) and listening to recordings made of his broadcasts and other radio programs. The Claude Sullivan Collection has been in the University of Kentucky Archives since 1978, when Alyce Sullivan donated 254 tapes made of Claude's sportscasts and additional recordings of his early broadcasts of UK sports events. An additional one hundred plus recordings, including some records that preceded magnetic tapes, were discovered in 1998, when Alyce moved out of the house that David and Alan had grown up in, and put into the collection. Forty-three transcription disks made by WHAS were transcribed in 2008 and added. Also in 2008, Alan used money from Alyce's estate to begin digitizing all the recordings that made up the "final" Claude Sullivan Collection, which took several years to do. When that was completed, UK had the "event" to honor both the Claude Sullivan Collection and the UK Digital Archives (or what is now called the Kentucky Digital Library), including the Big Blue Sports Archives. But then one more collection of tapes made overseas was found, donated by the Sullivans, and digitized—completing what the family knows of Claude's recordings to this point.

In 1970, Cecil Jones produced the vinyl album *Great Moments in UK Basketball* for the university's Committee of 101. For this album, Adolph Rupp was interviewed by Cawood Ledford, and the Sullivan family allowed recorded interviews of Claude to be used. A digitized version of it is in the collection.

Claude Sullivan contributed to three University of Kentucky publicity/fact books in the early to mid-1950s for director Ken Kuhn that are quoted in this manuscript. Those articles were used as the introduction to a particular University of Kentucky season and were not originally credited to Claude. Claude's original typed articles for those publications are in the Claude Sullivan personal collection—consisting of letters, fact books, memorabilia, photos, and various other materials. Claude also contributed to several articles in Wah Wah Jones's production *TV in the Bluegrass* in the mid- to late 1950s and early 1960s.

I. Baseball, 1963–1967

i. *Diamond Dope,* 1964–1965 (a series of interviews of baseball players, coaches, and managers that Claude did from 1964 to 1967 and were taped the day of the game for use during the game that day or evening)

Bobby Klaus, June 19, 1964
John Temple, June 20, 1964

Si Burick, June 21, 1964

Duke Snyder, June 22, 1964

Lou Smith, June 23, 1964

Del Crandall, June 23, 1964

Willie Mays, June 24, 1964

Bob Bailey, June 26, 1964

Fred Hutchinson, June 28, 1964

Michey Vernon, June 28, 1964

Ron Santo, June 29, 1964

Rip Collins, June 30, 1964

Bill McCool, July 8, 1964

John Callison, July 9, 1964

Jim Bunning, July 10, 1964

Gene Mauch, July 11, 1964

Don Heffner, July 12, 1964

Phil Seghi, July 12, 1964

Harry Craft, July 14, 1964

Mel Queen, July 15, 1964

Don Pavletich, July 16, 1964

Deron Johnson, July 17, 1964

Art Mahaffey, July 18, 1964

Clay Dalrymple, July 19, 1964

Ray Shore, July 19, 1964

Ryne Duren, July 20, 1964

Marty Keough, July 21, 1964

Ron Hunt, July 22, 1964

Roy McMillan, July 23, 1964

Smokey Burgess, July 24, 1964

Roy Face, July 25, 1964

Chico Ruiz, July 26, 1964

Tony Perez, July 26, 1964

Ed Bailey, July 27, 1964

Warren Spahn, July 28, 1964
Jojo White, July 29, 1964
Johnny Keane, July 31, 1964
Lou Brock, August 1, 1964
Reggie Otero, August 2, 1964
Bob Bragan, August 4, 1964
Dr. Richard Rhoade, August 4, 1964
Rico Carty, August 5, 1964
Hank Aaron, August 6, 1964
Wally Post, August 7, 1964
Harvy Kuenn, August 8, 1964
Jim Davenport, August 9, 1964
Tommy Davis, August 10, 1964
Alan Roth, August 11, 1964
Frank Howard, August 12, 1964
Mike White, August 14, 1964
Ken Johnson, August 15, 1964
Sam Ellis, August 16, 1964
Orlando Cepeda, August 18, 1964
Jim Otoole, August 19, 1964
Chico Ruiz, August 20, 1964
Dick Sisler, August 21, 1964
Maury Wills, August 22, 1964
Marty Keough, August 23, 1964
Jim Coker, August 25, 1964
Casey Stengel, August 26, 1964
Eddie Leashman, August 26, 1964
Bob Aspromonte, August 29, 1964
Jim Turner, August 29, 1964
Don Larsen, August 20, 1964
Walter Bond, August 30, 1964
Dick Elsworth, September 1, 1964

Jim Otoole, September 3, 1964

Gus Bell, September 4, 1964

Warren Spahn, September 5, 1964

Rico Carty, September 6, 1964

Red Schoendienst, September 7, 1964

Jim Ferguson, September 7, 1964

Jim Bunning, September 21, 1964

Dick Sisler, September 22, 1964

Gene Mauch, September 23, 1964

Bill Dewitt, September 25, 1964

Pat Harmon, September 25, 1964

Casey Stengel, September 26, 1964

John Callison, September 27, 1964

Richie Allen, September 28, 1964

Jim Turner, September 29, 1964

Fred Hutchinson, September 30, 1964

Danny Murtaugh, October 1, 1964

Jim Bunning, October 2, 1964

Dick Young, October 4, 1964

Warren Spahn, July 22, 1965

ii. Interviews, 1965–1967

Burger Beer intro and close, January 1965 (Burger Beer was the
    sponsor of the Cincinnati Reds games before Wiedemann
    Brewing Company took over in 1965 after Waite Hoyt retired)

Babe Dahlgren interview, August 13, 1965

Waite Hoyt interview, October 3, 1965

Sullivan with Reds vs. San Francisco Giants at Crosley Field,
    August 10, 1966 (rain delay)

Dave Bristol interview, March 1967

Joe Nuxhall interview, April 1967

iii. Reds Games, 1963–1966

Cincinnati Reds vs. Giants, August 13, 1963 (audition tape)
Cards vs. Dodgers air check, September 17, 1963 (audition tape)
Chicago White Sox vs. Cincinnati Reds, March 1964
Cincinnati Reds vs. Chicago White Sox, March 13, 1964
Cincinnati Reds vs. Philadelphia, April 30, 1964
Cincinnati vs. Atlanta Braves at Crosley Field, August 5, 1964
Cincinnati Reds vs. San Francisco Giants at Candlestick Park,
   August 19, 1964
Cincinnati Reds vs. San Francisco Giants, August 20, 1964
Cards vs. Reds Highlights, April 23, 1965
Cards vs. Reds Highlights, April 24, 1965
Giants vs. Reds, August 3, 1965
Dodgers vs. Reds, September 2, 1966

iv. "Golden Moments" (a sports moment Claude produced for
Wiedemann Sports Eye)

Story 5, June 6, 1962
Story 6, June 8, 1962
Story 7, June 9, 1962

II. Basketball, 1949–1967

i. Games Broadcast, 1949–1966

UK vs. Loyola, March 14, 1949, NIT
UK vs. Oklahoma A&M, NCAA Tournament, March 26, 1949
UK vs. Alabama, February 2, 1955
UK vs. Georgia Tech, January 30, 1956
UK vs. Duke, February 1, 1956

UK vs. Auburn, February 4, 1956
UK vs. Mississippi, February 11, 1956
UK vs. Mississippi State, February 13, 1956
UK vs. Vanderbilt, February 20, 1956
UK vs. Georgia, February 27, 1956
UK vs. Tennessee, March 3, 1956
UK vs. Washington & Lee, December 1, 1956
UK vs. University of Miami, December 3, 1956
UK vs. Temple University, December 8, 1956
UK vs. Maryland, December 15, 1956
UK vs. SMU, December 21, 1956
SMU vs. Dayton, December 22, 1956
UK vs. Illinois, December 22, 1956
UK vs. VPI, December 28, 1956
UK vs. Houston, December 29, 1956
UK vs. Georgia Tech, January 5, 1957
UK vs. Loyola, January 7, 1957
UK vs. LSU, January 12, 1957
UK vs. Tennessee, January 19, 1957
UK vs. Vanderbilt, January 26, 1957
UK vs. Georgia Tech, January 28, 1957
UK vs. Georgia, January 30, 1957
UK vs. Florida, February 2, 1957
UK vs. Mississippi, February 8, 1957
UK vs. Loyola, February 15, 1957
UK vs. Vanderbilt, February 18, 1957
UK vs. Auburn, February 25, 1957
UK vs. Pittsburgh, March 15, 1957, NCAA Regional
UK vs. Michigan State, March 16, 1957, NCAA Regional Final
UK vs. Duke, December 2, 1957
UK vs. Ohio State, December 4, 1957
UK vs. Temple, December 7, 1957, three overtimes

UK vs. St. Louis, December 14, 1957

UK vs. Utah State, December 23, 1957

UK vs. Loyola, December 30, 1957

UK vs. Georgia Tech, January 4, 1958

UK vs. Vanderbilt, January 6, 1958

UK vs. LSU, January 11, 1958

UK vs. Tulane, January 13, 1958

UK vs. Georgia, January 29, 1958

UK vs. Florida, January 31, 1958

UK vs. Mississippi, February 8, 1958

UK vs. Mississippi State, February 10, 1958

UK vs. Vanderbilt, February 17, 1958

UK vs. Tennessee, March 1, 1958

UK vs. Miami, NCAA, March 14, 1958

UK vs. Notre Dame, NCAA Region Finals, March 15, 1958

UK vs. Temple, NCAA Tournament Semifinals, March 21, 1958

UK vs. Seattle, NCAA Championship, March 22, 1958

UK vs. Temple, December 6, 1958

UK vs. Alabama, February 22, 1959

UK vs. Ohio State, December 28, 1959

UK vs. Georgia, January 27, 1960

UK vs. Auburn, February 20, 1960

UK vs. VMI, December 1, 1960

UK vs. Notre Dame, December 7, 1960

UK vs. Mississippi State, February 13, 1961

UK vs. Vanderbilt, February 21, 1961

UK vs. Kansas State, December 23, 1961

UK vs. Florida, February 2, 1962

UK vs. Mississippi State, February 12, 1962

UK vs. Auburn, February 26, 1962

UK vs. Duke, Sugar Bowl, December 31, 1963

UK vs. Auburn, February 22, 1964

UK vs. Alabama, February 24, 1964
UK vs. Tennessee, February 29, 1964
UK vs. St. Louis, March 2, 1964
UK vs. Northwestern, December 10, 1966

ii. Short Clips, 1957–1967

Adolph Rupp interview, February 15, 1957
UK vs. Maryland game clip, December 9, 1957
Forrest Allen interview, December 14, 1959
Partial sports broadcast, December 15, 1959
UK vs. Georgia game clip, February 7, 1961
Adolph Rupp interview, November 25, 1961
"Golden Moments," February 24, 1962
UK *Warmup Show*, December 18, 1964
Standard Oil Network intro and commercial, NCAA, re-recorded,
     March 1, 1966
UK vs. Texas Western, game audio with Rupp interview, March
     19, 1966
Before Cornell game, re-recorded, December 28, 1966
Before Georgia game, re-recorded, January 16, 1967
Before Auburn game, re-recorded, January 21, 1967
Before Mississippi game, re-recorded, January 30, 1967

iii. *Great Moments in Kentucky Basketball*, vinyl album recorded in
1970, produced by Cecil Jones for the UK Committee of 101

III. Claude Sullivan Sports Shows, 1949–1954

Today in Sports, April 19, 1949
Today in Sports, April 22, 1949
World of Sports, July 14, 1949

World of Sports, August 20, 1949
World of Sports, October 28, 1949
World of Sports, November 1, 1949
Today in Sports, November 16, 1949
World of Sports, June 15, 1950
Sports Parade, March 1951
Today in Sports, May 26, 1954

IV. Football, 1948–1965

i. *Bear Bryant Show,* 1949

September 12, 1949
September 19, 1949
September 26, 1949
October 3, 1949
October 10, 1949
October 17, 1949
November 14, 1949

ii. *Football Forecasts,* 1948–1949

Football Preview
November 19, 1948
September 24, 1949
October 1, 1949
October 29, 1949
November 5, 1949
November 12, 1949
November 26, 1949

iii. UK Football Game Broadcasts, 1948–1963

UK vs. Villanova, November 6, 1948
UK vs. LSU, September 24, 1949
UK vs. Georgia, October 8, 1949
UK vs. Tennessee, November 21, 1953
UK vs. Auburn, October 9, 1954
UK vs. Vanderbilt, November 6, 1954
UK vs. Memphis State, November 13, 1954
UK vs. Tennessee, November 20, 1954
UK vs. Tennessee, November 19, 1955
UK vs. Florida, October 6, 1956
UK vs. Auburn, October 13, 1956
UK vs. LSU, October 20, 1956
UK vs. Georgia, October 27, 1956
UK vs. Tennessee, November 24, 1956
Rebroadcast of UK vs. Georgia Tech, September 19, 1957 (October 23, 1954 air date)
Rebroadcast of UK vs. Mississippi, September 29, 1957 (September 24, 1955 air date)
Rebroadcast of UK vs. Florida, October 3, 1957 (October 6, 1956 air date)
Rebroadcast of UK vs. Memphis State, October 3, 1957 (November 18, 1954 air date)
Rebroadcast of UK vs. Auburn, October 17, 1957 (October 9., 1954 air date)
Rebroadcast of UK vs. Georgia, October 24, 1957 (October 27, 1956 air date)
UK vs. Memphis State, November 2, 1957
UK vs. Vanderbilt, November 9, 1957
Rebroadcast of UK vs. Xavier, November 14, 1957 (November 19, 1956 air date)

UK vs. Xavier, November 16, 1957

Rebroadcast of UK vs. Tennessee, November 21, 1957 (November 19, 1955 air date)

UK vs. Tennessee, November 23, 1957

UK vs. Georgia Tech, September 20, 1958

UK vs. Tennessee, November 22, 1958

UK vs. Tennessee, November 21, 1959

UK vs. Tennessee, November 19, 1960

UK vs. Auburn, October 7, 1961

UK vs. Tennessee, November 25, 1961

UK vs. Tennessee, November 24, 1962

UK vs. Baylor, November 16, 1963

iv. UK Football Interviews, 1952–1962

Bear Bryant Show, September 28, 1952

Homecoming Eve WVLK Mobile News, November 22, 1957

Sullivan Looks Them Over, interview with Andy Gustavson; review of stats before Miami vs. UK, September 23, 1961

Interview with Mississippi coach J. Vaught, September 30, 1961

Interview with Auburn coach S. Jordan, October 7, 1961

Interview with UK and Georgia coaches after the game, October 28, 1961

Review of football game scores around the country; interviews with UK and Florida State coaches after the game, November 4, 1961

Postgame (UK vs. Vanderbilt) interview with Coach Art Gueepe, November 11, 1961

Interview with Xavier coach E. Doherty, November 18, 1961

Interview with Bear Bryant on Coach Bradshaw; portion of Mississippi vs. Texas, January 1962

Interviews from Bradshaw Players Picture Day, August 31, 1962
Bradshaw's first interview of the season, September 1962
Bradshaw's last interview of the season, November 22, 1962
Interview with Tennessee coach Bowden Wyatt, November 23, 1962
Postgame (UK vs. Tennessee) interview with Coach Bradshaw, November 24, 1962

v. UK Short Clips, 1951–1965

UK vs. George Washington on Dempsey, November 17, 1951
UK vs. Mississippi, September 25, 1954
UK vs. Auburn, October 9, 1954
UK vs. LSU, October 18, 1958
UK vs. Mississippi State, November 1, 1958
UK vs. Vandy, last three minutes of the third quarter at Stoll Field, November 8, 1958
UK vs. Georgia, October 28, 1961
UK vs. Xavier, November 17, 1962
Pregame Miami vs. UK, September 22, 1961
Football Predictions, October 23, 1964
Standard Oil Network intro and commercials, September 1965
Football Predictions, November 6, 1965
Football Predictions, November 20, 1965
"Golden Moments in Sports": game highlights, predictions, and interviews, undated

V. High School Basketball, 1948, 1950

Holmes vs. Carr Creek Quarterfinals, March 1948
Clark County vs. Catlettsburg Sixteenth Regional Finals, March 11, 1950

VI. Highlights of Claude Sullivan's Career, 1949–1962

Hope Chandler interview, April 29, 1954
Keeneland featured race, October 15, 1949
Keeneland race Tim Tam, April 1958
Phog Allen interview, 1959
UK vs. Loyola, basketball, March 14, 1949
UK vs. Mississippi State, basketball, February 13, 1961
UK vs. Oklahoma A&M, basketball, March 26, 1949
UK vs. Tennessee, football, November 19, 1955
UK vs. Tennessee, football, November 19, 1960
UK vs. Tennessee, football, November 24, 1962

VII. Horse Racing, 1949–1962

i. Keeneland, 1949, 1958

Keeneland Fall Meet, October 15, 1949
Keeneland Spring Meet, April 1958
Nashua Retries, undated

ii. Red Mile, 1962

Lexington Trots, June 5, 1962
Lexington Trots, June 6, 1962
Lexington Trots, June 7, 1962
Lexington Trots, June 9, 1962

VIII. Journalism Hall of Fame, 2006

Combined audio highlights, April 11, 2006
Sullivan presentation, April 11, 2006

IX. Overseas Tours, 1957–1960

i. WVLK Tour, Soviet Union, 1957

Sullivan speaking from London, July 2, 1957
Sullivan speaking from Berlin, July 3, 1957
Sullivan speaking from Berlin, July 6, 1957
Sullivan and guide Andre Struic speaking from Berlin, July 7, 1957
Sullivan from Berlin to Warsaw, July 7, 1957
Rebroadcast of *Sullivan in Warsaw, Poland,* and the Palace of
    Culture music program, September 3, 1957
Continuation of Palace of Culture music program, July 7, 1957
Sullivan in Warsaw countryside, July 7, 1957
Sullivan's trip from Warsaw to Moscow, July 9, 1957
Sullivan sightseeing in Moscow, July 10, 1957
Sullivan in Leningrad, July 11, 1957
Sullivan in Leningrad, July 12, 1957
Sullivan in Leningrad, July 13, 1957
Sullivan in Karkoff, Ukraine, July 14, 1957
Sullivan in Karkoff, Ukraine, July 15, 1957
Sullivan in Tablisi, Georgia, July 16, 1957
Sullivan in Tablisi, Georgia, July 17, 1957
Sullivan in Sausci, Georgia, July 19, 1957
Sullivan in Yalta, Ukraine, July 22, 1957
Sullivan in Odessa, Ukraine, July 24, 1957
Sullivan in Odessa, Ukraine, July 25, 1957
Sullivan in Odessa, Ukraine, July 26, 1957
Circus in Ukraine, July 27, 1957
Sullivan on the way from Odessa to Lavoff, Ukraine, July 28, 1957
Sullivan in New York, original air date August 1, 1957
Sullivan on flight from Paris to New York, August 2, 1957
Pilot played football at UK, original air date August 2, 1957

Rebroadcast of *Sullivan in Kiev* and interview of Ms. Adell
  Hollingsworth, October 10, 1957

Rebroadcast of Sullivan on the way from Odessa to Lavoff,
  Ukraine, October 14, 1957

Rebroadcast of Sullivan on the way from Lavoff to Budapest,
  October 15, 1957

Rebroadcast of Sullivan in Vienna, Paris, and the return flight to
  New York, October 17, 1957

Sullivan interviewing the pilot on flight overseas, who happened to
  be former UK football player

Rebroadcast of Sullivan on flight from Paris to New York, October
  21, 1957

ii. WVLK Tour, Middle East, 1958

Reel 1 of 18: 1a—New York Weston Hotel, 1b—Airplane trip to
  Brussels, 1c—Tour member interviews. July 3–5, 1958

Reel 2 of 18: 2a—Brussels airport/hotel, 2b—St. Michaels and
  World's Fair, 2c—Tour of the World's Fair. July 6, 1958

Reel 3 of 18: 3a—Brussels to Cairo, 3b—Sabina flight from
  Brussels, 3c—Egyptian museum and desert. July 7–8, 1958

Reel 4 of 18: 4a—Camel ride to Sphinx and Pyramids, 4b—Cairo
  listening to local radio broadcasts. July 9, 1958

Reel 5 of 18: 5a—Trip to Jerusalem via Beirut, 5b—Jerusalem,
  Jordan, 5c—Jerusalem, Israel. July 10–12, 1958

Reel 6 of 18: 6a—Mt. Zion to Haifa, 6b—Tel Aviv. July 13–14,
  1958

Reel 7 of 18: 7a—Tel Aviv to Galilee, 7b—Tel Aviv to Istanbul,
  7c—Airplane trip to Istanbul. July 14–17, 1958

Reel 8 of 18: 8—From Tel Aviv by phone. July 16, 1958

Reel 9 of 18: 9a—Istanbul history guide interview, 9b—
Sightseeing in Istanbul, Turkey. July 18, 1958
Reel 10 of 18: 10—From Athens by phone. July 19, 1958
Reel 11 of 18: 11—Athens, WVLK edited. July 19, 1958
Reel 12 of 18: 12a—Trip from Istanbul to Athens, 12b—
Sightseeing in Athens. July 19–20, 1958
Reel 13 of 18: 13a—Athens and southern Greece tour, 13b—Call
to WVLK from Rome, Italy. July 21–23, 1958
Reel 14 of 18: 14a—Trip from Athens to Rome and sights, 14b—
Alyce Sullivan reports on trip. July 23, 1958
Reel 15 of 18: 15a—Rome sights and Mrs. Wiley, 15b—Sights,
shop, and pope in Rome. July 10–12, 1958
Reel 16 of 18: 16a—To Florence from Rome, 16b—Riveria, Pisa,
Genoa, 16c—Monte Carlo and sights. July 26–28, 1958
Reel 17 of 18: 17a—Monte Carlo to Grenoble, 17b—Grenoble into
France with guide. July 31–August 1, 1958
Reel 18 of 18: 18a—British radio broadcasts, 18b—More British
broadcasts. August 1958
Sullivan in Mt. Zion to Haifa, July 13, 1958
Sullivan in Tel Aviv, Israel, July 15, 1958
Sullivan and Ray Holbrook phone conversation from Tel Aviv,
Israel, July 16, 1958
Sullivan and Gig Henderson phone conversation from Athens, July
19, 1958
WVLK edited version of Sullivan and Gig Henderson phone
conversation from Athens, July 19, 1958

iii. WVLK Tour, Europe, 1959

Sullivan's tour of Europe, September 25, 1959
Reel 1 of 16: 1a—Intro to series, 1b—Portugal, 1c—Lisbon to

Madrid, 1d—Madrid and Spain, 1e—Intro to Spain cities and Paris. June 20, 1959

Reel 2 of 16: 2a—Paris, 2b—London/Scotland, 2c—Scotland/ Norway, 2d—Norway/Sweden. June 20, 1959

Reel 3 of 16: 3a—Sweden/Denmark, 3b—Germany/Holland, 3c—Lexington/New York City, 3d—Flight to Lisbon. June 21–25, 1959

Reel 4 of 16: 4a—Lisbon and sights, 4b—Bullfights, 4c—Lisbon and market, 4d—Tour old city. June 26–28, 1959

Reel 5 of 16: 5a—Trip to Madrid, 5b—Bullfights, 5c—Madrid sights, 5d—To Toledo, Spain. June 28–30, 1959

Reel 6 of 16: 6a—Madrid/Granada, 6b—Granada, 6c—Algecrias, 6d—Algecrias/Rock of Gibraltar. July 1–3, 1959

Reel 7 of 16: 7a—To Seville, Spain, 7b—Seville, 7c—Seville/ Cordoba, 7d—Cordoba/Paris. July 4–7, 1959

Reel 8 of 16: 8a—Paris and sights, 8b—Eiffel Tower, 8c—Paris/ Versailles, 8d—Paris, River Seine. July 8–10, 1959

Reel 9 of 16: 9a—Paris to London, 9b—London, 9c—Surry/ Windsor Castle, 9d—London sights. July 10–11, 1959

Reel 10 of 16: 10a—London to Stratford, 10b—Oxford/Scotland, 10c—Edinborough, 10d—Sterling Castle. July 12–15, 1959

Reel 11 of 16: 11a—Scotland/Norway, 11b—Norway mountains, 11c—Oslo sights, 11d—Oslo Viking ships. July 17–18, 1959

Reel 12 of 16: 12a—Rural countryside, 12b—Stockholm, 12c— Stockholm Canal, 12d—To Copenhagen. July 19–22, 1959

Reel 13 of 16: 13a—Kronborg Castle, 13b—To Hamburg, 13c— Hamburg/Holland, 13d—Amsterdam. July 23–27, 1959

Reel 14 of 16: 14a—From Lexington to Amsterdam via London and home, September 4, 1959

Reel 15 of 16: 15—Tour highlights with music departure, September 25, 1959

Reel 16 of 16: 16—Tour highlights with music departure,
     September 25, 1959
Germanic music, likely recorded during 1959 tour, possibly 1959

iv. WVLK Tour, 1960

Tour promos, July 1, 1960
Sullivan on plane, New York to Amsterdam, August 6, 1960
Sullivan in London, August 8, 1960
Sullivan in London, August 9, 1960
Sullivan in London, August 10, 1960
Sullivan in Amsterdam, August 11, 1960
Sullivan in Amsterdam, August 12, 1960
Sullivan in Brussels, August 13, 1960
Sullivan in Brussels, August 14, 1960
Sullivan in Luxembourg, August 14, 1960
Sullivan in Germany, August 14, 1960
Sullivan in Rome, Olympic basketball, August 26, 1960
Sullivan in Rome, Olympic basketball, August 27, 1960

X. Waite Hoyt Sports Shows, 1949

Hoyt Sports Review Preseason, March 1949
Sports According to Hoyt, October 17, 1949
Sports According to Hoyt, November 1, 1949

XI. General, 1944–1967

Baer Kaminski fight, 1940s
BBC Olympics telephone report, August 2, 1948 (interview with
     Adolph Rupp)
Choo Choo Justice interview, 1949

Dempsey interview, 1951

Dempsey–Miskey fight, 1920s

Gay Brewer interview, 1949

Grizzard's interview of Claude Sullivan after surgery, January 11, 1967

Knute Rockney story, undated

Lebanon crisis report, July 19, 1958

Part of sportscast, May 6, 1958

President Eisenhower speech at the Bureau of Advertising (Publishers), April 22, 1954

Re-recorded *Wave Honey Krust News*, October 27, 1944

Sports segment, September 22, 1949

Sports segment, September 23, 1949

Sports segment, September 30, 1949

Sports segment, October 19, 1949

Sports segment, October 20, 1949

Sports segment, October 27, 1949

Sports segment, December 14, 1949

Sports segment, December 15, 1949

Sports summary, 1949–1961

Standard Oil intros and commercials, undated

Sullivan interviews of Bob Hope and A. B. "Happy" Chandler, April 29, 1954

Sullivan's interview of Governor A. B. "Happy" Chandler, September 1955

Sullivan's interview of Mrs. A. B. Chandler, September 1955

Sullivan's voice/practice test, August 14, 1967

Sullivan's voice/practice test for TV, July 9, 1967

Today in Sports, Dempsey tape, undated

Twelve Years of Kentucky Sports, 1961 (an audition tape that had a summary of recordings of games from 1949 to 1961)

Bibliography

Archives and Personal Collections

Claude Sullivan Collection

Digital Collection (recordings). University of Kentucky Archives, Lexington. A complete listing of the collection is given in the appendix.

Personal Collection. Correspondence, programs, notes, photos, and other personal materials. Privately held by the Sullivan family.

Books

Note: Some of these books are mentioned and quoted in the text, and others were useful mostly to double-check aged memories.

Bryant, Paul W., and John Underwood. *Bear: The Hard Life and Good Times of Alabama's Coach Bryant.* Boston: Little, Brown, 1975.

Chandler, Dan, and Vernon Hatton. *Adolph Rupp: From Both Ends of the Bench.* N.p.: Dan Chandler and Vernon Hatton, 1972.

Ledford, Cawood, and Billy Reed. *Hello Everybody, This Is Cawood Ledford.* Lexington, KY: Host Communications, 1992.

Maraniss, David. *Rome 1960: The Olympics That Changed the World.* New York: Simon and Schuster, 2008.

Nelli, Bert, and Steve Nelli. *The Winning Tradition: A History of Kentucky Wildcat Basketball.* 2nd ed. Lexington, KY: University Press of Kentucky, 1998.

Ragland, Shannon. *The Thin Thirty: The Untold Story of Brutality, Scandal, and Redemption for Charlie Bradshaw's 1962 Kentucky Football Team.* Louisville, KY: Set Shot Press, 2007.

Rice, Russell. *Kentucky Basketball's Big Blue Machine.* Huntsville, AL: Strode, 1976.

———. *The Wildcats: A Story of Kentucky Football.* Huntsville, AL: Strode, 1975.

Rosen, Charlie. *Scandals of '51: How the Gamblers Almost Killed College Basketball.* New York: Holt, Rienhart and Winston, 1978.

Wallace, Tom. *University of Kentucky Basketball Encyclopedia.* New York: Sports Publishing, 2012.

Articles

Anderson, Wayne. "Shop Talk." *Atlanta Journal,* January 17, 1950.

Ashford, Ed. "It Says Here." *Lexington Herald,* March 22, 1952.

———. "Grid Victory Makes Wildcat Fans Lose Interest in Basketball Scandal." *Lexington Leader,* October 21, 1951.

Bailey, Rick. "Memories." *Lexington Herald,* December 8, 1967.

Birdwhistell, Terry. "Remembering Kentucky's Claude Sullivan." *Speaking Volumes,* fall 2009, 1 and 7.

Boeck, Larry. "Of Adolph Rupp." *Courier-Journal Magazine,* January 19, 1964.

Bryant, Paul W., and John Underwood. "A Run-in with Rupp and Trouble Down in Texas." *Sports Illustrated,* August 22, 1966.

Darack, Arthur. "Baseball as I See It." *Dimension Cincinnati* 2, no. 4 (1964): 8–10.

Fitzwater, John. "Claude Sullivan, UK Voice, Now after 500th Contest." *Kentucky Kernel,* January 15, 1960.

Gallaher, Mary Jane. "Through Pre-Sputnik Russia, We Drew a Crowd Wherever We Went." *Louisville Courier-Journal Magazine,* October 27, 1957.

Harmon, Pat. "Prediction: Sullivan Will Succeed Hoyt." *Cincinnati Post and Times-Star,* October 22, 1965.

Kimbrough, Babe. "[Title unavailable.]" *Lexington Herald,* March 15, 1949.

McGinty, David. "Time Out." *Lousiville Times,* November 11, 1967.

Rice, Russell. "Reluctant Rupp Hesitates but Deplanes First." *Lexington Leader,* February 5, 1964.

"Russia's Invitation to Tourists Has Aroused Little Business Here." *Louisville Courier-Journal,* "Traveling Around" section, May 20, 1956.

Shropshire, Larry. "Down in Front." *Lexington Leader,* April 28, 1949.

"Thanks for the Memories" (photo with Bob Hope on his one hundredth birthday). *Lane Report 2003,* August 2003.

"Thirty, Mr. Sullivan—Big Man, Bigger Loss." *Kentucky Kernel,* December 8, 1967.

Personal Interviews

Note: These interviews were conducted by Alan Sullivan and recorded (unless noted otherwise) and are included in the Claude Sullivan Collection Oral History at the University of Kentucky Archives. In addition to the interview of Jim Host listed here, Host also granted use of his oral history collection at the University of Kentucky.

Hacker, Ralph. May 9, 2011, Lexington, KY.

Hagan, Cliff. August 31, 2011, Lexington, KY.

Hammond, Tom. February 19, 2011, Lexington, KY.

Holbrook, Ray. January 15, 2011, Versailles, KY.

Host, Jim. March 1, 2012, Lexington, KY.

Huddleston, Dee. January 27, 2011, Bardstown, KY.

Jones, Wallace "Wah Wah." May 10, 2011, Lexington, KY.

Mobley, Terry. August 31, 2011, Lexington, KY.

Newton, C. M. November 11, 2011, Tuscaloosa, AL (correspondence).

Parilli, Babe. November 11, 2011, Lexington, KY.

Reed, Billy. June 3, 2011, Louisville, KY.

Rupp, Herky. April 23, 2011, Lexington, KY.

Sullivan, Alyce. November 28, 2004, Lexington, KY (microcassette).

Sullivan, David. April 2, 2011, Lexington, KY.

Tsioropoulos, Lou. January 23, 2012, Louisville, KY.

Vance, Van. Interviewed by Leslie Lyons. February 24, 2011, Louisville, KY.

Wellman, Ferrell. August 31, 2011, Versailles, KY.

Yessin, Humzey. May 9, 2011, Lexington, KY.

Websites

Scott, Jon. Kentucky Wildcat Basketball. At http://www.bigbluehistory.net/bb/wildcats.html.

Note: I have only the highest praise for this groundbreaking website. Not only is Scott's information almost infallible, but he has more of it and it is better organized than any other reference source on Kentucky basketball. I pity everyone who wrote about the topic before Scott's site existed.

Index

Bradshaw, Charlie, 236, 251;
hiring of as UK football coach,
166–68; and integration of
SEC football, 207; and 1962
football season, 178–79; and
1963 football season, 181; and
1964 football season, 195, 196;
and 1965 football season, 205,
206, 207; and 1966 football
season, 228, 229; and 1967
football season, 238; and
recruiting of David Sullivan,
229–30; and training methods
of, 176–77
Brewer, Gay, 254
Bristol, Dave, 225, 233
Browning, Omar, 38
Broyla, Vince, 38
Bruno, Al, 59, 60, 75
Bryant, Paul "Bear," 52, 102, 103,
166; and career after UK
coaching job, 118, 250–51;
and departure from University
of Kentucky, 73, 91, 93, 97;
and hiring as UK football
coach, 29; and membership in
UK Athletics Hall of Fame,
3; and 1946 football season,
29; and 1947 football season,
33–34; and 1948 football
season, 41; and 1949 football
season, 47–50; and 1950
football season, 59–62; and
1951 football season, 75–77;
and 1952 football season,
86–87; and 1953 football
season, 93–97; practice habits

of, 32, 49, 76, 176; and
revitalization of UK football
program, 31
Burchett, Carroll, 174
Burrow, Bob, 104–5, 106, 109

Calipari, John, xi, 250, 256, 257
Calvert, Gerry, 119, 122
Cardenas, Leo, 203, 225
Carlisle, Ralph, 102, *103*
Carr Creek High School, 24–26
Casey, Mike, 238, 240, 249
CBS, 51, 145, 246
Chamberlain, Wilt, 120, 121
Chandler, A. B. "Happy," 102–3,
188–89, 211
Chapman, Wayne, 197
Cincinnati Reds, 248; and 1964
season, 191–95; and 1965
season, 201–3; and 1966
season, 223–26; and 1967
season, 234
Claiborne, Jerry, 49, 166, 168, 251
Clark, Emery, 77
Clark County High School, 26,
81, 235
Clay, Cassius, 155, 156; as
Muhammad Ali, 192
Clemente, Roberto, 192
Coffman, Bernie, 143, 144, 149,
151
Cohen, Sid, 143, 144, 149
Coleman, Gordy, 180, 192, 201
Collier, Blanton, 207, 251, 254;
and academic requirements
for athletes at University of
Kentucky, 142; and firing as

Visit **www.VoiceoftheWildcatsBook.com**
for exclusive audio recordings, images, and videos from
Claude Sullivan's family and professional archives, including:

- Broadcasts from University of Kentucky basketball
  and football games (1948–1963), as well as from the
  Cincinnati Reds (1964–1967)

- Claude Sullivan calling the 1949, 1958, and historic
  1966 University of Kentucky Basketball National
  Championship games, as well as the 1957 game in which
  Vernon Hatton's iconic 47-foot shot took the University of
  Kentucky basketball team into a second overtime for an
  eventual victory over Temple University

- First airings of the *Bear Bryant Show*

- Exclusive interviews with Adolph Rupp, Hank Aaron,
  Jack Dempsey, Phog Allen, Governor A. B. "Happy"
  Chandler, Bob Hope, and many others

- Radio programs from the 1948 and 1960 Olympic Games
  and multiple European tours with WVLK